ACKNOWLEDGMENTS

I would like to thank the many people who have helped me over this book. First those who encouraged me to look for a new publisher, and my thanks to the publishers for accepting the work and their help. Mrs Wendy Brown for all her ever ready help with the computer, and all the work she put in to get the Champion list correct and on a disk, also her valuable work helping me to compile the index.

My vet Mr David Frere Cook who has been so helpful and ever willing to answer my questions. Mrs Anne Pickburne and Mrs Diana Harding for their help in checking over certain chapters. Mrs Grace for her diagrams. Jean Luc Paul Lambert, for his superb photographs, and drawing of the Shih Tzu in action. All who have generously lent their photographs. Not least my husband John for his patience.

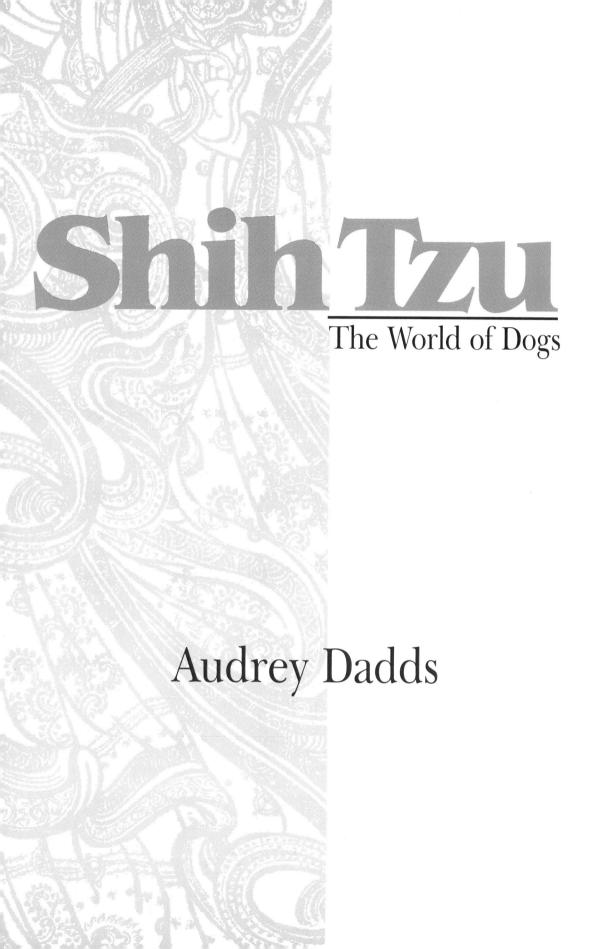

Shih Tzu

The World of Dogs

Audrey Dadds

ISBN: 1-85279-005-9

GB-003

Published by Kingdom Books
PO Box 15
Waterlooville PO7 6BQ
England

Designed by Add Graphics
PO Box 15
Waterlooville PO7 6BQ
England

CONTENTS

APPENDICES

INDEX

CHAPTER ONE

EARLY HISTORY – CHINESE and TIBETAN

Tibetan background

The origin of the Shih Tzu is somewhat obscure. It is classified as a Chinese dog, since it was bred there for many hundreds of years, but is considered to have originated in Tibet, where it was kept in the temples and occasionally given to emperors of China as a tribute gift.

According to Snellgrove and Richardson's A Cultural History of Tibet, records suggest that Tibet was a barbaric country inhabited by nomadic tribes of eastern Asian descent. Myth and superstition abounded; the founder of the Yarlung dynasty was said to have come from heaven on a 'sky-cord', leaving no mortal remains on earth. He preceded the great King Srong-brtsan-sgam-po (AD 627-50), who established his palace at Lhasa in AD 639 and from whose time written historical records began.

The T'ang Annals give an account of the relationship between China and Tibet from the seventh to ninth centuries, during which period the two countries were in close contact. From the seventh century onwards, Tibet entered upon a new period of growth and development. On one occasion, Tibetans captured the Chinese capital Ch'ang-an-(Sian), and were considered a formidable threat, even from the viewpoint of learning. Following a request from a Tibetan envoy for copies of the Chinese classics, a Chinese minister commented, 'They have a war-like nature, yet are steadfast in purpose, intelligent and industrious, intent on learning undistractedly.'

King Srong-brtsan-sgam-po was a force to be reckoned with, and in 640, he and one of his heirs were given Chinese princesses as brides. Occasional marriages may have also taken place between Tibetan nobles and Chinese brides, since the granting of princesses to neighbouring 'barbarian' rulers formed part of Chinese diplomacy. This is not intended to be a historical account of Tibet, but a small part of the early history does illustrate the close association between the two countries and the consequent possibility of an interchange of dogs. There are records of dogs in Tibet from early times. For example, there were Tibetan mastiffs guarding towns and caravans, and small house dogs with good hearing used to alert the ferocious mastiffs. Both types had thick, shaggy coats.

Myth and superstition

Buddhism and the mythological lion play a large part in the development of the lion dogs. Introduced from India, Buddhism took the form of Lamaism, and eventually spread throughout Tibet; this form was not adopted in China until the time of Kublai Khan in 1253. In Tibet, dogs are sacred animals, and people believe the souls of erring priests enter them. The small lion dogs are kept for temple duties and as house pets, where they live as members of the family. The great worship of the lion which forms part of Buddhism, and is particularly prominent in its more mythical form of Lamaism, is considered to be bound up with other, earlier religions. The Buddha Manjusri, the god of learning, is said to travel the four continents as a simple priest, accompanied by a small 'ha pah' (pet) dog. In an instant, the dog can be transformed into a mighty lion with Buddha riding on its back.

There are true or 'spirit lions' and 'dog lions'. Images of the spirit lions occur in sacred places such as carvings on the pillars of temples, while the dog lions are the earthy beasts known as the menagerie. The Lamas teach that the true lion is a mountain spirit, which possesses the power of instantaneous projection through space, can become visible or invisible at will, and is similarly capable of infinite expansion or reduction in size. According to the Samye-Ling Tibetan centre, established in Scotland in April 1967, 'The Shih Tzu, which is a house pet in Tibet, as is the Apso, has a very strong resemblance to a symbolic creature, the Gang Sing or snow lion, and is part of Ancient Imagery in which he is considered the King of Animals, and is so powerful that when he roars, seven dragons fall out of the sky. The three powers which he has are, the ability to leap, then turn in an instant and come back, to walk in mist and clouds, and his voice, the voice of the Middle Way (if truth and fearlessness) subdues all.' (Manchu News Letter)

Photo of Chinese Scroll showing Pug (top), Shih Tzu (middle) and Peke (bottom) owned by Alan Roger
Photo: Alison Snell

This could well be a description of the present-day Shih Tzu. It can be assumed that the Tibetan Lamas encouraged the tendency to breed these dogs to resemble their 'lions', and undoubtedly their best specimens would have been selected to be taken as tribute gifts to China.

The lions were not indigenous to China, but from AD 87 were imported as gifts to the emperors. Few artists had access to these beasts, and therefore modelled their lions on their own conceptions allied to the use of Buddhist and Lamaist representations. The Lamaist lion is depicted with a harness, to exemplify the subjection of the fiercest passions to the gentle influence of Buddhism, and also has an orb or cub under its foot, which have their own symbolic meaning. The earlier Chinese lions have neither harness, ball nor cub.

Tribute gifts
To be given a lion dog was a great honour, and the last tribute gift to the Chinese emperors was made in 1908 when the Dalai Lama visited the Empress Dowager some months before her death, bringing several dogs. According to Collier in Dogs of China and Japan in Nature and Art, these were seen by several foreigners who described them as being similar to the breed of lion dogs then in Peking, and known by authentic testimony to have existed there for at least 40 years previously. The journey from Lhasa to Peking would take eight to ten months by caravan.

Earlier gifts to Manchus
In 1644, Peking was captured by the Manchus, who had already embraced the Lamaist form of Buddhism. They conquered Tibet in 1645, and the Dalai Lama visited the Emperor of China in Peking in 1653. It was considered that the popularity of the 'lion-like' dogs at the court of the Manchu Emperors was due not only to their affection for animal curiosities but also because of the association with Buddha and his pet dog. The emperors, being regarded as the personification of the Sun and Sons of Heaven, were seen by the flatterers who surrounded them as symbols of Buddha. This comparison was encouraged by the Tibetan Lamas, and Chinese authorities maintain that they originated the dynastic name of Manchu, basing it on the Tibetan name Manjusri for Wen Shu (the Chinese Buddha), and hence calling the rulers the Man Chu Hsi Li Emperors.

The emperors were continually followed by their small pet dogs, who heralded their entrance by barking; this was the signal for all servants to avert their faces.

It is believed that the custom of sending these 'shock' dogs from Tibet originated in the early period of the Manchu Dynasty.

Early Chinese dogs
There are certain authenticated facts making it possible to follow to some extent the breeding of dogs in China which could possibly be the ancestors of our Shih Tzu.

From the time of Confucius, around 500 BC, there are records of 'small' and 'short-faced' dogs in China. In the British Museum, there is a skull of an early short-nosed dog which has the bones of the nose natural and unbroken; this seems to disprove the assertion that the Chinese broke the nose bones of young puppies with a chopstick to make them short.

There are clear records of small dogs being imported from Turkey, Persia and Russia, and one of the most interesting is given by both Collier in Dogs of China and Japan and Lauffer in Chinese Pottery of the Han Dynasty. It seems that in AD 624, a pair of small dogs were imported from Fu Lin in

Turkey, and right up to the 17th century, their descendants were referred to by the Chinese literati as dogs of Fu Lin. Their measurements are given as six (Chinese) inches high by one (Chinese) foot long, i.e. seven by 12 of our inches, according to Collier. It is said they were remarkable for their intelligence and understood how to drag a horse by the bridle and carry a torch in their mouths. These imported dogs outdid the Chinese dog in popularity; one of their colloquial names was 'ha pa' and another, according to Lauffer, was Shih Tzu Kou or 'lion dog'. 'Ha pa' was translated as 'pet' or 'lap' dog with short legs. Lauffer considered he could not authoritatively state how the dogs came to Turkey, but Collier writes that there are records to show the type was probably Maltese in origin, dogs from Malta having been imported to Turkey and become very popular there.

The 'pug' dogs of Shantung Province were also referred to as 'Turkish' and 'ha pa' dogs. In the description of the prefecture of Shan t'ien, the following passage occurs: 'The long haired among them are designated 'monkey-lion dogs' (nae — a long yellow-haired monkey). The people of the locality call it 'Shih nung-kou' (nao, nung, or nang — a fierce, shaggy-haired watchdog).'

Reference is also made to H Ramsay's Western Tibet, and Lauffer comments, 'It is interesting to note that the Chinese pug-dogs were introduced as far as Lhasa. In Tibet, they are called 'Lags K'ye' (hand dogs) because it is believed that if a human being lays hands upon a young eagle when freshly hatched, the bird is transformed into a dog of the Chinese pug breed.' As used here, the word 'pug' could have been a purely literary translation.

Another 'pug' is, however, recorded in a work of the Sung Dynasty; this is the Lo-chiang dog, which comes from the Ssuch'uan Province. In AD 990-94, they were sent in tribute to the Emperor, described as very small, intelligent, always tame and docile. They sat beside the Imperial couch, and at every audience, they were supposed to wag their tails and bark first so people would be properly respectful. A later work, written at the end of the 11th century, mentions one of these dogs as having a red colour. It is not clear to which 'pug dog' Ramsay refers when he says the Chinese pug was exported as far as Lhasa.

Chinese sleeve dogs
The height of the lap-dog cult was reached in the reign of Tao Kung (1821-51), at which time dwarf dogs were reared which had been cruelly stunted by artificial means. When large sleeves became fashionable, these dogs (of various breeds) took the added name of sleeve dog. Collier, writing in 1921, says this name was then unknown to dog fanciers in Peking, and the cult of dwarfing had not existed for the past 70 years. The Empress Dowager Tzu Hsi objected to the artificial dwarfing of such small dogs, which were always in the nature of freaks.

Restriction of food was apparently one of the methods adopted and another is said to have been the practice of enveloping small puppies in close-fitting wire cages, which were not removed until maturity.

Breeding
There were no written standards, but careful records were kept on scrolls and by means of pictures in the dog books. Emperors and empresses also had illustrations of their favourite dogs painted by the court artists, and in these ways, fashions were dictated to which the eunuchs would breed. The scroll among my illustrations portrays the three Chinese breeds together — the Pekingese, the Pug and the Shih Tzu; this is the rare type of Shih Tzu which was bred in China.

It is reported that eunuchs (numbering at least 1,000, once reputed to be as many as 4,000, and living in the 'Forty-eight places' in the Palace) would try to outdo each other in breeding the best specimens. At this period, the only dogs obtainable from the Palace were inferior specimens sold in the market, but dog breeding is known to have been practised in the homes of the people for hundreds of years.

Hon Mrs Bruce. Patron of The Shih Tzu Club with her Pug and Shih Tzu

According to Collier, a Chinese historian describing the Imperial menagerie in the time of Kublai Khan remarked that 'the lions (which were kept in the Palace and paraded for the Imperial guests) are of the same colour and astonishingly like the golden-coated nimble dogs which are commonly bred by the people in their homes'. Another reference made by a Chinese chronicler in the same period says 'there was a civilian named Shen Heng Chi who bred a 'Chin Ssu' (literally 'golden-silk') dog in his home. This dog was not more than a foot long, and was very intelligent. When guests were presented, the dog lay beneath the table.'

The Empress Dowager was said to supervise personally as many as 100 dogs. According to Miss Carl, who lived in the Chinese court for 10 months, one of her great favourites which followed her around was an animal of the long-coated variety which the Empress called Tibetan, but she was not successful in breeding this type. Miss Carl also mentions the Empress was particularly interested in symmetrical marking, and like her predecessor, encouraged the lion dog appearance to perpetuate the comparison between the emperors and Buddha. In Lhasa Lion Dog by Madame Lu Zee Yuen Nee, there are various references to the Shih Tzu being delicate and difficult to breed in the Palace, and also to their difficulty in whelping. We have not experienced this problem with our English stock; in fact, Lady Brownrigg was always most anxious to preserve the breed's ease of whelping.

According to Collier, the Tibetan lion dogs existing when he was in Peking were sometimes as diminutive as the common Pekingese, but usually somewhat larger. He adds that Chinese breeders distinguish two varieties, which is borne out by the Chinese scroll illustrated and in paintings. There is the ordinary shock-headed dog with hair standing out on the face and bridge of the nose, and then the extremely rare 'nae y' ou', of which the forehead only is shaggy, the lower parts of the face being short-haired; the Chinese lion dogs (Shih Tzu Kou) are longer-nosed than the flat-faced Pekingese. Collier also mentions that nowadays, the breed is sometimes crossed with Pekingese with a view to introducing length of coat into the latter. Many Chinese Pekes are portrayed in scrolls as having short body hair, and do not have the flat nose of our modern variety; also the mouth of the Shih Tzu is drawn wider than that of the Peke. I find it surprising that no reference is made to the 'rare Shih Tzu type' by foreigners in China during the 1920s and 1930s. They must have been very rare indeed — could they have become extinct?

The Chinese 'lion dog' is so called chiefly on account of the length and shagginess of coat. Many superstitions are held by the Chinese regarding colours and markings — fortunate markings could bring honour to a family, and every colour had its value. Some of the 32 superior marks of Buddha were encouraged in the dogs, such as:

4) 'Between the eyebrows a little ball shining like silver or snow' (the white top-knot).
12) 'The tongue large and long' (this was encouraged in the early Peke, and it was customary to pull continually on the tongue of a puppy to make it hang out, though this practice caused it to hang from the middle of the mouth instead of the side where it should have been).
13) 'The jaws those of the lion' (i.e. broad, as portrayed in their lions).
17) 'The skin having a tinge of gold colour' (yellow and gold-coated Shih Tzu were highly prized on this account).

Lady Brownrigg

The saddle marking was also prized, because of the connection with Buddha when he rode on the back of his transformed 'ha pa' dog. The Comtesse d'Anjou was considered to be an authority on the breed in China, although it has been implied she was only interested in tiny Shih Tzu, and that in the Imperial Palace no animals weighed more than 12lb. According to Mrs Audrey Fowler, 'In 1954, Count d'Anjou wrote out a standard of the breed for France, taken from the booklet by Madam Lu Zee Yuen Nee and approved by the French judge Monsieur Frick and Monsieur Chayet, who was a judge at dog shows in Peking and states he was a breeder of half a hundred Shih Tzu.' The Comtesse wrote a resume of this standard for the newspaper La Vie Canine Paris. Among other things, she says, 'Regarding the assertion of rumours circulated that the Tibetan Shih Tzu are a Peke cross, this is utterly false. They are a pure breed originating from Tibet and were presented to the Emperors of China two or three hundred years ago.' With reference to weight, she refers to a standard weight of 5-10 kilos (11lb 3oz-22lb 9oz), 'et meme un peu plus' (even a little more).

There are many other experts, including Dr Walter Young (quoted in This is the Shih Tzu) and Madame Lu Zee Yuen Nee (The Lhasa Lion Dog), who consider the Shih Tzu to have been a pure breed in Tibet. There is a Tibetan pastel drawing (1932) of an indisputable gold and white Shih Tzu owned by Mrs Olive Grindey, and also the reference of Lauffers (Ramsay) to 'dogs of the Chinese pug breed being exported as far as Lhasa', which could have accounted for the short nose.

It is, however, very likely that the longer nosed Apso was taken into India, which was no longer a strongly Buddhist country. The dogs seen there are mostly of that type and Sherpa Tensing owned about 30 at the time of the conquest of Everest. The shorter-nosed lion dogs were mainly sent to China, where this species was so highly valued.

Later Chinese

Following the death of the Empress Dowager Tzu Hsi in 1908, there was no one to supervise dog breeding in the Imperial Palace, for the puppet Emperor, Pu-Yi, was not interested in the Palace dogs. Many of them were given away by the eunuchs to important Chinese families and high-ranking foreign officials, while others were sold in the dog markets of Lung Fu Ssu and Hu Kuo Ssu, both old Lamaist temples. Dog breeding continued outside the Palace in both Chinese and foreign families; the lion dogs were jealously guarded and it was believed that the Chinese would go to great lengths to prevent live dogs and puppies from leaving the country. This was confirmed by Mrs Audrey Fowler; when she handed her puppies into the care of the ship's butcher (which was obligatory), she was told. 'Oh, they will only live a few days.' On asking why, she was told, 'The Chinese always give these puppies powdered glass just before they leave as they do not want them to leave the country.' You can imagine how relieved she was that her puppies had not been bought from a Chinese family!

Breeding within the Palace continued to a lesser degree, for there are records of Palace dogs being given away as late as 1928. According to Easton in This is the Shih Tzu, all but 50 of the 1,000 eunuchs were dismissed in 1923. Three dowagers were left, one of whom died soon after the dismissal of the eunuchs, while the other two were turned out in 1924, some days before the flight of the Emperor to Tientsin.

From my own experience of breeding, and realising the changes which can be accomplished in a very short time, it is hard to understand why — at a time of great unrest and disturbance — Palace stock should have been thought superior to dogs bred outside the Palace, where breeding had also been carried on for hundreds of years.

We know from many people in China in the Twenties and Thirties, and also from Soerby (Editor of the Chinese Chronicle, and a dog judge) that the Tibetan breeds were all grouped together under the following names:

> Tibetan Poodle
> Shih Tzu Kou (literal translation, Lion Dog)
> Lhasa terrier
> Apso
> Ha pa or ha-par'rh kou
> Lion Dogs

There was great confusion in distinguishing between the breeds, and this was eventually accomplished with the aid of the English Kennel Club, which had already divided the Tibetan breeds into their correct categories.

Sowerby told in the Chinese Chronicle of 1930 (Manchu News Letter) how he was a judge at the China Kennel Club show in Shanghai classifying 'the Lhasa Terrier or Tibetan Poodle'. It was no secret, he said, that he experienced considerable difficulty in deciding how to adjudicate, for there was no guiding information laid down concerning the breed. This is hardly surprising, for the breed would seem to have been wrongly named so far as the China Kennel Club was concerned. Mr Sowerby continuously urged that the breeds be clarified. In 1933, he described the difference between the Peke and the Apso by referring to the latter as having 'very long rather stiff outstanding hair (not a flat coat as in the Pekingese) all over the body, legs and face'. He goes on to say that crossing has been taking place, as some dogs coming from Peking and winning prizes had, on investigation, been the offspring of pure Pekingese bitches sired by so-called Tibetans. In 1934, the Peking Kennel Club was formed, and their standard was drawn up in 1938. According to Alan Roger (who knew her well), Madame de Breuil, a Russian refugee, was largely instrumental in drawing up the standard, and other owners involved included the Comtesse d'Anjou. The main points are given here:

Chinese Standard 1938

Long Ears: Heart-shaped (the longer the hair on the ears, the better). Long Apron and Pantaloons: (long hair difficult to find on hindlegs and all the more appreciated).
Size: 13-18 in.
Weight: 10-15 lb.
Height: 9-12 in.
Eyes: Large and clear (hair should fall over them and cover them completely if possible).
Toes: Well-feathered, paws broad and flat.
Front Legs: May be slightly bowed (controversy about this). Hindquarters: Slightly higher than the back.
Hair: As glossy as possible; apron and pantaloons wavy. Skull: Broad and flat.
Tail: Well-plumed, carried gaily over the back.
Colours: All colours permissible, single and mixed. Tawny or honey-coloured highly favoured.

Some eyewitness accounts of the Shih Tzu in Asia

Monsieur Graeffe (Belgian Minister at Teheran, Iran) and his wife had a number of Shih Tzu which they had brought from Peking, their previous post, between 1941 and 1945. These were seen by Alan Roger, and also by Mrs Sheila Bode, who later became an English breeder. Alan Roger remembers them as being brown and gold in colour, and it was acquaintance with these dogs that made him determined to own some himself when the war was over. Unfortunately, this strain died out, but they varied in size and were probably 14-20lb in weight. Strangely enough, within three days of his arrival in Hong Kong after its liberation from the Japanese in 1945, he saw a small bedraggled dog rush out of the sea towards him, and recognised it as a Shih Tzu. The colouring was grey, white and black. The dog's master said he knew of no others in Hong Kong, this one having been saved from the

Comtesse de'Anjou showing Shih Tzus in China. 1929

Japanese by a faithful house boy in Shanghai, and brought from there after the end of the war. After an interval of three years, a dog puppy was acquired out of parents from Peking; he was almost pure white with apricot ears. Soon after this, Alan Roger acquired a grey and white bitch from a Chinese who was returning to China (where pet dogs were not permitted by Communist authorities) and wanted to find a satisfactory home for his much-loved pet.

The parents of the dog puppy were brought to Hong Kong by Mr and Mrs Harman, the former having been Consul-General in Peking. It is believed the dogs retained by the Harmans went with them to the USA, and under the conditions prevailing at that time, were no doubt metamorphosed into Apsos! Dr Nesfield, who was medical officer for the Younghusband expedition in 1904, wrote to Mrs Fowler in February 1956 about the dog which was given to him by the Dalai Lama:

Venerable Ato Rinpoche with his wife and Shih Tzus.

'I cannot tell you how this dog originated. I know the breed is very old. I got mine in Lhasa in 1904 during the Younghusband expedition. She came back with me to India and died in Gemilet, Assam, in 1910 from fever. There is no dog I imagine more faithful and more affectionate. She would not go to anyone else. They are believed to bring good luck, hence the honour in receiving one. My dog came from the Dalai Lama, who at that time had fled from Lhasa. The thirteenth Dalai Lama gave these dogs as special gifts to the old Empress of China. That is why specimens are found in Peking. My dog is gold and white. The face was not like a Peke, i.e. stumpy.'

Mrs Fowler's interest in these dogs stems from Dr Nesfield, who was her family doctor in Sussex, and it was his account of them which made her determined to obtain one herself. While on a visit to friends in China during the winter of 1936-7, she tried in Hong Kong and Shanghai without success. However, she met the Comtesse d'Anjou in Peking, where she was fortunate in obtaining a gold and white bitch puppy and a little honey-coloured bitch from Miss Frances Beiber, who was a great authority on the myth of the sacred lion of Buddha. A saying of the Chinese is that the Shih Tzu is 'an honoured member of the family with its head on the pillow'. She describes the dogs in a show held at Peking in 1936 as being of average size and various colours, although the golden ones were the most highly prized. Another description, according to Gay Widdrington in The Shih Tzu Handbook, is written on a scroll depicting a parti-coloured Shih Tzu with the caption 'from Tibet and very rare, its character is that of a human being'.

I have related the facts I have been able to ascertain, although I am sure there must be many more untapped sources of information which will eventually come to light. We may all form our own opinions as to the origin of this little dog, but I hope I have made it quite clear that it has always been regarded as an honoured member of the family, and I feel that it is only by treating it in this way, with love and respect, that the true character of the breed will be retained.

Later confirmation that the Shih Tzu was bred in Tibet came to me through The Venerable Ato Rinpoche, who escaped from Tibet in 1956 during the Chinese invasion, he informed me his father owned and bred all the Tibetan dogs. Though the small ones were called 'Apso', they were distinctly different. The dogs were bred within the family, but occasionally, some were given as presents when visiting distant villages. They were kept as pets and guards, their job being to alert the big dogs, and were never friendly to strangers. They were all sizes but character was of greater importance than size, and they were highly intelligent. The tiny ones were never bred from as this had always been disastrous.

The strong reflection of the snow caused early 'blueing' of the eyes, which was worse if there were white patches round the eye or the white cornea showing in the eye. Pink rims were also bad as these gave weak eyes. The eyes were round but not prominent. The colours were mainly grey and white, there were some solid blacks, few black and whites, and gold and honey colours were all looked upon as Apsos. Jaws were undershot. The chests were broad and deep; there was no waist. The legs were not bowed, but were short and straight. The Tibetans did not like a rangy dog and so they had to be 'all in one piece with the head and tail held high'.

On caravan journeys, the Shih Tzu, being very special, was never permitted to walk, but was carried in the panniers on the backs of the mules.

CHAPTER TWO

THE SHIH TZU COMES TO EUROPE

Great Britain - Pre-War

Although specimens of the breed had occasionally been brought into this country in the early part of the century — and even exhibited — no breeding took place here until Miss Hutchins brought in one pair of her own dogs and another pair belonging to General and Mrs Douglas Brownrigg (later Sir Douglas and Lady Brownrigg).

In 1958, 30 years after the Brownriggs acquired their first Shih Tzu in China, Lady Brownrigg wrote an article on 'How it all began', in which she recounted the difficulty she had experienced in obtaining the good specimens she wanted. She saw many dogs which were too large and coarse, and these she was careful to avoid. Some resembled the Lhasa Terriers she had seen at championship shows, and she felt convinced that they were a separate breed; in this she was quite correct, although it was some years before this was generally recognised and accepted.

My Lord Of Tibet. imported to Lady Constance Butler in Ireland by the Kauffmanns

By the time Miss Hutchins and the Brownriggs met and became friendly, the former had already bought her dog, Lung Fu Ssu. It was seeing Miss Hutchins's dog which made Lady Brownrigg even more determined to possess her own.

The bitch Shu Ssa was the first to be found, and this is how Lady Brownrigg described her: 'She was white with a black patch on her side, root of tail and head. This (latter) had a white topknot or apple mark. Her hair was not as long as it became, but stuck up all round her face, and with her large eyes she looked like a fluffy baby owl or perhaps a chrysanthemum! She quickly enslaved us and was extremely clever!' The Shih Tzu is sometimes known as the 'Chrysanthemum' dog.

Two points which were always of particular importance to Lady Brownrigg were character and ease of whelping. She found her Shih Tzu even more intelligent and sporting than her standard poodle Ch. Polaire, who was gun-trained and a very good retriever.

A mate for Shu Ssa was subsequently found — Hibou, whose master (a French doctor) had returned home. Hibou was of a lighter build than either Shu Ssa or Miss Hutchins's Long Fu Ssu, was described as 'very active, a great character and sportsman'. Shu Ssa was exceptionally fond of swimming, but Hibou did not like water! Shu Ssa had her first litter by Hibou in China.

Mrs Hutchins returned to England in 1930, taking with her the Brownriggs' dog and bitch, her own Lung Fu Ssu and another bitch called Mei Mei. Unfortunately, Mei Mei was killed by a Sealyham after coming out of quarantine, but Shu Ssa's second litter was born while she was in quarantine. The Brownriggs returned to this country in 1931.

The weights of the early specimens were 12.1lb, 13.10lb and 14.9lb. This was the ideal weight and size range so far as Lady Brownrigg was concerned; she did see some very small animals, and was well aware that a different range existed in China, but said very small dogs were not used for breeding.

It was at about the same time that Colonel and Mrs Eric Bailey imported several dogs from the border of Tibet, calling them Apsos. The Brownrigg dogs were still called Tibetan Lion Dogs, the name most frequently used in China. When the Brownriggs went to see two of the Baileys' dogs, they 'found that apart from colour (they were brown

Dogs belonging to Madeline Hutchin's in Ireland

or golden and one black) they had narrower heads, longer noses and smaller eyes than our dogs'. However, the Shih Tzu were accepted into the ranks of the Apsos. The Apso and Lion Dog Club was later formed, and they were recognised by the Kennel Club. When first shown alongside the Apsos in 1933 at the West of England Ladies Kennel Society championship show, it was realised they were quite distinct breeds — in 1934, it was ruled by the Tibetan Breed Association that the Tibetan Lion Dogs which the Brownriggs had imported were in fact a separate breed.

In consultation with Mr Croxton-Smith, a prominent member of the Kennel Club at that time, it was decided to adopt the Chinese name for the breed, Shih Tzu, and in September 1934, the application to change the title of the Apso and Lion Dog Club to Shih Tzu (Tibetan Lion Dog) Club was granted. This was finally altered to the Shih Tzu Club the next year.

At this point, complete co-operation existed between Miss Hutchins and the Brownriggs over the breeding of the Shih Tzu in England. Minute details of every new puppy were supplied and each available litter was inspected; any pups which did not conform to the highest standards were either not registered or were sold as pets.

The club went from strength to strength, with General Brownrigg as treasurer and his wife as secretary, and registrations were increasing. The total up to the end of 1939 was 183, and there were

47 new registrations during that year. Two bitches were exported to the USA in 1938, to be re-registered there as Apsos. Amoy — by Yangtze out of Tsu Hsi — was exported to Mr Walter Ekman in Sweden in 1935 and lived to be 21. Mr Ekman subsequently became the Swedish Consul-General in Holland, and after the war, Lady Brownrigg visited the family and saw Amoy in good health.

There were other imports before the war, but unfortunately, most of these lines died out. Imports included:

Hitsui by Mrs R Bourke-Burrowes.

Taragul by Mrs B Manico-Gull.

Ping Erh by Mrs Hull.

Dol Ma (breeder Madame Wilden) by Hon J Hare and Hon J Fox-Strangeways. Although there were two litters here, the line died out.

My Lord of Tibet (breeder Mme Kauffmann) by Lady Constance Butler. Descendants could be in Ireland, as there were two litters ex Ah Tishoo of Way (Tumbler).

*Choo Choo half-brother to the above, imported to Queen Elizabeth. *Tashi of Chouette (breeder Mrs Morgan, Canada), by Lady Brownrigg and Miss Reoch; also two dogs, who died. The bitch Tashi went to Lord Essex.

Fu Tzu Niu San (breeder Comtesse d'Anjou) brought from China by Mrs Audrey Fowler in 1937, but left no progeny.

*Ming from China by Mrs Telfer-Smollett in 1939; also a dog and two of their puppies which died in quarantine.

*Lines which have been continued.

Minutes of the last committee meeting of Shih Tzu Club held at Olympia on 7th Oct 1937

Present:
> Miss Reoch (in the chair)
> Major General Brownrigg
> Lady Constance Butler
> Mrs Cowley
> Miss Crabbie
> Mrs Eaden
> Miss Hutchins
> Hon. John Fox-Strangways
> Mrs Moulton
> Mrs O'Connor

Apologies received from:
> The Countess of Essex (President) by telegram received just after the meeting.
> Miss Penrose Fitzgerald
> Hon. Mrs. Robert Bruce
> Mr Brocklehurst
> Mrs Monkland
> Mrs Woodward

Minutes of the last General Meeting:
Read approved and signed by the chairman

Treasurer's Statement of Accounts:
Read, showing a balance at Lloyds Bank, 6 Pall Mall, of £18.14.6. supported by the bank to this affect. Accounts passed.

It was agreed to support the following shows in 1938.

Crufts.
Cheltenham
L.K.A.
Richmond
Kennel Club
Taunton (two classes guaranteed by Mrs O'Connor) (Taunton was then Ch. venue.)

Following classes to be put on at Crufts:

Novice D or B
Undergraduate D or B (guaranteed by Miss Hutchins)
Open D (guaranteed by Mr Fox-Strangways)
Open B (guaranteed by Miss Reoch)

It was agreed to leave details of classes to be supported at other shows until a meeting was arranged to settle these points at Crufts. Judges

Proposed by Miss Reoch that Mr Crufts should be asked who are the ALL-ROUNDERS available.

Also that Mr Garrow should in any case be asked. Passed.

Advertising:
Proposed by General Brownrigg and seconded by Mr Fox-Strangways that the Club was too much in its infancy for any central arrangements to be made yet awhile for advertising. Passed.

Dog Papers:
Mrs Moulton urged members to take in Our Dogs and the Dog World, in which Shih Tzu notes written by her appeared most weeks. Mrs Brownrigg pointed out how much of her correspondence would be reduced if members would do this.

Other Business:
Cups offered:
1. By Lady Constance Butler, for best D or B of 15lb weight at Richmond
2. Mrs Eaden, for best puppy at L.K.A.
3. Mrs O'Connor, to be won three times but not by the same exhibit.

New Members:
Lady Langman.
The Countess of Ilchester
Mrs Moulton
(Signed) Mona Brownrigg (Hon. Secretary)

At the outbreak of war in September 1939, activities ceased, and there were no more imports until hostilities ended.

In 1939, Mee Na of Taishan was sold to Mrs Garforth Bless (later Mrs Widdrington). The bitch was of a larger size than was desired and slightly mismarked over one eye, but very sound and of good quality. Although she was large, it was always made clear that tiny or toy dogs were not desirable. Mee Na became the foundation bitch of the Lhakang Kennel, and after the war won several prizes at Championship shows.

Mee Na of Taishan

During the pre-war years, the Club sponsored classes at many championship shows, and dogs were extensively shown in 'any other variety' categories in Scotland and England. The breed always attracted a great deal of attention.

Lady Brownrigg sought out every import she heard about, and inspected and advised on as many puppies as was practicable. Details of whelping and puppies were sent to her and it is interesting that although no mention is made of difficult whelpings, there was a high mortality rate among puppies. It was doubtless careful culling (plus the loss of the weaker puppies because veterinary science was not so advanced) which kept the breed so strong, for there were no signs of weakness caused by inbreeding.

Enquiries came from all over the world. In China, matters were confused, for the breeds had not been distinguished and were judged together without any standard. It was not until after our standard had been drawn up in England that the Peking Kennel Club was formed in 1934, and standards were then drawn up for the various dogs.

In 1940, the breed was granted a separate register, having been registered under 'Any Other Variety' since 1932. It now became eligible for Challenge Certificates, but none were actually awarded until after the war.

During the war years, Lady Brownrigg was very busy with Red Cross work, and breeding practically ceased. Wool from the grooming of the dogs' coats was made into yarn, and used for knitting articles which were sold in aid of the Red Cross. Between 1940 and 1946, registrations dwindled to five, with a total of 51 during those years.

Great Britain - Post-War
After the war, Mrs Garforth Bless (Widdrington) helped Lady Brownrigg to get the Club back on its feet; they acted as treasurer and secretary respectively, and the future outlook for the breed was hopeful.

In 1945, the following letter was sent out by Mona Brownrigg to the members:

48 Thurloe Square London, S.W.7. July 1945

Dear Member,

I feel that the time has come when we should begin to think of future activities.

The war has torn such a gap in our lives that it is perhaps best to start quite fresh, rather than be bound by the decisions of the last General Meeting held at the Kennel Club in December 1938 -most of which decisions are obviously inoperative.

The Rules of the Club lay down that the annual subscription shall be ten shillings, payable to the Treasurer by 5th July every year. May I therefore ask members to send their subscription for 1945 to me or to my husband at the above address?

The Club Account shows a credit balance of £39.9.0. (£23.10.1. being the credit balance at Lloyds Bank, and the rest being cash in the hands of the Treasurer).

Lady Essex has consented to remain President of the Club and, although Miss Hutchins lives in Ireland, I have asked her to continue as Vice-President - seeing that she introduced the first Shih Tzu to England in 1930. I am glad to say she has agreed to remain. I myself am willing to continue as Secretary, and my husband is willing to remain as Treasurer.

I suggest therefore that we renew our activities with the following officers:-

> *President: The Countess of Essex*
> *Vice-President: Miss Madeline Hutchins*
> *Hon Secretary: Lady Brownrigg*
> *Hon. Treasurer: Lt General Sir Douglas Brownrigg.*

Members of the committee:-

> *Hon Mrs Bruce*
> *(Lt Colonel Brocklehurst*
> *(Mrs Eaden*
> *(Hon J Fox-Strangways*
> *(Mrs Hawkins (formerly Mrs Moulton)*
> *(Miss Reoch*

Will the above-named kindly signify their willingness to serve, when sending their subscriptions.

In conclusion may I remind you that, when the last General Meeting was held in December 1938, the Shih Tzu was only recognised by the Kennel Club under the heading 'Any Other Variety'. In May 1940, however, the Kennel Club officially recognised the Shih Tzu as a separate breed; and the breed now has championship status. Statistics about the Shih Tzus are to be found in the Kennel Gazette and in the dog papers.

Trusting that you will continue to support the Club and help the breed to a new lease of life.

> *I am,*
> *Yours sincerely,*
> *(signed Mona Brownrigg)*

GENERAL MEETING OF THE SHIH TZU CLUB TO BE HELD AT 15, THURLOE SQUARE, LONDON, S.W. ON 10TH. MARCH. 1947

1. To elect a Chairman of the Committee.
2. To read the Minutes of the last General Meeting, held in December, 1938.
3. To record with very deep regret the passing of the Hon. Treasurer, Lt.General Sir Douglas Brownrigg, and to express the greatest appreciation to his invaluable work for the Club.
4. To record with deep regret the passing of Mrs Hawkins (formerly known as Mrs Moulton) and to express the greatest appreciation of her help to the Club, as a member of the committee and as a correspondent to the dog papers.
5. To approve the appointment of Officers arranged provisionally by circular letter of July 1945, as follows:

   President   The Countess of Essex.
   Vice-President Miss Madeline Hutchins.
   Hon. Secretary Lady Brownrigg
   Members of the Committee
           Hon. Mrs Bruce.
           Lt.Col.Brocklehurst
           Mrs Eaden.
           Hon. J. Fox-Strangways
           Miss Reoch.
6. To appoint an Hon. Treasurer in the place of Sir Douglass Brownrigg. (it is proposed to suggest Mrs. Gabrielle Garforth-Bles, who has been acting as treasurer pro.tem.)
7. To appoint a successor to Mrs. Hawkins as a Member of the committee. (it is proposed to suggest Mrs. Cowley.)
8. To receive a statement of account to be submitted by the Hon. Treasurer from December, 1938 (the date of the last General Meeting) to date.
9. To appoint an Hon.Auditor of the accounts to hold office until further notice. (it is proposed to suggest Mr M. Garforth-Bles A.C.A.)
10. To receive nominations for, and elect, any new Members.
11. To discuss shows to be supported in 1947.
12. To choose Judges who would be asked to officiate.
13. To discuss the best means of advertising and popularising the Breed.
14. To discuss the possibility of importing new stock.
15. To record all names and addresses of Members, and to stress the importance of recording any change with the Hon. Secretary.
16. to remind Members to register all puppies with the Kennel Club, and any transfer of ownership of same.
17. To receive all unpaid subscriptions due on 5th July, 1946.
18. To accept any offers of cups or prizes for Shows.
19. To accept circulation of club rules and Standard Points of the Shih Tzu.
20. To read and amend (if necessary) the existing rules and, in particular to waive the requirements of Clause 4 as to election of the Committee for the year 1947/8 only.
21. Any other business.
22. To decide upon a date for the next Meeting of the Committee. 4th March. 1947.

At their next meeting, in London on March 20, the committee got down to business. The Hon Secretary was asked to obtain a list of Championship Shows being held during the ensuing year with a view to putting on a class for Shih Tzus at one or two of them. (The Metropolitan and Essex, and Kennel Club shows were suggested). It was also hoped that members would enter their dogs in as many Variety classes as possible.

The following judges were approved:- (in those days, the Clubs chose the judges and sent a list up to the Show Society who would usually put those judges on for them.)

Mrs Barber, Mr Beynon, Mrs Eaden, Mr Cowley, Mr Garrow, Capt T H Hudson, Miss Reoch, Mr Tom Scott and Mr Leo Wilson. This was a selection of both all-rounders and specialists.

They decided to advertise the breed in the Christmas number of Our Dogs and that the cost of this should come out of Club funds.

There was the welcomed news that Maj-Gen. Telfer-Smollett was importing two Shih Tzus from China.

Miss Reoch stressed the importance of getting new buyers to join the Club, and for all members to record any change of address with the Hon Secretary and to register all births or transfers of their dogs with the Kennel Club.
Donations for special Prizes were received.

You can tell how hard these pioneers of the breed worked to get it going again. General Telfer Smollett's imports arrived and others, as below.

Ishuh Tzu from China in 1948 by Major-General Telfer-Smollett.
Pjokken Dux from Norway in 1948 by Mrs Widdrington.
Jungfaltets Jung Ming from Sweden in 1959 by Mrs Longden.
Hsi Li Ya from China in 1952 by Mrs Dobson.
Wuffles imported from Tientsin in 1948 by the Fraser Buchanans and Mai-ting in 1949.

Mee Na with Yalu, Kosi and Kuchi
Photo:J W Foreman

The last two mentioned in this list had one litter, producing the bitch Piu Yaou. Wuffles was run over and killed. Mrs Widdrington gave Ku-chi (featured in the picture with Mee Na) to Mrs Morris of the Lunghaw Shih Tzus to replace him as a sire for her Mai-ting. A daughter from those two, Gun-Uiang of Lunghaw, was given to Mrs Widdrington, and she was able to incorporate this breeding into her main lines.

Shih Tzu at pre-war show, Olympia

In 1949, Ta Chi of Taishan was made the first Champion of the breed. She was black and white, and came through on the imported lines of Swedish Choo Choo and Canadian Tashi of Chouette as well as our original lines. She was a very fine specimen of the breed, and is even now considered to be the type to aim for by most of the knowledgeable breeders in this country

Lady Brownrigg remained Secretary of the Shih Tzu Club until 1954, when she became President, and was still taking a very active interest in the breed when she died in April 1969. The Hon Mrs Bruce, her childhood friend, remained our patron until her death. The latter obtained her Shih Tzu from the earliest litters, and was influential in encouraging the breed in Scotland. Her beautiful Sungari, by Hibou out of Shu Ssa, was a small bitch, and came from the first litter born out of quarantine.

The 1950s brought new breeders and many changes. The Antarctica kennel of Mr and Mrs K B Rawlings entered the Shih Tzu show ring in 1950 with Perky Ching of the Mynd; this kennel brought a vast improvement in coats and general show-ring presentation. In 1951, Miss E M Evans, of the Elfann kennel, who was a highly successful Peke breeder, acquired Fenling of Yram — later Elfann Fenling of Yram — bred by Mrs Haycock.

During this decade, top show honours in the breed went mainly to the three kennels of Taishan, Lhakang and Antarctica. However, there were also a great many other good dogs belonging to smaller kennels which were limited in their showing and therefore did not have so great a chance to make up champions.

The Taishan Kennel bred only one litter of importance in the 1950s. This was by Ch. Choo Ling out of Ch. Pa Ko of Taishan, and following a bad start with distemper, this litter produced three champions. One was English Ch. Wang Poo of Taishan, whose smaller brother Pei Ho won two CCs and two reserve CCs in England before being taken to Australia as foundation stock by his owners, Mr and Mrs Dobson. He became an Australian Champion. The third brother was exported to Italy, where he also became a champion. After this, Taishan faded out of the breeding programme, only having one more litter in 1962 in an effort to obtain a bitch from her own line for Lady Langman.

Champion Ta Chi of Taishan. 1949
Photo: Thomas Fall Ltd

Lady Langman, who had been a Lady In Waiting to the Queen, owned Fu of Taishan, the only bitch to have been mated to the Queen's Choo Choo, and she had written to Lady Brownrigg to say how attached she had been to 'Fu' and how she would dearly love another one. This spurred Lady Brownrigg, with my co-operation, into mating a daughter of Ch. Wang Poo of Taishan to my Snaefells Huckleberry Finn. The bitch was whelped at my home, where Lady Brownrigg stayed with me and had the dam in her room that night. Whelping certainly did not seem too far off but in the short time Lady Brownrigg was having her bath, two puppies were born so quietly that she was still unaware there were any until the third pup squeaked! There was one bitch in the litter of six which was similar to Fu of Taishan — named Fu Wang, she was earmarked for Lady Langman although not quite the pick of the litter. Lady Brownrigg delayed the puppy's departure for as long as possible, which in Lady Langman's case was unfortunately too long for, unhappily, she died just before Fu Wang was permitted to go to her. The remainder of the litter eventually went to old friends and families of early breeders, but I do not think any of them were used for breeding, so unfortunately the line has died out. Fu Wang was the biggest escapist we have ever known, and was named 'the devil dog'. When Lady Brownrigg died, she and her dam — the only ones left in the kennel — came to live with me, and even than at nearly 10 years of age, she was still a remarkable escapist!

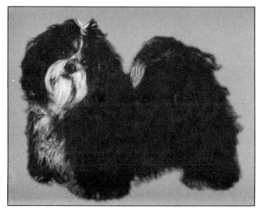

Wu Chen of Lhakang 8 months. 1953
Photo: C M Cooke

Maya Wong of Lhakang 8 months 1953
Photo: C M Cooke

There was a period in the 1950s which saw so much trouble and unhappiness within the Club and breed that I would gladly have left it unrecorded, but as this is a true history, I feel it must be set down.

The Peke Cross, 1952

Miss E M Evans, a Peke breeder of high repute and breeder of many champions, had come into the breed in 1951. She considered that certain faults were creeping in, and specified 'over-size, narrow heads, over-long noses and snipey muzzles, terrier legs with narrow fronts, loose jointedness, poor coats, small close-set eyes and bad carriage'. What a depressing picture this conjures up! There were some extremely fine specimens around at that time, according to show reports and pictures. However, Mrs Widdrington, who had imported Pjokken Dux from Norway (he died in quarantine), wrote that she considered the cross would bring in fewer faults than an imported Shih Tzu of unknown pedigree.

The crossing of the Shih Tzu to the Peke at that time would not necessarily have been a bad thing for the breed if the faults mentioned above really had become prominent, but this was disputed by many other breeders. The fact that this crossing was undertaken by a newcomer into the breed, however experienced, and without prior consultation with the Breed Club whose main object was to protect and improve standards, caused untold trouble for years to come. It was not until after the puppies of the first cross were born that a letter was written explaining the motives involved. Lady Brownrigg did not give her approval, although she did permit her Ch. Choo Ling to be used on the bitch of the first cross. We cannot tell whether this was to make the best of a bad situation, or whether she would have been in agreement with the cross had she been consulted beforehand.

PEKE CROSS PEDIGREE

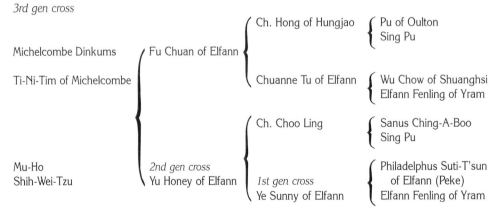

It cannot be sufficiently emphasised that nobody should ever undertake such a step again. The modern Peke does not resemble the original Chinese Peke, and there would in fact be more attributes to breed out than in. Present-day Pekes, with their exaggerated features and totally different build, complete lack of nose (set higher up than in the Shih Tzu), can do nothing but harm our healthy and active little Shih Tzu. We do not want dogs with noses which are too short, for this can cause many problems to health; neither do we want the noses set too high, for the hair of the Shih Tzu (which grows up on the nose) can cause eye trouble. We do not want the bowed legs; many of the early dogs did have this feature thrown through Shu Ssa, but it was being bred out. The Shih Tzu's elbow is ideally on a level or just above the brisket line, and the shoulders lie close to the rib cage. I appeal to all would-be 'experimenters' to leave the breed alone, and if you should feel that there is room for improvement, and outside blood needed, please first have consultation with the breed clubs.

The Peke chosen was a championship show-winning specimen, red/white parti-colour, selected because of his rather straight legs and level jaw, excellent dark pigment and large eyes. The dam was Elfann Fenling of Yram, a nice type of Shih Tzu bitch descended from two champions (Choo Ling and Shebo Tsemo of Lhakang). This cross was correctly registered with the Kennel Club. In each succeeding generation, one bitch puppy only was mated back to a Shih Tzu, until the third generation — still cross-breed — when six puppies were registered, four of which were bred from. The progeny of these matings were eligible for first-class registrations as pure Shih Tzu. The names of the third-generation crosses were:

Peke and Shih Tzu owned by Mrs Sheila Bode.

Ti-ni-Tim of Michelcombe (d) transferred to Mrs Widdrington in the north of England, who also had Michelcombe Pee-Kin-Pus (b). Elfann Shih Wei Tzu (b) transferred to Mrs Murray Kerr, a Scottish breeder. Mu Ho (d) transferred to Mrs Thelma Morgan in the Midlands. Michelcombe Fucia (b) and Michelcombe Dinkums (b) remained with Miss O I Nichols of Devon, who had the dam Yu Honey (cross-breed). From the above, the dogs Ti-ni-Tim and Mu Ho and the bitches Michelcombe Dinkums and Shih Wei Tzu were used for breeding.

Extensive breeding then went ahead, the animals being so well distributed throughout the country that in a few years it became difficult to find sufficient stock without this line to avoid inbreeding. Consequently, the majority of kennels soon had this line in their animals.

Cross or no cross, the dogs of 1973 — 20 years after the cross was first perpetrated — were much more uniform in size; the larger type which had earlier become too big was seldom seen in the show ring. In the main, the smaller size was not much below 12lb, of good solid type, and well-constructed. Both the Swedish and the Peke lines helped to reduce the overall size. The most difficult Peke feature to breed out was the over-bowed front. Now a further 20 years on, size is variable. Each year, the size of the new young stock is inclined to change. There is no doubt we do have more animals at the top end of the weight than at the lower end. I would hazard a guess that no 10lb animal has been shown and won. Whereas many which must weigh above 18lbs have won well, it is a fact that the larger animal usually stands a better chance for winning the group. Food for thought!

According to Burns and Fraser, the achondroplastic (short leg) gene — as in the Peke — affects heavy bone more than fine bone, making it more difficult to get a short-legged dog with straight legs if the bone is heavy than if it is light, '...heavy bone, being soft, bends more easily, and is also more liable to inherit rickets'. There has never been anything in the Shih Tzu standard to state that the bone should be heavy, only 'muscular with ample bone, and should look massive on account of the wealth of hair'. On the other hand, too fine a bone is not desirable either — it is quite possible to obtain a medium thickness.

After this upheaval over the Peke cross, another was to follow when the Lhakang Kennel began to specialise in breeding 'tinies'. At an Annual General Meeting, the interested parties won a majority vote to have the weight altered to 'up to 18lb, ideal weight 9-16lb. Coming after the schism of opinion over the Peke cross, this split the Club and breed in two.

The principal objection to breeding miniatures was that this would produce a toy breed and cause unnecessary suffering during whelping, whereas one of the main features of the breed had always been ease of whelping. Also, so many breeds have come near to ruin due to breeding down in size. Had some provision been made in the standard for a minimum weight of even 9lb — though 10lb was more likely to have been acceptable — all might even then have been well. Lady Brownrigg wrote to the Kennel Club, imploring them not to allow such a small size in the breed; the Kennel Club disallowed miniatures, but permitted 'tinies' and accepted the revised standard. Lady Brownrigg then asked if there could not be a division into two sizes, but this was refused on the grounds that numerically, the breed was too small. Provision was then made for the lower size range, and weight classes were then put on at shows to accommodate the smaller dogs; these classes were guaranteed by the Shih Tzu Club. However, in 1971, the standard was altered to impose a minimum limit: '10-18lb, ideal 10-16lb'.

Champion Pako of Taishan. 1954

In 1956, a private club was started by Mrs Longden to encourage the small size. Application was made to the Kennel Club for the right to have its own title, but since the aims of the club were 'to foster a small size', this was not granted. In 1962, on the intervention of Owen Grindey (later Chairman), the aims of the club were changed to 'to promote and protect the breed and preserve it on the right lines according to the Kennel Club standard of 1958'. The same official standard was also to be used. The Manchu Shih Tzu Club was now officially in being, with Mrs Widdrington as President, Mrs Bode as Secretary and Owen Grindey as Chairman.

This is all past history now, but nonetheless forms a vital part of the breed's progress and had to be recounted.

In 1958, Mrs Longden exported Fu Ling of Clystvale to Mrs Jungefeldt in Sweden, where he became a leading stud. In exchange, she sent Mrs Longden Jungfaltets Jung Ming. There will be more about this line in the chapter on lines and families later in the book.

The advent of the 1960s saw the breed going ahead well. Registrations rose from 540 in 1967 to 1,526 in 1970. Exports also increased from 113 in 1967 to 554 in 1970, the majority going to the United States. More than 100 animals were exported to Japan between 1967 and 1969; while we have every sympathy for the heartbreak experienced by the unsuspecting breeder when the conditions then existing were realised, no good breeder or dog lover can feel anything but contempt for those whose one motive was a quick cash return. It should be placed on record that few of these exporters were regular breeders of this enchanting dog, though some regrettably were. I regret that in 1993 there is much a similar situation over large exporting of all toys dogs to unknown homes in the East, where they are now in great demand. Much of this sad business is brought about by numerous 'puppy farms', who have no thought for the welfare of their animals and export them under very stressful conditions.

Ireland is well back in the picture and the quality of their dogs is improving all the time. Northern Ireland now has The Ulster Shih Tzu Club, and southern Ireland has had a club for many years. There is much more competition with the British dogs at their Irish shows, both in the north and south, and there are several Irish Champions in England. There are also Irish dogs which have been exported to Australia and become Australian champions.

Ch. Ling Fu of Antarctica. 1964 owned and bred by Mr and Mrs K.B. Rawlings

In the 1980s, the breed expanded alarmingly, with registrations reaching into the thousands each year. There are now six clubs, including the latest Northern Irish one, who co-operate well with each other. The Shih Tzu Club of Scotland was recognised in 1980, the Northern Counties Shih Tzu Club in 1981, the Shih Tzu Club of South Wales and Western Counties in 1984 and the Northern Irish Club in 1990. In 1985, the original and senior Shih Tzu Club celebrated its Golden Jubilee. The Manchu Society celebrated their Silver Jubilee in 1987.

With the great expansion in numbers and popularity in the breed, more dogs of varying quality are entered into the show scene to try their luck. There are many dogs of great quality, several of which frequently win groups and higher awards. Presentation of the dogs in the show ring is improved beyond recognition, and coats in minor puppy classes reach to the ground, sometimes to the detriment of their action, and possibly due to over-confinement. Many very good dogs have been exported to other countries and become Champions. Unfortunately, commercialisation and puppy farm breeding has crept in, which in its wake can bring in poor breeding, with dogs unfit for this purpose being used. This happens in all breeds. The future will tell whether we have made good use of our latest imports, which have been from Sweden, Finland, Norway ,Canada, Australia and the USA. Details are given in the next chapter.

Norway

Dogs were imported into Norway in 1932 by Henrik Kauffmann, than Danish Minister to China, and his wife. They were the brown female Leidza and white bitch Schander*, and black and white dog Aidze*. In 1933, Queen Maud of Norway brought one of the Kauffmanns' puppies to England for the Duchess of York (later Queen Elizabeth, now Queen Mother). Letters which passed between Madame Kauffmann and Lady Brownrigg in 1934 show exactly how the Kauffmanns obtained their dogs. When Madame Kauffmann knew the Shih Tzu had been accepted as a separate breed in England, and that a standard was being fixed; she wrote:

*These are the English Kennel Club's interpretations of the names Schauder and Aidzo.

Dear Mrs Brownrigg,

I was much interested in your letter and the photograph of your dogs. There is a light coloured dog in one of your pictures, I believe called Tai Tai – I wonder whether it is brown or white? – they all look so beautifully brushed. Tzu Hsi looks especially good, isn't she? I am also much in favour of getting a standard fixed for them – particularly because I believe one of mine to be among the very best of her kind either in China or in Europe.

We got our three in Peking. Our brown bitch, whom you see in the snapshot, was brought from an old palace eunuch and I know her to be from the palace stock. The black and white male, also begging, took me a year and a half to find, having seen dozens of dogs - because he is just as small as the brown one. For that reason I think he must come of good stock too, and had perhaps been stolen or given away - but I really know nothing about him.

Two years later we found the other little female, also black and white, having again had trouble about the size. I think she is not quite so good, being a bit higher from the ground, but not bad. She is in the background of the snow picture.

Madame Kauffmann continues by commenting on the number of people who have said the brown bitch is very good, saying she is adopting her as a criterion, and adds:

... so far none of her puppies have been quite her equal, unless a little black and white one I recently sent to London. I have just sent another one to England to Lady Constance Butler, which has a white spot on the nose. [This was My Lord of Tibet.]

I have a Chinese Amah with me here who has been much interested in the dogs always, and she has learned a lot about Chinese standards in regard to them and told it to me. I wonder whether you have ever met a Mrs Bailey who bought something like twelve dogs at Lung Fu Ssu within a few days and took them back to England to breed?

My Lord of Tibet, who was prominent at shows in 1936 and 1939, was used at stud to Ah Tishoo of Way (Tumbler). There was one smooth haired puppy in the litter. The line may have died out subsequently, or there may still be descendants in Ireland. My Lord of Tibet's sire was Law-Hu II, a son of Aidze and Schander. Incidentally, it is interesting here to note that Spratts' boarding charges in 1934 were 12/6d per week (62p)! The price of a good Shih Tzu specimen was £20, and the first prize at a championship show was £2, the same as in 1978! In 1939, Crufts paid £2.10s. as a 1st Prize. With boarding kennel fees now costing as much per day, illustrating the terrific rise in the cost of food, wages, etc, and entry fees to show now at £3, one wonders how they could have made a show pay in the past. (Since first drafting this chapter, championship fees have risen to £14 and there is now no prize money.)

Choo Choo, who was imported to the then Duchess of York, was a son of the original imported pair from China, Aidze and Schander. When the Duchess became Queen, she put Choo Choo into the care of her brother, the Hon David Bowes-Lyon, and in 1937, he was with Lady Strathmore. He was mated to Lady Langman's Fu of Taishan, and the ensuing litter was reared by Lady Langman at North Cadbury Court, Yeovil. Mrs Bowes-Lyon was most interested in Choo Choo's puppies and came to visit them; one went to Princess Margaret, although Princess Elizabeth spoke of him as hers. The bitch Li Ching Chao figures in all pedigrees.

At this time, the dogs were still registered in Norway as Lhasa Terrier, the name they had had in China, but in 1939, the Norsk Kennel Club wrote to Lady Brownrigg:

> *Some years ago, Mrs Kauffmann imported some dogs we here call Lhassa Terrier from China, where she had stayed some years. One of these dogs was brought by our Queen to the Duchess of York, now Queen Elizabeth. As we have some of these dogs left here, I would appreciate very much to know what you call these dogs in England.*
>
> *Could you be so kind as to forward to us the standard for Lhassa Terrier and the Shih Tzu?*

An important distinction regarding the Kauffmann imports appears to have been concerning the jaws. Where puppies were exported by Madame Kauffmann with 'slightly undershot jaws', she mentioned this as a fault. However, in a later letter dated 1937, she wrote 'I must write and explain that none of my dogs have receding lower jaws — what you call 'even' was what I called 'receding' because the lower teeth fit in behind the upper ones.'

In June 1936, Madame Kauffmann wrote that one of her dogs 'died in March, just before she was to have puppies. I think the poor thing had too many puppies, but it seem absolutely unpreventable. The only bitch I have left now is the honey-coloured one who is at least 10 years old, so I don't think she will have any more.'

It should be appreciated that notes were regularly compared between the Kauffmanns and the Brownriggs, Madame Kauffmann having a great respect for Lady Brownrigg's opinion. It was mainly through the latter's intervention that the breed ever became registered as Shih Tzu in Norway. Both had chosen their imports with the greatest care; Lady Brownrigg had not wanted the smaller Scandinavian dogs since according to her, the very tiny ones had not been bred from in the Imperial Palace in China. It was not until Madame Kauffmann returned from China that she became seriously interested in the breed.

CHAPTER THREE

THE STANDARD

The first standard of the breed was drawn up in 1935 by the Shih Tzu Club, under the guidance of General Sir Douglas and Lady Brownrigg and with the help of Mr Croxton Smith, an important member of the Kennel Club. It was approved by Miss Hutchins, who had imported her dogs at the same time as the Brownriggs. This standard was then approved by the Kennel Club as the breed's approved standard. The Kauffmanns in Norway, who had imported their dogs at about the same time as the Brownriggs, had been in correspondence with them and, having compared notes and photographs, were agreed about the main points.

The standard was then considered to be 'suitable for a beginning', the idea being that it should be fairly loose in concept to allow scope for improvement within the breed. At that time, there was a total of 43 registrations.

Although the breed had been in this country for 15 years and was much more firmly established, a severe setback had occurred during the war years. A new standard was drawn up in 1948:

Breed Standard 1948

Head: Broad, round, wide between the eyes; shock-headed with hair falling over the eyes; good beard and whiskers, the hair growing upwards on the nose giving a distinctly chrysanthemum-like effect.

Eyes: Large, dark and round. (By 1949, it was considered necessary to include 'but not prominent').

Muzzle: Square, short, but not wrinkled like a Pekingese, flat and hairy.

Ears: Large, and carried drooping, so heavily coated that they appear to blend with the hair of the neck.

Body: Body between withers and root of tail should be considerably longer than the height of withers, well ribbed up.

Legs: Short, straight and muscular, heavily coated, with feet big and hair between pads. (Notice the word 'straight', which was in the standard from the beginning, and was always aimed for. In 1953, the word 'straight' was deleted from the standard, since it was realised that the leg bones were not straight when compared with those, for example, of a terrier. As this alteration followed on the Peke cross, it is natural that people assumed it was removed to permit a bow which might have been introduced by the cross. Unfortunately, nothing replaced 'straight' to show the bow was not permitted, although it is an understood point. There were some bad fronts before the cross, but this was not considered to be correct, hence the insertion of 'straight' in the original standard.)

Tail: Heavily coated and curled well over back, set on high.

Coat: Long and dense but not curly; looks harsher than it feels to the touch.

Colours: All colours, but a white blaze on the forehead and a white tip to the tail are highly prized.

Size: About 11in at the withers, but considerable variation from this standard is permissible, provided other proportions are correct and true to type. (It was recognised by those who had seen the dogs in China that there was a great variation in size, and it was considered more important to get the dog firmly established and to conform to the standard than to throw out good specimens on grounds of size alone).

General Appearance: Not toys, very active, lively and alert, with a distinctly arrogant carriage.

There were a few minor subtle changes made to help get things more uniform and clearer. In 1950, it was expanded to include 'forequarter, hindquarters and feet'. It was said that feet should be big with hair between pads. The feet should look massive on account of the wealth of hair. Under Colour, allowances were made for liver — 'liver dogs with liver marking may have liver noses and lighter eyes'.

In 1953, there were considerable changes made:

Head and Skull: Head broad and round; wide between the eyes. Shock-headed with hair falling well over the eyes. Good beard and whiskers; the hair growing upwards on the nose and short, but not wrinkled like a Pekingese; flat and hairy. Nose black for preference and about one inch from tip to stop.

Forequarters: Straight was removed.

Body: Body between withers and root of tail should be longer than height at withers; well-coupled and sturdy; chest broad and deep, shoulder firm, back level.

Hindquarters: Legs short and muscular with ample bone. They should look straight when viewed from the rear. Thighs well-rounded and muscular. Legs should look massive on account of the wealth of hair.

Tail: Heavily plumed and curled well over back. Carried gaily, set on high.

Colour: All colours permissiable, but a white blaze on the forehead and a white top to the tail are highly prized. Dogs with liver markings may have dark liver noses and slightly lighter eyes. Pigmentation on muzzle as unbroken as possible.

Ideal Weight and Size: Weight between 14-19 lbs. Height at withers, not more than $10\frac{1}{2}$ inches. Type and breed characteristics of the greatest importance and on no account to be sacrificed to size alone.

Faults: Narrow heads, pig-jaws, snipeyness, pale pink noses and eye-rims, small or light eyes, legginess, sparse coats.

In 1958, the only change was in Weight and Size. Lowering the top weight to 18 lb and Ideal Weight to allow for small ones was altered to 9-16lb.

In some ways, breeding to type in the early pioneer days must have been easier, since the sole aim of those concerned was to improve the breed. This was watched over with a careful eye by Lady

Brownrigg who travelled around inspecting as many of the puppies as possible. If she could not see them, letters were sent, giving minute details. Whenever possible, puppies were placed with people who would breed or show, and faulty dogs were sold cheaply as pets. Sometimes points which are not nowadays regarded as faults were then considered undesirable, and however good the animal was otherwise, it would be sold as a pet. One example of this was to show the white cornea of the eye, which was referred to as a squint — it was not considered good to show any white. The latest KC standard has now introduced this.

The main objective was to keep the breed to the original size — a medium 12-14lb in weight. Lady Brownrigg had, after all, selected her dogs with considerable care, refusing to buy any larger or smaller ones offered to her.

Each fresh import has brought in good and bad traits, and each year sees different points change for better or worse. It is the breeder's responsibility to recognise this, and not to be 'kennel blind', for a dog is usually judged as a whole and not on individual points. In this way, a bad feature can very easily seep imperceptibly through a breed, carried by a prolific champion stud dog. The only way to prevent this happening is to know the standard thoroughly and to be able to recognise good and bad in one's own dogs — should you think your dog is perfect, remember it may be only in your eyes!

The unwritten part of a standard, or the implications behind it, are as important as the features actually written into it.

From 1958, the standard was as follows with just one small change in Weight and Size in 1980. In 1986, the Kennel Club reviewed all breed standards, changing them to a uniform pattern. The breed clubs were consulted and agreed together before the standard was submitted to the Kennel Club for final approval. This was accepted with one or two small changes by the Kennel Club, not all of which were fully approved by breeders.

Breed Standard 1958-1986
General Appearance: Very active, lively and alert, with a distinctly arrogant carriage. The Shih Tzu is neither a terrier not a toy dog.

Head and Skull: Head broad and round, wide between the eyes. Shock-headed with hair falling well over the eyes. Good beard and whiskers; the hair growing upwards on the nose gives a distinctly chrysanthemum-like effect. Muzzle square and short, but not wrinkled like a Pekingese; flat and hairy. Nose black for preference and about one inch from tip to stop.

Eyes: Large, dark and round but not prominent.
Ears: Large, with long leathers, and carried drooping. Set slightly below the crown of the skull; so heavily coated that they appear to blend with the hair of the neck.
Mouth. Level or slightly underhung.

Forequarters: Legs short and muscular with ample bone. The legs should look massive on account of the wealth of hair.
Body: Body between withers and root of tail should be longer than height at withers; well-coupled and sturdy; chest broad and deep, shoulders firm, back level.

Hindquarters: Legs short and muscular with ample bone. They should look straight when viewed from the rear. Thighs well-rounded and muscular. Legs should look massive on account of the wealth of hair.

Feet: Firm and well-padded. They should look big on account of the wealth of hair.

Tail: Heavily plumed, curled well over back; carried gaily, set on high. (Note: this was not intended as a pig tail.)

Coat: Long and dense, but not curly, with good undercoat.

Colour: All colours permissible, but a white blaze on the forehead and a white tip to the tail are highly prized. Dogs with liver markings have dark liver noses and slightly lighter eyes. Pigmentation on muzzle as unbroken as possible.

Weight and Size: Up to 18lb, ideal weight 9-16lb. Height at withers, not more than 10^1/$_2$in. Type and breed characteristics of the greatest importance and on no account to be sacrificed to size alone.

Faults: Narrow heads, pig jaws, snipeyness, pale-pink noses and eye-rims, small or light eyes, legginess, sparse coat.

Note: Male animals should have two apparently normal testicles fully descended into the scrotum.

Here follows today's standard, reproduced by kind permission of the Kennel Club:

Current Breed Standard   *(The Kennel Club ® March 1994)*

General Appearance: Sturdy, abundantly coated dog with distinctly arrogant carriage and chrysanthemum-like face.

Characteristics: Intelligent, active and alert.

Temperament: Friendly and independent.

Head and Skull: Head broad and round, wide between eyes. Shock-headed with hair falling well over the eyes. Good beard and whiskers; the hair growing upwards on the nose giving a distinctly chrysanthemum-like effect. Muzzle of ample width, square and short but not wrinkled; flat and hairy. Nose black but dark liver in liver or liver-marked dogs, and about one inch from tip to definite stop. Nose level or slightly tip-tilted. Top of nose leather should be on a line with or slightly below lower eye rim. Wide-open nostrils. Down-pointed nose highly undesirable, as are pinched nostrils. Pigmentation on muzzle as unbroken as possible.

Eyes: Large, dark, round, placed well apart but not prominent. Warm expression. In liver or liver-marked dogs, lighter eye colour is permissible. No white of eye showing.

Ears: Large, with long leathers, and carried drooping. Set slightly below the crown of the skull; so heavily coated that they appear to blend into the hair of the neck.

Mouth: Wide, slightly undershot or level. Lips level.

Neck: Well-proportioned, nicely arched. Sufficient length to carry head proudly.

Forequarters: Shoulders well laid back. Legs short and muscular with ample bone; as straight as possible. Consistent with broad chest being well let down.

Body: Longer between withers and root of tail than height of withers; well-coupled and sturdy; chest broad and deep, with shoulders firm and back level.

Hindquarters: Legs short and muscular with ample bone. Straight when viewed from the rear. Thighs well-rounded and muscular. Legs looking massive on account of wealth of hair.

Feet: Rounded, firm and well-padded, appearing big on account of wealth of hair.

Tail: Heavily plumed, carried gaily well over back. Set on high. Height approximately level with that of skull to give a balanced outline.

Gait/Movement: Arrogant, smooth-flowing, front legs reaching well-forward; strong rear action and showing full pad.

Coat: Long, dense, not curly, with good undercoat. Slight wave permitted. Strongly recommended that hair on head is tied up.

Colour: All colours permissible; white blaze on forehead and white tip to tail highly desirable in parti-colours.

Weight and Size: 10-18lb (4.5-8.1kg). Ideal weight 10-16lb (4.5-7.3kg). Height at withers not more than 10½ inches (26.7cm). Type and breed characteristics of the utmost importance and on no account to be sacrificed to size alone.

Faults: Any departure from the foregoing points should be considered a fault, and the seriousness with which the fault should be regarded should be in exact proportion to its degree.

Note: Male animals should have two apparently normal testicles fully descended into the scrotum.

Clarification of the standard

General Appearance and Characteristics: These two can be taken together. They are self-explanatory, for alertness should be seen in the show ring, and the Shih Tzu should be quick and ready to move. To see the conformation of the Shih Tzu can be deceptive because of its heavy coat. The standing position shows the outline and balance. Hands on the dog are needed to assess the width of chest, and thickness of the bone. It should not be so narrow in chest and fine of bone as a terrier, and not as dainty as a toy. It should be solid and heavy for its size. It needs to be seen on the move and should move arrogantly holding its head up and striding out in a lively fashion. However, this should not be confused with rushing or running the dog round the ring at speed; that is not a show of arrogance. Neither should it plod along in a sluggish manner — this frequently means that the legs are too short.

A dog which is only good when 'set up' is not of good intrinsic merit. It must also be assessed on the move; this is the test for its conformation. The standing position should be adopted naturally, and the animal should be capable of holding its tail in a 'pot handle' over its back. It should not be necessary to 'top and tail' Shih Tzus once they are out of puppy. This, unfortunately, is something which has been creeping into the handling of Shih Tzus in the show ring of latter years, and is to be deplored. It is up to the exhibitor to handle their dogs to their best advantage and so disguise their faults if possible. Where puppies are concerned, it is excusable to help to position them, for they are still learning, and many find the atmosphere of the ring unnerving.

Temperament: Friendly and Independent This at first may sound a trifle contradictory. The Shih Tzu is a very friendly dog, but not all respond in this way to those whom they do not know. In Tibet, it was used as a guard dog, and many still have that instinct. An arrogant Shih Tzu male will freqently show disdain for the judge by turning its head away, rather than showing its 'happy' expression when bags of sweets are rustled in front of its face, unless it happens to have been trained with bait. It is undoubtedly an independent little dog with a mind of its own.

Head and Skull: The size of the head should be in balance with the body, and — together with the neck — in balance with the tail, hence the saying 'you can't tell which end is which'.

A well-dressed head can do much to improve a dog's appearance and disguise its real size. Height and breadth can be altered with good furnishings, and the way in which the head has been dressed. The length of the nose and width between the eyes can appear different according to how the top-knot is tied. It is essential to examine the head closely from all angles, for a ring-side view or a photograph can be very deceptive. A good head is of the utmost importance, and should resemble neither the Apso nor the Pekingese. The chrysanthemum-like effect is seen best in the puppy around three months old.

The muzzle should be broad and square, as depicted in the Chinese 'lions', and definitely not a 'spoon' shape. The stop of the nose should start on a line with the lower eye rim. Nose length has to vary a little depending on the size of the dog, hence 'about' one inch from tip to stop. Too long a

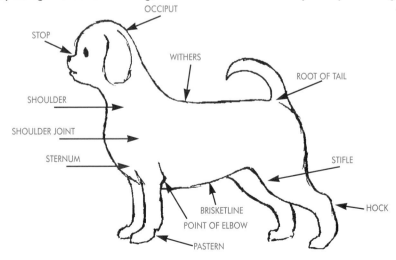

Figure 1: Body outline with anatomical points.

nose and too short a nose are equally undesirable, it can be level or slightly uptilted. A down-pointed nose is very bad as it gives a totally different expression to the face. Wide nostrils have been added, as tight nostrils will cause breathing difficulties. It is, however, not infrequent for puppies' nostrils to tighten during teething and widen later. It is preferable that the pigmentation on the muzzle is unbroked.

The standard makes it clear that liver-coloured dogs are permitted a liver-coloured nose. Some gold colours come on the same gene line as liver (other golds are the second colour to black) and, unfortunately, these have been known to have a lighter coloured nose. In winter, many golds have an off-

Figure 2: The Head.

The Shih Tzu. Correct head.

The Pekingese. For comparison. Flat skull, large prominent eyes, ears set high on skull.

The Lhasa Apso. For comparison. Narrower head, nose a little lower and longer.

Figure 3: The skull.

(a) correct skull; good stop; slightly uptilted nose; proportions approximately from nose to stop and stop to occiput as 1 is to 4 or 5.

(b) incorrect skull; nose long and turned downwards; stop too shallow.

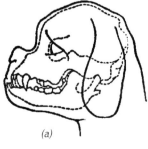

(a)

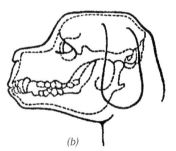

(b)

colour nose. Referred to as a 'winter nose', it occurs in many breeds and should not be penalised.

Eyes: The standard says 'large', but size must also be in proportion to the head. It also permits the lighter eye of the liver dogs, which is sensible as they are genetically unable to have a dark eye. It has always been recognised that 'white of the eye showing' is undesirable. It is now in the standard. Unfortunately, during the intervening years when it was taken out of the standard, it became strongly established in some lines. It should be pointed out that there are degrees of the amount of white showing. Sometimes, it is an unsightly ring all round the eye or it may be just a small amount in the corner of one eye in an otherwise good specimen. It is up to the judge to assess the degree of the fault. Also, many dogs will show the white of eye when they are anxious, or excited, both of which frequently occur in the show ring, particularly on the judging table.

A warm expression to the eye: This is the first time any expression of the eyes has been mentioned. Again, this is good. Some very large eyes are quite expressionless and blank. The Shih Tzu's eyes should be full of a soft, gentle expression.

Ears: The standard for the ears is self-explanatory. It is preferable to have a thick ear leather as this adds width to the head.

Muzzle: A little more has been added but it is still insufficient. There is nothing to encourage breeders to improve the teeth and bite; this is a weak point with many of our Shih Tzus. It does say that the mouth should be wide, which is important, and lips level. An up-tilted nose will frequently have a strong undershot jaw, but so long as the teeth are not showing and the lips are level, that will not be penalised, as it gives a more arrogant expression. A straight nose is more likely to be lacking in chin. A wry jaw is definitely a fault.

Teeth: These do not get a mentioned in the standard. There should be six incisors —the front teeth between the canines — in each jaw. Some dogs have only four, which I think is common to brachy-cephalic or short-faced dogs. Fewer than four incisors is definitely undesirable, and these animals should not be bred from as it could be hereditary; too few teeth will give a narrow jaw. Measurements of the head are about 4-1 of the nose length from the stop to the occiput of the skull. The head of the male is larger than that of the female, and should appear more masculine. The bitch has a defi-nitely feminine expression, and it is usually possible for a knowledgeable person to tell the difference between the sexes at a glance. Pastel-shaded dogs should not be referred to as 'bitchy' purely on grounds of colour.

Neck: This is a new introduction to the standard. We do not want a 'swan neck', but neither do we want a lack of neck, which is equally bad. I think the standard describes it well — 'sufficient length

Figure 4: Jaws.

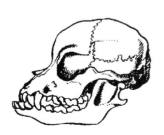
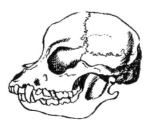

correct undershot or level.   *incorrect overshot.*   *correct square jaw.*

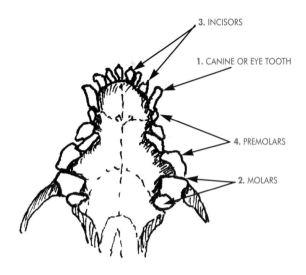

3. INCISORS

1. CANINE OR EYE TOOTH

4. PREMOLARS

2. MOLARS

Crowded upper jaw from inside the mouth.

to carry head proudly'.

Forequarters: Neck and forequarters need to be considered in conjunction with each other, for the neck, set-on of head and shoulder placement are each relative to the other. First, the dog needs to be standing correctly. It should not be strung up by a tight lead. The set-on of the head and placement of the scapula are most important. There have been many arguments over the length of neck; some people maintain that it should be short, and fear that a long neck will give a long back, but geneticists say this is not so and that although the bones of the thoracic and cervical vertebrae go together, the various parts of the spine have their own genes. In cases where both the cervical and thoracic bones are short, the front action is unlikely to be very free, and the dog will be either short in length or too long in loin.

For a 'well-laid-back shoulder', the neck and chest need to be of sufficient length; the muscles of the scapula (shoulder blade) are attached to both and when they are long, the attachments of the scapula pull them further back to give a well-laid-back shoulder. The attachment of the scapula muscles is also relative to the importance of the action, a good forequarter being essential for the correct front action.

To come to the leg, the standard says 'short', but the question is, how short? This is where the danger lies. It is common in breeding to exaggerate specified points when there is no maximum or minimum measurement. The good of the breed must always be considered from a health angle as well as 'show angle'. As the legs are shortened, so is the pelvic cavity, the space from above and below becomes narrower leaving less space for a large head to emerge. A leg which is too short will put the dog out of balance. Lady Brownrigg called these 'walking caterpillars'. Also, if its chest is extra wide, it cannot

walk with a free-striding front action. The Shih Tzu was never designed to have a 'Peke barrel chest' and ultra short legs. This is just the converse of a terrier front, and both are equally bad.

Figure 5

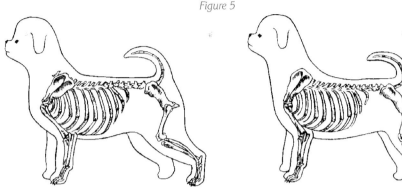

(a) showing correct lay back of shoulder.   *(b) incorrect upright shoulder blade.*

So far as balance is concerned, the dog should be longer from withers to root of tail than its height at the withers, not from the point of the shoulder as in the Apso. The elbows are ideally level with or very slightly above the brisket line, the elbow joint coming directly under the withers with the foot directly under that. The distance from elbow to withers is a little greater than that from elbow to ground. In fact, it should be possible to draw a perpendicular line from the withers to the foot. The scapula and upper and lower bones of the leg should be about equal in length. If the humerus is short, the action is sure to be affected, since the elbow will be too far forward; this will make the dog down in front unless accompanied by a too upright shoulder. The legs should appear massive on account of the wealth of hair, the bone being ample rather than massive. The legs should not be bowed. The feet should point straight ahead when in action, which they seldom do if there is any bowing, although this discrepancy is frequently concealed by the long coat coupled with 'stringing'* the dog.

Figure 6: Forequarters

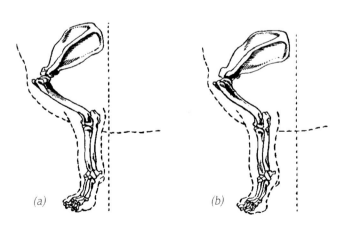

a) correct; line through withers to foot perpendicular.   *b) incorrect; humerus too short; elbow too far forward.*

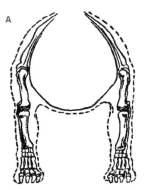

a) correct; elbow level with brisket; broad deep chest; legs with slight curve.

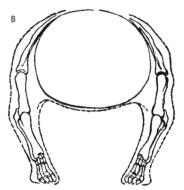

b) incorrect; barrel chest out at elbows, bowed front feet turned in.

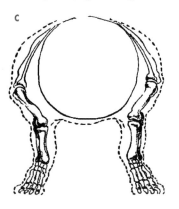

c) incorrect; 'Peke-type'; 'Queen Anne' legs; toes turned out.

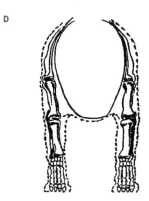

d) incorrect 'Terrier-type'; front too narrow; legs too straight.

*Walking the dog on a tightly drawn lead. In this way, extra support is given to the muscles of the forequarter.

The well let-down chest should not have its widest part at the elbows of the dog, for it is broad and deep. The elbow joint, if in the correct place, is below the widest part of the chest, unless the dog has a Peke barrel, in which case there is more likely to be bowing of the front legs.

Body: The length of the body from withers to the root of the tail should be greater than the height at the withers. The body should be short coupled, which is very different from being 'cobby' or short in length — how often does one hear the comment 'he is so nice and short', which is clearly not what is wanted? Short coupled means that the coupling — which is the distance between the last rib and the hindquarters - should be short; therefore to give the Shih Tzu its length the chest should be long. This point should not be exaggerated in a brood bitch, as she needs more length of loin to enable her to turn to lick herself during whelping. It is not desirable for a Shih Tzu to be too long cast, for this has been known to give rise to disc trouble. On the other hand, too short a back will not permit the typical action.

The chest should be broad and deep, not barrel as it is in some cases inaccurately described. Too much barrel will give the undesirable Pekingese front roll. The Shih Tzu rolls with its whole body when it rolls, this is usually to be seen when it is moving slowly. The body of the Shih Tzu does not have a waist, neither should it be 'tucked up' nor tapered behind. The underline should remain nearly parallel to the upper line. The body should be muscular rather than fat, and in hard condition; it should be possible to feel the ribs, but they should not feel too thin and bony.

Figure 7: Top Lines.

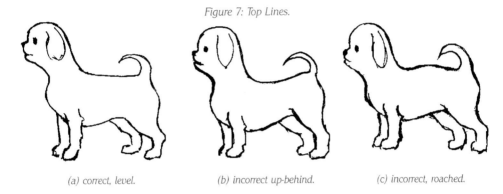

| (a) correct, level. | (b) incorrect up-behind. | (c) incorrect, roached. |

The top line should be level, which means there should be no roach, dipped in the middle, 'sway backed' (this is sometimes to be seen in very long dogs) nor up behind. The latter is frequently disguised by the tail or by the legs being stretched out too far behind when stationary conformation is being judged. There are varying degrees of being up behind, and, whereas this can occur to a very slight degree and may be a small point compared with others, when more pronounced it is usually accompanied by other faults such as straight stifle or incorrect ultra short forequarters. A growing 'teenage' puppy may well be up behind and then level out as an adult.

Hindquarters: It is important to have some bend of stifle, since too straight a stifle will give a stilted action and, as I said previously, cause the dog to be 'up behind'. The legs should appear straight and parallel from behind when standing, and feet should turn neither in nor out. There should be no 'cow hocks' or bowing.

Feet: Rounded has been added. It must be noted that with the longish hair on the feet, they do not always look round. It is not correct in this country to trim round the feet, just under between the pads. The pads should be thick and firm.

Tail: More emphasis has been placed on the height of the tail, which should give balance to the dog. The standard says it should be approximately level with the height of the skull. It is seldom so high that it is level with the height of the top of the skull, unless the dog is lacking in neck; one has to presume it means level with the base of the skull. The weight of the furnishings usually pull it lower, falling to the side of the dog. Many a six-month-old puppy's tail will be pointing straight up in the air — it should be well over by the time it is a year old, and should not require to be held down by its furnishing. However, that is something which the judge should be able to detect.

Figure 8: Hindquarters.

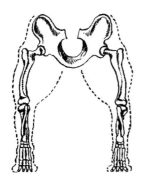 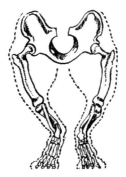 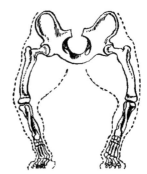

(a) correct legs straight.   (b) incorrect cowhocks.   (c) incorrect wide and bowed.

Sometimes, you see it being brought over and pushed flat on the back. This should not be — one does not judge on its length, except as how it affects the overall balance of the dog. It should be a 'teapot handle' tail, with just the tip touching the back or going slightly to one side. A tight tail is

Figure 9: Feet.

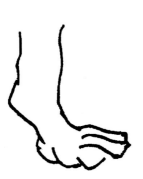  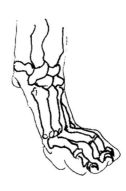

(a) incorrect slack pastern.   (b) correct pastern   (c) anatomy of the foot.

incorrect, and although this is a point which can be bred out easily, and is in no way detrimental to the well-being of the animal, it is nevertheless heavily penalised in the show ring when it spoils the balanced picture of the dog, which it usually does.

Gait/Movement: The ideal action should be free, the front leg stretching well forward. The legs should go straight, the feet turning neither in nor out. The latter should not be swung forward like a terrier, but neither should they throw them upwards, which can be due to being down on the pasterns or

figure 10: Tails.

a) correct; pot-handle tail   b) incorrect;   c) incorrect;   d) incorrect;
(over back hanging to one side.)   low set.   flat to back.   skew too tight.

short in the upper arm. The head is held arrogantly high, without the need to be 'strung up'. In the hind action, the legs should look straight, and be flung out behind with a strong thrusting action and a slight kick showing the whole pad. They should not be too wide apart, as the legs should converge on movement. The faster they move, the closer the legs, but never so close that they brush against or go in a straight line with each other.

A stilted action is quite incorrect; there should be no weaving, plaiting or padding, dragging of one leg or frequent hopping — the action must be clean and straight. A slight roll is permitted, owing to the broad, deep chest, and this can also occur when a dog walks too fast — for a split second, all four legs are off the ground and the animal comes down into a roll (this can best be seen in slow motion).

If the dog is not put together correctly, it will not walk correctly. Should the hindquarters be particularly good, and the forequarters only indifferent, he may not walk in the right way. In this case, it may

Figure II: Gait

(1) Good balance and elegance; correct centre of gravity, with correct heights of head and tail. Front and back are in unison. This gives the best effortless movement.

(2) Good all over balance, with correct head and tail. Front movement is too short but excellent behind with good thrust. This is the movement seen on most dogs.

(3) Lacks balance; tail too low set. Similar to 2 but not so good.

(4) Incorrect. Bad balance; set on of both head and tail incorrect; causing the head to push forward. The tail is too low set. The movement will not be good and will lack proudness.

be better if both ends were mediocre. Each bone, joint and muscle is related to the other, and synchronisation between front and rear is all important.

Coat: The texture of the coat is still not described in the standard, which is as well, for there are so many different textures with each colour it is even possible to find black-and-white hairs alternating on one strand, each of a different texture such that the difference can be felt as one passes it through the fingers. In the early days, it was considered to be 'harsh to the touch'. That is not always so now with the frequent bathing and preparations which are used on the show dog. A slight wave is permitted, but it must not be curly. Whereas the majority of our early dogs had a slight wave in their strong coats, now people seem to prefer them to be straight — it certainly helps to give more length. A long, flowing coat is to be desired, but overemphasis on the coat to exclude other points will be the downfall of the breed. A good undercoat as stated in the standard is important, though some colours never have carried a very thick undercoat. An extra thick woolly undercoat just makes hard work of grooming, which frequently means the dog gets its coat cut off when not shown. This applies to both breeders and pet owners.

Colour: All colours are permissible The solid gold dog usually has a black mask and ear fringes. The range of colour particularly in the gold shades adds much glamour. Too pale a gold can be insipid.

Figure: 12 Relationship of coat to dog underneath.

It is a lovely sight to see a large class of beautifully coated Shih Tzus of varying colours; one colour setting the other off. There are pastel shades intermingled with the beautiful black and whites, the greys and the silvers, and the few solid blacks. They look their best outside on the grass, especially if the sun is shining. Justice is not done to the colour at some indoor shows with yellow lighting and asphalt or yellow flooring. It is a bonus if you have 'even' face marking, though uneven colourings round the muzzle seldom deflects from the good looks of the dog, and is not a fault. However, unevenness right round the eyes, is definitely bad, particularly as in some cases where there is white fur round one eye. You are liable to get pink pigmentation, which is most unsightly, and should never be considered as a show specimen.

Weight and Size: There is no change here. There has always been a considerable variation in the size of the Shih Tzu, and this has been accepted, although some countries have their preferences, particularly when listed in the 'toy group'. The Shih Tzu should be heavy for its size, and weight comparisons are not therefore very significant. According to many authorities, there were both small and large dogs in China and Tibet. All sizes within the standard of 10-18lb and up to 10 $\frac{1}{2}$ in in height are permissible. It is more difficult to breed a good small dog than a good large specimen, since proportions must be more exact when the size is small. Also, a small dog must be quite solid and not just the smallest dog in a litter.

There is a demand for all sizes. It should always be remembered that weight and size are relative to each other, and that the standard lays down that 'type and breed characteristics are of the greatest importance and on no account to be sacrificed to size alone'. In my opinion, it is high time this was removed, as with the large entries we have, there should be sufficient good ones to choose from within the standard.

Faults: This has been changed. Actual faults have been listed in the appropriate place in the standard. It is left to the judges' discretion to penalise according to the degree of the fault and the quality of the dog as a whole.

It should be appreciated that a standard is only a guideline, since no dogs are absolutely perfect, and interpretation of a standard always varies. It would be quite impossible to include minute details and expect nature to conform. Therefore, there will always be some variety of type, and of course, people also vary considerably in their preference for one feature or another. This is why individual strains differ, so it is sensible to decide on what one considers to be ideal within the standard and to breed to this. It is well-known that some people are liable to interpret a standard to the likeness of the breed of dogs they have previously owned, and while I do not feel this can really apply where breeds are totally different, it can happen when similar breeds are involved, and is very much to be deprecated. Another failing is to identify perfection with one's first and often best-loved Shih Tzu, blinding oneself to its faults and — rightly or wrongly — breeding to this type. This is kennel blindness.

CHAPTER FOUR

KENNELS AND DOGS

The future of our breed does not only rely on the dogs and bitches of the present generation, so some understanding of the science of genetics is essential to a breeder. There are many good books written on the subject and it is to your advantage, and certainly the dogs', if you at least learn a smattering of the subject.

Much depends on the dogs of the past, not just the present generation, though it is the first four generations which are the most influential. However, those animals received their genes from their antecedents, and although breeders may try to improve certain points and lose the bad ones, they cannot tell what genes all animals carry, particularly the recessives.

Breeding would be a lot easier if dominant and recessive genes fell into neat little compartments, so you could be sure which was which. They hardly do, and often combine with others to complicate the situation. The recessives have a way of rearing their ugly heads just when you think you are going to have a perfect litter. They hide away for umpteen generations and you are often unaware that they are there. These are usually the bad points, such as 'blue eyes', the things which you do not want. Sometimes it is very difficult to tell whether a gene is dominant or recessive. The recessive genes do not appear unless they are in both animals, and then not all in the litter may have them. When aware that an undesirable gene is carried by our animal, many of us are careful to try to breed to others we hope do not carry it. This is where knowledge of past dogs comes in, and the older breeder and well-established kennel has this advantage.

Mrs Fowler of Chasmu was one of the earliest breeders, establishing her kennel in 1938. Having no progeny from her early gold and white specimens imported from China, she was determined to establish a gold line. Since this was the first attempt at any specific colour breeding, I feel it is of historical interest to give an account.

The foundation dog was gold/white Sui Yan — a grandson of the Queen's imported Scandinavian Choo Choo, who, although registered as black/white, did have some brown on him in the early days. Sui Yan was bred to the chocolate and white bitch Madam Ko of Taishan (grand-daughter of the brown/white Canadian imported Tashi of Chouette), and the ensuing litter included two bitches — black/white Ta Chi of Taishan (later the first champion of the breed) and gold/white Yi, who became the foundation bitch of the Chasmu strain. Yi was mated to Ch. Choo Ling, the only offspring being a white and brindle bitch called Om Mani Pudni. Being bred back to her white/gold grandsire, Sui Yan, she produced many solid honey and honey/white colours with good black pigmentation, among which was the dog Ki Ming. Om Mani Pudni was then mated to the black Shebo Schunde of Hungjao, of the solid-coloured Ishuh Tzu line. There were some honey-coloured specimens, but in those where the gold had darkened, it also blended with the black. Most of the puppies were a sold dark gold/brindle, and one was a solid black (Kepong). In 1954, one of this litter, a white/honey bitch called Golden Salween, was mated to her half-brother, Ki Ming, and produced the desired beautiful clear gold in the dog Tasmin, who on being mated to an equally clear gold bitch, Lhakang Mimosa of Northallerton, established this colour. The breeding is sufficient to show that this gold is a recessive colour.

General colour breeding will take some clarification, for every new line has brought in a different colour, and fading genes to add to the range. I rather hope colouring will never be too rigidly classified, since it is the diversity of colour changes which makes the Shih Tzu so beautiful and interesting. However, it is true that colour is becoming an increasingly important factor as competition in the show ring becomes stiffer.

Do not underestimate the excellent quality of our dogs and showing in earlier days. When I look back at my old catalogues, I see a long list of formidable breeders and their dogs. Many of these really good breeders still participate today, but have had to cut down on their dogs and breeding. This was inevitable, but a pity, for they had so much to give to the breed.

It was no mean competition in those days. To win above these breeders gave great satisfaction. After the fading out of the Taishan kennel of Lady Brownrigg and the Lhakang kennel of Mrs Widdrington, who became less interested in showing, the Antarctica kennel of Mr and Mrs Rawlings took over as top breeders. They would bring five, six, and sometimes nine dogs with them, always showing two champions of each sex. At that time, there was other very strong competition. Ch. Ellingham Kala Nag (born 1959) was a top winner owned by Mrs Jean Lovely. Then came the kennel of Cathay, owned by Mrs Grindey. This kennel must have been the biggest challenger to the Antarctica kennel, having made up the first solid black champion — Ah Hsueh Li-Chan of Cathay.

Mr and Mrs Leadbitter of the Greenmoss kennel then entered the scene, with many of their first dogs from Miss Freda Evans. This kennel did a lot of exporting and the Greenmoss prefix is well-known throughout the world. Their best-known dogs must have been Ch. Greenmoss Chin Ki of Meo (silver and white) and Ch. Greenmoss Glory Bee (solid gold).

Other good kennels soon became interested. There was Whitethroats of Mrs Eunice Fox, who died so tragically of breast cancer at a relatively young age. Her first champion was from the Lhakang kennel — Jen Ki Ko of Lhakang — and many more followed his footsteps. Her last dog, Whitethroats Jarvis, unused and unseen in this country, was exported to Sweden, where he has made his mark. His lines have been returned in our latest imports.

Other top kennels include Keytor of Mrs E.M and Miss Susan Johnson, who made many champions, and the Richardsons' kennel of Bellakerne, which made its debut with Patsy Do of Hyning as their foundation bitch. There was also the Crossleys' Santosha kennel and the Crowvalley kennel of Les Williams and his wife Stephanie, who also died tragically of cancer at a young age. The Lansu kennel of Tom and Sylvia Hoyle exported dogs to Sweden, where they were used extensively at stud. One was Kurts Boy of Lansu, the top stud of all breeds in Scandinavia for 1978, '79 and '80. With Tom's death, the kennel ceased much of its breeding, but a pair were sent from Sylvia's (now Rawlings) last litter in 1990.

The Scottish kennels were coming back into the picture with Jim Peat of Kareth, Vickie and Jim Grugan of Jhardu, Tom and Freda Harvie of Lharings (though sadly Tom died and Freda kept the kennel going), and Andersons of Tatsanna all pushing ahead with winning dogs.

There are many other good kennels who bred excellent dogs, but if I mention them all, it would take up the whole book. I must give details of our earliest dogs as I was told about them by Lady Brownrigg, who, as a very honest breeder, not only criticised other people's dogs in sometimes a slightly hurtful and straightforward manner, but was equally harsh on her own.

Shu Ssa (b). Imported 1930. Weight 12lb 2oz. white and black, predominantly white. She was smallest of the three, rather more 'Pekey' in type. Her tail was rather too tight over her back, and in her photos she looked up-behind and rather straight in stifle. She had good dark eyes and good square jaw.

Hibou (d). Imported 1930. Weight 13lb 10oz. Black and white. Predominantly black. The predominant colour was always said or written as the first colour. He was lighter in bone and higher on the leg than Shu Ssa. He had a very good tail carried well over his back, a good large head and broad jaw.

Lung Fu Ssu (d). Imported 1930. Black and white, weight 14lb 9oz. A coarser coat which was inclined to be wavy. A good head and his tail was long, but on the looser side. His coat must have been very thick for he looks bigger than his weight.

From the description of our first imports, you should note that large good heads, broad jaws and well-held tails were very important to Lady Brownrigg. The dogs were referred to as 'coming and going, head and tail' dogs, for you could not tell which end was which. This is something she instilled into other breeders, so it is still of great importance to the look of our English dogs. We do not like tiny heads, particularly on males, nor do we like flat tails, something many foreigners do not understand. You should note other differences in coat texture, height of leg and thickness of bone; we still get these differences within the breed.

Choo Choo (d). Imported in 1933 to The Duchess of York (our present Queen mother) from the Kauffmans in Norway. Black and white, but when young had brown colouring, as well. His parents were smaller than he; he had too long a nose (a correct length nose was a most important point with Lady Brownrigg). He also had an overshot jaw, something permitted in the earlier Scandinavian dogs.

Tashi of Chouette (b). Imported 1939 from Canada. A small white and brown bitch, she brought in the chocolate colouring.

This was the small pool of dogs they had to breed from before the war, with only one bitch until 1939, but some very good and sound dogs were produced. There were no more imports until:

Ishuh Tzu (b) in 1948. She was a dark solid colour; the blacks came through on this line, also solid clear golds. This line was the first to bring in the solid colouring.

Hsi-Li-Ya (b). Imported 1952 from China. According to Mrs Widdrington, she brought in a pretty pale gold and white which seemed less recessive than the red-gold and could be brought out by breeding to pastel grey. Nostrils were inclined to be getting tight in the breed and Hsi-Li-Ya helped to improve this important point. Pigment, which was frequently not fully filled in, was also improved.

Jungfaltets Jung Ming (d). Imported 1959 by Mrs Longden, who, in exchange, exported a dog to Sweden. He was black and white with an excellent coat, exceptionally sweet intelligence and gentle temperament. Very good pigmentation, dark eyes and wide nostrils. He had a good, level back and true action. Many of our dogs were oversized at that time so the introduction of a smaller size did no harm, and our dog's teeth and bite certainly needed improving as they were frequently too undershot and crooked, but we did not want a lack of chin and scissor bite. He was mated to Elfann Tara of Clystvale, but only two dog puppies survived. One was Chi Ma Che of Antarctica who became a champion. He was quite a large black and white dog, and sired large-ish puppies of good quality. The other was Snaefells Huckleberry Finn, who was much a smaller and lighter build, but also black and white. He had excellent puppies of a smaller size.

As with so many imports, the line was condemned by many people for the faults it could bring in. These were a smaller size, lighter bone and higher leg, a scissor bite and a tight tail. With careful breeding, these points were not bred in, whereas his many virtues improved the stock. Some of his Champion son's (Ch. Chi Ma Che of Antarctica) puppies had a thinness of hair on their legs until their second coat came in. Che Ma Che sired two Champions — Ch. Chan Shih of Darite and Ch. Kuang Kuang of Antarctica. The line followed through to Ch. Dominic of Telota and Chs. Chesake and Che Ko of Antarctica. Snaefells Huckleberry Finn gave me much that I wanted in my line. He sired Ch. Dott of Gorseycop and is grandsire to my Ch. Newroots Nankipoo of Snaefell and many other excellent animals. He was also used in the Lhakang line of Mrs Widdrington with advantage.

This was a few years after the Peke cross and those dogs were now recognised as pure bred, but the Peke front needed watching and I found that this Swedish line was an excellent in counteracting this.

The Lunghwa line: A daughter, Piu Yaou, of the two imports, Wuffles and Mai-ting (imported in 1948 and 1949), was mated to Ku-chi of Lhakang, and was not incorporated into the main line of English stock until 1962, through a black and white bitch — Gun-yiang of Lunghwa — a grand-daughter of the original pair. This line brought in a dense, lasting black and white with occasional fawn shades from Wuffles. Puppies were often born with complete pigment. This is a sound and intelligent line with plenty of natural instinct, but length of nose had to be watched in early generations.

51

Sw. and Fin Ch. Kurts Boy of Lansu. Exported to the Anibes kennel in Sweden by Mr and Mrs Tom Hoyle. Became top stud all breeds in Scandinavia 1978, '79 and '80.

Liliencrons Lady Kaskada (b) and her half-brother, **Shin-Moon Opus One**, were imported by Mrs Willis in 1973. They had one litter before being re-exported. A dog in the litter was Springett Opus Minor, whose line continues. A bitch in the litter was Lady Fayre of Novaskaya. She had two litters when owned by Mrs Joyce Ellis, the first to my Ch. Buttons of Snaefell, who came through on the earlier imported Swedish line, and the second to Ch. Spring Bandit of Fernell. The little bitch was very heavily in whelp and required a ceasarean, when she died. Her large litter was hand-reared and one dog became a champion — Ch. Fernell Mista Magic. Both these lines continue.

There were no further imports until 1983, which I feel was another landmark in our history. So I will try to bring you up to date with some of the more influential earlier dogs.

Chen Fei (b). Born in 1938, she was bred by the Earl of Essex, and owned by (then) Mrs Brownrigg. She distinguished herself by going best of all breeds at a wartime City and Suburban show. She was a daughter of the imported Tashi of Chouette, and sired by Jung Lo, a son of the original imports Lung Fu Ssu (ex Shu Ssa). Tashi, as mentioned earlier, was imported by Lady Brownrigg and Miss Reoch, and later went to Lord Essex. Chen Fei was the granddam of Ch. Ta Chi of Taishan. Black and white herself, she carried the chocolate colouring.

Ch. Yu Mo Chuang of Boydon was the son of the bitch Hsuah Li Chan of Taishan (born 1937), who was mated back to her father Yantsi of Taishan and who sired four champions in one litter to the bitch Ch. Mao Mao of Lhakang, and another — Ch.Pako of Taishan — when mated to Ch. Sing Tzu of Shebo.

Ch. Shebo Tsemo of Lhakang (d). Born in 1948, he was by Pu of Oulton out of Lindi Lu of Lhakang, bred by Mrs Widdrington and owned by Mrs Sheila Bode. His early colour was red/brindle/white, later changing to grey/white. For some years, he stayed with the Antarctica kennels of Mr and Mrs Rawlings, where his strong

The latest two from Sylvia Rawlings (nee Hoyle's) last litter 1990.

Ch. Pan Wao Chen of Antarctica winning Best In Show at WELKS 1963, with owner Betty Rawling (l) and judge Judy de Casenbroot in the foreground.   Photo: C M Cooke & Sons

influence was shown particularly on the male side. Tsemo produced two champions, the bitch Ch. Shu-Ssa of Michelcombe out of Chuanne Tu of Elfann, and a dog, Ch. Yi Ting Mo of Antarctica, when mated to the bitch Tang of Oulton.

Ch. Yi Ting Mo headed a long line of champions for the Antarctica kennel, giving us his grandson Ch. Pan Wao Chen of Antarctica who made history in the breed by going Best in Show at W.E.L.K.S. in 1963. His great-grandson Ch. Fleeting Yu Sing, great-great grandson Ch. Ya Tung of Antarctica and great-great-great-grandson Ch. Kuire Hermes, the top-winning CC winner of his time, then followed. He was bred by Mrs Josephine Johnson, coming through on the Telota line of Mrs Newson as a grandson of Ch. Domese of Telota. The first three champions of my own breeding also come through on Tsemo's line, namely Ch. Sindi Lu of Antarctica, who was a grand-daughter. Ch. Li Ching Ku of Snaefell and Ch. Su Si of Snaefell, a grandson and grand-daughter respectively. Another Australian Ch., Hia Nan of Snaefell, is also a grand-daughter. From this male Champion Antarctica line, there is also Ch. Philwen Mi Boi of Antarctica and the bitches Ch. Sou Shang of Antarctica and Ch. Bowstones Crowvalley Shan Tang.

Wen Shu of Lhakang (d). Bred by Mrs Widdrington, and the first influential dog from the Peke-cross line, he was the fourth generation and the first to be given a first-class registration. He sired Ch. Choo Choo of Cathay and Ch. Shebo Wen Yin of Lhakang, and was instrumental in improving the quality of many of his progeny.

Choo Choo and Ten Sing of Telota. Remarkably good stock has come through these two quite small dogs, both owned by Mrs Newson and bred by Miss Gill and Mrs Newson respectively. Choo Choo's sire was Lundhouse Pong and the dam was Coral of Airlea. Ten Sing was sired by Tackla Sahib of Lhakang from the dam Chin Shih of Elfann. Ch.Greenmoss Chin-Ki of Meo is a grandson of Choo Choo, and another well-known name is Ch. Tensing of Shanretta, a grandson of Ten Sing of Telota.

Ch. Domese of Telota: Born 1963, a black and white. She always put her stamp on her puppies and should be given credit for starting a line of her own! She produced Ch. Dominic

Ch. Ya Tung of Antarctica. Owned and bred by Mr and Mrs K.B. Rawlings.   Photo: Sally Anne Thompson

of Telota and Ch. Don Juan of Telota, also two Irish Champions, and the leading Canadian Champion in 1972 — Ch. Choo Lang of Telota. Ch. Kuire Hermes of Antarctica is a grandson of Ch. Domese.

Ch. Dominic of Telota: Born in 1968; was dark grey and white. He was bred and owned by Mrs Olive Newson; a son of aforementioned Champions Antarctica Chan Shih of Darite (a grandson from the Swedish import Jungfaltets Jung Ming) and Domese of Telota, and is the sire and grandsire to several Champions. Ch. Montzella's Tsi Chou (dam Shu-Shu-Ming of Montzella's), is the son of Ch. Dominic of Telota and continued the strong line by siring two Champions for the Montzella kennel of John and Sylvia Carter — Ch. Montzella's Chink to Chen (dam Montzella's Lu-Chia) and Ch. Montzella's Rosa Lin (dam Montzella's Chinta Tou). Other Champions of Dominic's are Pensmoor Jade Prince (dam Mandu Annette), Ch. Telota Simon Chen (dam Telota Ta-Mah) and owned by Miss Greves of the Wentres kennel), Ch. Meriadoc Kaherdin (dam Meadow Blue Mary Poppins), Ch. Chelhama Ajax Olympius (dam Ch. Queensfield Tootsi Wong of Chelhama, and owned and bred by Valerie Goodwin of the Chelhama kennel), Ch. Gorseycop Splendid Summer (dam Gorseycop Georgette; owned and campaigned by Mrs Pickburn of the Janmayen kennel), and Ch. Gorseycop Turnip Top (dam Gorseycop Araminta), both of which were bred by Mrs Margaret Hoare of the Gorseycop kennel.

Ch. Telota Anouska: Born 1976 (sire Telota Dominga dam Telota Domdarshe) and a grand-daughter of both Ch. Dominic and Ch. Domese has started her line with two Champions in her litter to Tarrelenka Chung Tien of Trisula — Ch. Harropine China Town and Ch. Harropine Super Trooper. Trooper was unfortunately sterile so left no progeny.

Ch. Greenmoss Chin Ki of Meo, bred by Mrs Reynolds and owned by Mr and Mrs Leadbitter. Silver/white but carrying both strong black/white and gold/white genes; was a very prolific stud and strong force in the breed, producing in all six champion dogs and seven champion bitches, with some variation of type and colour depending on the bitch line to which he was bred. His Champion sons have produced more Champions and have started lines of their own in other kennels. Notable ones are:

Ch. Ching Ling of Greenmoss (dam Hsiang Chieh of Liddesdale) gave good black/white and strong gold/whites. Before being exported, he sired the following influential dogs and bitches:

Ch. Patsy Do of Hyning, who went as foundation bitch to the Bellakerne Kennels of Tom and Sheila Richardson, who came into the breed in the 1970s. She has been one of the notable producing bitches in the breed while managing to hold her own in the show ring — no mean achievement. She started a line of good black/white, producing two Champions in her litter to Hyning Yes Sir — a dog Bellakerne Zippity Do and a bitch Bellakerne Inca Do, then two Champions — Bellakerne Melisa Do and Bellakerne Zoe Do — in a litter to Ch. Greenmoss Chinki's Fling (Chinki of Meo's son). This kennel has continued making further champions while retaining their original type. Their latest champion was Bellakerne Misty Do in 1993.

Ch. Keytor Midas (dam Marrietta of Shasheen) was a strong gold/white from Ch. Chin Ling, for the Keytor Kennel, and has been used to good advantage.

Ch. Chin Ling of Greenmoss has been a strong force in the Santosha kennel. Mated to Brownhills Teresa of Elfann, he produced Tomtru of Lhakang, who, although not a Champion, has figured extensively in these kennels, being the sire of Champion Santosha Bewitched (dam Santosha Double

Ch. Kadwen Yan Tsi. Born 1974. Owner Mrs Margory Devine, breeder Mrs sellers. *Photo: Diane Pearce*

Ch. Crowvalley Tweedledum. Born 1973. Was reserve Utility Group two years running at Crufts. Bred and owned by Mr and Mrs LesWilliams. *Photo: Lionel Young*

Dimple) and grandsire of Ch. Santosha Genevieve and Ch. Santosha Bewitching of Janmayen. He also sired Ch. Khumar China Silk of Darralls (dam Khumar Kobweb). Ch. Chin Ling also sired Champion Sandown Yolande (dam Yen-Ting of Sandown), Ch. Santosha Rambling Rose (dam Marnie of Myarlune) and Ch. Kusha Palhi of Shasheen (dam Shawala Kula).

Back to more of Chin Ki of Meo's sons, who include Ch. Zeus of Bridgend (dam Tricina Kylin) for the kennel of Tricina. He begat my Ch. Buttons of Snaefell (dam Flame of Snaefell) who begat Ch. Snaefell Charm (dam Newroots Pitti Sing of Snaefell, herself a daughter of Chin Ki of Meo), who was mated back to Chin Ki's son Ch. Newroots Nankipoo of Snaefell and begat Ch. Snaefell Katrina of Janmayen. Zeus also sired Ch. Elfann Golden Posy (dam Chin-EE-Lee of Elfann).

Ch. Newroots Nankipoo of Snaefell (dam Ho Yan of Newroots). A Son of Ch. Chin Ki of Meo and sire and grandsire of several Chs: Khumar Kiss Me Kate (dam Khumar Kismet), Snaefell Katrina of Janmayen (dam Ch. Snaefell Charm). Snaefell Imperial Imp (dam Snaefell Queen of the Snow), who produced a champion in each of her two litters, namely Snaefells Imperial Rose of Janmayen and Int Span Port Ch Snaefells Little Flower. His son, Snaefell Carry On Regardless, has continued the Champion line with his daughters Ch. Janmayen Bianca (dam Bowstones Tzulah of Janmayen) and Ch. Harropine Christmas Carol (dam Tanzu Mi-E-Clare of Harropine).

Wysarge Chin Ki Tuo of Greenmoss was another son of Chin Ki's, mated to Khumar Toffee Royal, begat Ch. Kareth Krishna for Mr Jim Peat's kennel in 1972, a keen new Scottish kennel.

A son of Ch. Chin Ki's who has been influential but did not make Champion status in England was exported to Italy, where he became an International Champion. This was **Greenmoss Gaylord of Elfann** (dam Elfann Sunshine of Greenmoss). He was the sire of the influential dog Ch. Greenmoss Glory Bee (dam Chantilly Lace), who begat Cherholmes Dipperty Do (dam Cherholmes Golden Samantha). Cherholmes Dipperty Do sired Juling Ming's Han Sum Sun, the sire of Ch. Shirwen Hansum Bee, who sired Ch. Hyning Barnaby Bee of Rabart. Han Sum Sun figured in the line of Valardy, being the sire of Ch. Valardy Chan-Ting (dam Valardy Chantana) and Ch. Shirwen Hansum

Ch. Patsy Do of Hyning. Bred by Mrs Rowlings.
Owned by Tom and Sheila Richardson.
Photo: Diane Pearce

Ch. Misty Do of Bellakerne.
Bred by Tom and Sheila Richardson.
The two photos show the first and latestt
Champions of the Bellakerne Kennell.
Photo: Carol Ann Johnson

Bee (dam Susie Bee of Greenmoss). He was grandsire to many a good producing animal.

Champion bitches have not been so influential in this line of Chin Ki's but they do not get the opportunity like the stud dogs as many of their years are spent in the show ring and, of course, they do not have the chances of a stud dog. I do not know about his non-champion daughters except my own Pitti Sing, whose Champion line has already been mentioned.

Ch. Greenmoss Glory Bee well deserves description as an influential dog, having sired six Champion bitches and four Champion dogs. He has also been a dominant sire, throwing very recognisable puppies. To the bitch Wysarge Jade Lotus Bud, he sired three Champions in different litters: Ch. Greenmoss Bee in a Bonnet (b), Ch. Greenmoss Surely Bee (b) and Ch. Greenmoss Bees Knees (d). This rather dispels the theory some people hold that repeat matings are unsatisfactory. His other Champions were Grandavon Maeli (b) (dam Jankeri Jazebal of Grandavon), Keytor Trishe Trashe (b) (dam Tricina Ross of Keytor), Unistev Mei Wey (b) (dam Ch. Simone of Sandown), Ch. Jardhu Wuffles Wu (d) (dam Wen Chengsian Of Glengall), Jorkecas Kevins Feeling (d) (dam Jorkecas Baby Jane), Yakee Chang Yeh (b) (dam Keytor Singing Wind of Yakee) and Ragoosa Golden Raffles (dam Furara Florsho of Ragoosa). Both Ch. Bees Knees and Yakee Change Yeh went on to produce Champions.

Ch. Buttons of Snaefell. Owned by the author, bred by Ivy May.

Ch. Santosha Sunking. Owned and bred by David and Susan Crossley.

Ch. Wendolyn Witchfire. Bred and owned by Mrs Wendy Wood-Jones. One of the only two champion daughters of Ch. Sunking.
Photo: Squires of Sandbach

Ch. Firefox of Santosha. Top-winning Shih Tzu with 35 CCs. bred by Mr Bert Easdon and owned by Mr David and Mrs Susan Crossley.
Photo: Jean Luc Lambert

Ch. Greenmoss Golden Peregrin of Elfann (sire Sing-Hi of Lhakang, dam Golden Bobbin of Elfann) threw some useful stock in this country before being exported to Italy, where he produced more Champions and became an International Champion.

Ch. Crowvalley Tweedledum (d) was born in 1973 (dam Crowvalley Yameeto) and won reserve in group at Crufts two years in succession — no mean achievement. He was renowned for his great glamour and showmanship, which he imparted to his offspring. He heads a line of champions. His son Ch. Poseidon (dam Ch. Crowvalley Minerva) was exported, but not before he also achieved a Utility Group win. He is grandsire to Ch. Pegasus (dam Tricina Kay) and Ch. Delridge Golden Gemini of Crowvalley on his dam's side and great-grandsire on his sire's side. He is also great-grandsire to Ch. Claropie Peter Pan of Crowvalley (dam Claropie Pandi). His other Champions are Wentres Jaycee Valency (dam Marizan Ziska), Ch. Bowstones Shu Shan (dam Ch. Bowstones Crowvalley Shang Tang, and Ch. Crowvalley Perdita (dam Ch. Crowvalley Jessica). Several dogs from this kennel were exported.

Lhakang Babu of Bodinic (sire Win-Sun-Sing of Elanzo, dam Shantung of Witches Knowe) has started a new line, with two Champions to his credit — Ch. Kareth Khoir Angel (b) (dam Santosha Serephin) and Ch. Santosha Sun King

Ch. Harropine Chaka Khan of Antarctica wins the Utility Group at Crufts in 1987. Picture shows Betty Rawling with Mr Bill Jobson, Group Judge and Katie Boyle presenting the Utility Group Cup .
Photo: Dalton

Ch. Rosaril the Chimney Sweep . Owned and bred by Eunice Stephenson.

(d) (dam Santosha Sunset), who became a leading stud for that kennel, producing both solid golds and blacks. The lines of Babu on his sire's side are quite old lines, bringing in the beautiful original gold of the Chasmu dogs.

1980s - 1993

In the early 1980s, honours were distributed fairly evenly throughout the kennels. There were no top dogs or bitches which stood out until the latter half of the 1980s. The established kennels still held their own and were winning very well, though I am unable to mention them all except for the leading winners.

Santosha was in the lead with a string of champions. Ch. Firefox of Santosha now became the leading CC-winning dog, with 35 CCs. and a group win to his credit. Ch. Santosha Sun King was producing good solid gold and blacks, one of which was Stevenson's Ch. Rosaril The Chimney Sweep, who became an excellent stud. This kennel was now well to the fore. Other Sun King progeny and champions of the Santosha line in the Scottish kennels of Jardhu were winning, as well as his only two Champion daughters — Ch. Wendolyn Wild Ginger, owned and bred by Mrs Wendy Wood-Jones, and Herbouchen Wonder Woman, owned and bred by Mrs Linda Ripley.

The glamorous gold and white bitch Senousi Be Bop Delux was born at the end of 1985. She won everywhere, and had three CCs before she was out of puppy, thus requiring one more after her first year before she could claim her title. She soon won this and went on to the climax of her career — Best In Show at Blackpool Championship Show.

Changes were ahead for the breed in the show scene. There had been great expansion and new kennels were coming into the breed, some with intent to start at the top rather than learn and work their way up. Earlier exhibitors felt that a few years' apprenticeship was important. These exhibitors were expert at the presentation of their dogs. Unfortunately, this also brought in more gamesmanship and a cut-throat atmosphere, following the trend of many sports today. Entries at shows often exceeded 200.

Ch. Senousi Be Bop de Lux. owned and bred by Mr David Iley. Best in Show Blackpool Championship Show 1988.
Photo: Diane Pearce

Both Harropine and Weatsom were winning with stock mainly from Ch. China Town, which took both the old lines of Antarctica and Telota. Ch. Harropine Chaka Khan of Antarctica, (s. Sistasu Silver Bullet. d. Harropine Odyssey) bred by Michael and Dee Harper and owned by Ken and Betty

Ch. Greenmoss Glory Bee. Owned and bred by Mrs and Mrs A. Leadbitter. Photo: Diane Pearce

Ch. Harropine China Town. Owned and bred by Michael and Dee Harper.

Rawlings, won the utility group at Crufts in 1987. Sadly, Betty died later that year, having celebrated her Golden Wedding earlier in the year.

Judy Franks (Hashanah), a new breeder, acquired a black and white pair from Weatsom Kennel, with whom she quickly made champions — Ch. Weatsom Little Big Man of Hashanah (Ch. Harropine China Town. ex Weatsom A Dream Come True.) and Weatsom My Fair Lady of Hashanah. (Tanzu Perfect Partner at Weatsom. ex Weatsom Magic Moment), who was a grandaughter of China Town. These two produced her Ch. Hashanah Take Me To The Top, a bitch, and Ch. Hashanah Hot Pursuit. With these two Champions, she won groups at Championship Shows. The same two, in another litter, produced the third champion, Hashanah No Jacket Required.

Ch. Sebastian of Keytor (d). (s. Keytor Tom Fool. d. Keytor Jibba Jabba) gold and white. Bred by Mrs Beecham and owned and Mrs E.M. Johnson and Miss S. Johnson, this dog was a big winner who won the Utility Group at Windsor Championship Show in 1989 and the reserve in group at Crufts in 1990. Later that year, at the height of his career, he died of leukaemia, which was a terrible loss for that kennel.

In the 1990s, Ch. Harropine Icarus took over as leading dog. He was a solid gold brindle son of Ch. Sun King and Harropine Thorn Bird, and has won 32 CCs to date and a Utility Group.

While these dogs were taking the stage, plans for importing stock were going on behind the scenes. By the 1990s, results from recent imports were beginning to show, and by 1993, I think their influence could be assessed.

Gwyn Goodwin, another new breeder, quickly came to the top by winning Reserve Best In Show at Blackpool Championship Show in 1992 with her home-bred bitch Cabbala Beautiful Dreamer, sired by my half American dog Ch. Snaefells Limited Edition, out of She Who Dares At Weatsom. This was also her first CC, and she soon won her Champion title after this.

The latest big winner is Ch. Harropine Chasing Rainbows, (Ch. Harropine China Town ex Am. imp. Dragonfires Scarlet O'Hara), who gained her title at South Wales Championship Show, where she also won the group and Reserve Best In Show.

Ch. Harropine Icarus. Winner of 32 CCs and a Group winner. Owned and bred by Mr and Mrs Harper. (s. Ch. Santosha Sunking. d. Harropine Thorn Bird.)
Photo: Carol Ann Johnson

Ch. Chanikos Yu Kizzy of Tomolly. Top bitch 1991. Bred by Mrs Anne Spooner. Owned by Mrs Carol Hennesy Smith. (s. Legusano Fu Wun. d. Chanikos Oh Diana.)

A young winner to hit the high spots in 1993 is Jardhu The Rebublican (Bellakerne Dandy Do at Jardhu ex Huxlor Personality Plus of Jardhu), a grandson of the American import Louwan Rebel Tu At Huxlor. He was top puppy of 1993. He won his first CC while still a puppy, and has two CCs to date. He has won a large puppy Stakes class at a Championship Show.

Latter Day Imports

Importing dogs to this country is both expensive and hazardous. Six months of incarceration in a quarantine kennel, however good, can destroy a dog physically and mentally, and it is not something undertaken without great thought toward improving our breed. It is a great asset to know the animals behind the import and what benefits they have to offer.

Ch. Weatsom My Fair Lady of Hashanah. Bred by Margaret Strangeland, owned by Judy Franks. Dam of three champions. (s. Tanzu Perfect Partner at Weatsom. d. Weatsom Magic Moments.)

Ch. Hashanah Take Me To The Top. Bred and owned by Mrs Judy Franks. (s. Ch. Weatsom Little Big Man of Hashanah d. Ch. Weatsom My Fair Lady of Hashanah.)

Ch. Hashanah Hot Pursuit. Bred and owned by Mrs Judy Franks. (s. Ch. Weatsom Little Big Man of Hashanah. d. Ch. Weatsom My Fair Lady of Hashanbah.) Photo: Carol Ann Johnson

Ch. Cabbala Beautiful Dreamer. Bred and owned by Mrs Gynneth Goodwin. Reserve Best In Show Blackpool 1992 (s. Ch. Snaefells Limited Edition d. She Who Dares at Weatsom.)

Michael Harper, who has had many imports, feels it is a great benefit in enlarging the gene pool, and Mrs Pat Lord is delighted with the temperament, which is so very important. Of course, unwelcome genes as well as welcomed ones are likely. It is most likely to be the stud who gets the blame and credit, though both parents are equally responsible. This is where careful breeding by knowledgeable owners comes in. Recessives genes long hidden may reappear, for English bloodlines are behind these dogs, and it is just as likely that they are carried in the imports and will combine to show themselves again when matched with ours.

It is by making use of the good that these dogs can give that we can improve our own lines. Our dogs are sufficiently strong to counteract exaggerations of others. No dog is perfect. Where others have gone too high on the leg, have not some of ours gone too low? Many of our top winners have also been higher on the leg. Where others have gone too narrow, have not some of ours become too broad, veering too much to the Peke? Do we not also have some too narrow? Sometimes the bone is heavier than the standard has ever demanded. Points will come through from both sides of the pedigree, but before breeding, we need to know just what we are trying to bring in or improve, and

Ch. Jardhu The Republican. Bred and owned by Mr and Mrs Grugan. Puppy stakes winner. (s. Bellakerne Dandy Do d. Huxlor Personality Plus of Jardhu.)

Ch. Harropine Chasing Rainbows. Bred and owned by Mr and Mrs Harper. (s. Champion Harropine China Town. d. Dragonfires Scarlet O'Hara — imp.)

what is important to retain. Haphazard breeding to any dog, let alone an import, does no good in the long run. One day, quarantine regulations will be fully relaxed, and our dogs will be in competition with the world dogs. Give the future some thought.

There have been many other imports which have not been mentioned. As far as I know, they have played no significant part in breeding.

It was a help to Harropine and Kynos that their owners either own or manage quarantine kennels, giving them contact with their dogs all through the six months.

Wyvern On A Promise (s. Canadian and Bermudan Ch. Carrimount Ah-Ting-Ting ex-Dorwent Ms Mosa's Debutant). A gold and white dog imported from Canada in 1983 by Mrs E.M and Miss S. Johnson. He was very carefully selected to bring back certain old English lines of Greenmoss which had been exported and lost to this country, and were wanted for the breeding programme at the Keytor kennel. They searched in many countries on the continent, Sweden and USA, before finding the breeding they felt would be best. The sire they wanted was a top winner and producer in Canada. In 1977, he won 30 Best Of Breeds, 20 Groups and 10 Best In Shows, and his Greenmoss breeding on his sire's side was very valuable to Keytor. There was a snag — he was now 12 years old. Nonetheless, he was mated to two bitches, but died very suddenly soon after the puppies were born, having been apparently in good health. His son, Wyvern On A Promise, was five months old when he came to Britain. His dam's lines are Santosha breeding. Ch. Keytor Any Questions is from his first litter, and the sire of aforementioned bitch Ch. Senousi Be Bop De Lux. The Johnsons were pleased and felt the dog was a great asset to the breed. His temperament was fantastic and he was well-constructed and sound, these being the main things they wished to impart before glamour.

Anibes Puttin On The Ritz (s.Whitethroat Jarvis. d. Nord Int Ch. Yinghs No Stuffed Shirt For Anibes)..A gold and white bitch imported from Sweden in 1985, and co-owned by her importer, Glynis Dolphin and her Swedish breeder, Anita Bergren. Jarvis was the last dog exported to Sweden

European Multi Ch. Putting on the Top Hat. Son of the imported bitch Anibes Putting On The Ritz. Owner Linda Reinelt-Gebauer (Germany.)

from the Whitethroat kennel of the late Eunice Fox. He had not been shown or bred from in England. This bitch had three good English lines and one Swedish line. The bitch as I remember her had great elegance and superb action and was of a medium size. She very quickly won her way to Championship status. A puppy from her first litter was returned to Sweden, where she was mated to an English import, Int and Nord Ch. Greenmoss Titfer-Tat, and a dog from that litter, Anibes Wishful Thinking, was imported to England in 1990. These lines have been used at limited stud, largely to maintain type and strengthen points which are strong in the Swedish lines, such as excellent bite and teeth and well-textured coats. Frozen semen was imported by Mrs Widdrington from a hernia-

free line of Nord & Sw. Ch. Boreas Golden Overlord in Norway. A litter was raised, but not permitted to be registered by the KC as permission had not been obtained. However, one straw remains unused. Permission may be given for its use when a suitable bitch is found.

Boreas' Chinese Spirit (d) and his sister **Boreas' Chinese Starlett of Lhakang** (b) (s. Int. Ch. Boreas Manchu Lancer. d. Nord Ch. Boreas Imperial Romance) Imported from Norway in 1887. These two were black and white. Both have been used for breeding and their progeny is in this country. The dog died young of heat stroke. Their special features were a very strong black and white coat, and particularly well-spaced dark eyes. Mrs Widdrington imported the bitch to try to get back her black /white coat from a line descended from Ch. Jen-Ki-Ko of Lhakang and Jolyon.

Boreas' Chinese Starlett of Lhakang. imported by Mrs L. G. Widdrinton from Major Hasle in Norway. s. Int Ch. Boreas Manchu Lancer. d. Int. Ch. Boreas Imperial Romance.

Dragonfire's Scarlet O'Hara (b) (s. Ch. Dragonfires Red Raider. d. Dragonfire's Great Draceana). Imported from USA in 1987 by Mr and Mrs Harper. A red and white bitch. Scarlet O'Hara was an impressive bitch who immediately did well in the show ring before unfortunately deciding she did not like showing. Misfortune struck again with her second litter (to Ch. Harropine China Town). All but one in the litter died of parvovirus, and Scarlet has not produced again. However, her surviving bitch puppy became a top winner. She was Harropine Chasing Rainbows, black and white like her sire. She won her champion title in 1992 and, in 1993, really hit the top, winning groups and a reserve Best In Show.

Dragonfire's All American Boy (s. Ch. Dragonfires's Red Raider. d. Ch. Dragonfire's Dang Sai Dickens). Imported from the USA in 1988 by Mr and Mrs Harper. A gold and white dog.

These two are of very similar blood lines, with just one line different on the bitch's side. They are both grandchildren of the very famous American dog Ch. Louwan's Rebel Rouser, a top winner and producer who brought red colouring into the American Shih Tzus. All American Boy has so far won one CC, but is seldom shown while his kennel rival Ch. Icarus is totting up the CCs!

Litter of puppies out of Starlett, sired by Wendolyn Joshua The Firelord of Wupino. Born 1991. Breeder Gay Widdrington.

Louwan Winning Colours At Huxlor (d) (s. Ch Louwan Rebel Rouser ex Louwan Tootsie) imported from USA 1988 by Mrs Lord. A gold and white dog who won his champion title in 1992. There are hazards when you import, and unfortunately, this dog has not managed to produce any progeny to date.

Louwan Rebel Tu at Huxlor (d) imported from USA in 1989 by Mrs Lord. Registered gold and white, actually a beautiful deep orange gold (s. Ch. Louwan Rebel Rouser. d. Louwan Ginger). Alhough he has not been shown, he has produced progeny — his outstanding winning grandson is the gold and white Jardhu The Republican.

Dragonfires All American Boy. imported from USA by Michael and Dee Harper. s. Dragonfires Red Raider. d. Dragonfires Dang Sai Dickens.

Ch. Din Ho Rupert T. Bear (d) (s. Mandalay's Blockbuster. d. Din Ho Oriental Poppy Mei Shan) was a pale gold and white dog much smaller than the majority of our English dogs. The English imported line in that pedigree was as far back as great-great-grandfather on the dam's side — Ch. Talifu Bobby Dazla. Rupert had excellent old American lines which had been bred for conformation rather than glamour. They had beautiful and large heads, level backs and

Ch. Louwan Winning Colours at Huxlor. Imported from USA by Pat Lord. s. Am Ch. Louwan Rebel Rousser d. Lou San Tootsie.

excellent action. I felt this complemented my own line, where I had always considered conformation of the greatest importance.

The American line also had great showmanship and this was something I wished to acquire in my line, while not losing other points for which I had bred. I was first attracted to use Rupert as I was looking for an out-cross and fell in love with pictures of his progeny in America. I was fortunate that the breeding to my Snaefells Irma La Douce paid off and produced my Ch. Snaefells Limited Edition, who was top Shih Tzu puppy in 1989 and has won 10 CCs. He produced Ch Cabbala Beautiful Dreamer.

Rupert's lines are quite different from the other American imports in this country, inasmuch as Am Ch. Louwan Rebel Rouser does not figure in his pedigree. As these two American lines are so different, it is a point that should be of great importance in breeding. Rupert was carefully bred through the lines of Ch. Winwards Wheeler Dealer and Ch. Long's Chiny-Chin Ah-Chop-Chop on his sire's side, with Ch. Ming Toi P V Spunky and Ch. Parquin's Pretty Boy Floyd on his dam's. These animals did not have the exaggerated features of the ultra-long neck and small heads of some of the American dogs.

Cherokee Idle Gossip Shalimar (s. Mei Ting Devil Made Me Do It. d. Shalimar Fancy Cherokee). The English import on this line was the red/gold Nutmeg of

Lu Wan Rabel Tu. With owner in quarantine kennel. Imported by Mrs Lord. s, Am Ch. Louwan Rebel Rousser ex Louwan Ginger.

Greenmoss, who was the great-great-grandsire on the sire's side. Idle Gossip was a very small exquisite pale gold and white bitch who took the eye of every judge, but was a little too different from our own larger and heavier built bitches to gain her title here. She was soundly made, with perfect Shih Tzu action and always looked glamorous with her beautiful coat so well presented. Our people found her too small and too light in bone. However, she did win the reserve in the Utility Group at Windsor Ch. Show. Rebel Rouser was her grandsire on her sire's line.

Am .Ch. Din Ho Rupert T Bear. Imported by owner Mrs Jane Couch. s. Mandalay's Blockbuster. d. Din Ho Oriental Poppy Mei Shan.

Cherokee Cause to Pause had the same sire as Idle Gossip. Her dam was Louwan Honeybee, who was a daughter of Rebel's. This gave her the red on both sides of her pedigree. She was a red bitch of a larger type and had a very beautiful and correct head with expressive dark eyes, and certainly not the tiny head so often associated with modern American dogs. Her tail end was her downfall, but she was a very sound bitch.

Both bitches produced a litter to Rupert in this country before they returned to America in 1992. A dog from each litter was retained. One Shalimar American Gigalo, out of Idle Gossip, was a silver and white, while the other, All the Rage at Shalihi (out of Cause to Pause), was a red and white. Both were large-bodied dogs with large heads, but their tails were not as we like them. Both dogs were used at stud and their lines remain.

Cheroke Idle Gossip Shalimah. Imported by co-owner Mrs Jane Couch; bred and co-owned by Mrs Anne Crisp. s. Mei Ting Devil Made Me Do It. d. Shalimar Fancy Cherokee.

It is early days yet to assess the full impact of this imported stock. I can only say that the animals who have come through from these American lines have been winning well, and certain points have noticeably come through to them all, such as good top line, showmanship and strong driving action, something which has been lost to some of our dogs in recent years. I have found the temperament quite enchanting; it has brought in some of the amusing Shih Tzu tricks I knew in earlier Shih Tzus. One should think to the future when quarantine restrictions are eventually lifted. The English type of Shih Tzu must not be lost, with its beautiful and large head, and high tail, but there are always improvement to be made, and it is up to you who breed to do this, so that our dogs will win among the best in the world when barriers are down.

CHAPTER FIVE

CHARACTER AND EARLY TRAINING

Character

This chapter on the Shih Tzu character should really be read in conjunction with the chapters on breeding, for it is not sufficient to breed for looks alone. Although the dog can be a delightful object of beauty when seen poised in the show ring with its long flowing coat superbly groomed, it doesn't stay that way for long! After a few mad turns rushing round the garden or park, or on the lawn in a heavy dew, you realise it is the character of the dog which really matters. The big question in judging is 'which comes first — soundness or type?' but to the breeder, soundness, type and character should all be of equal importance.

One needs to distinguish between inherited character and environmental character, as well as taking account of family characteristics within the breed. Here, I quote from Clarence Pfaffenberger's Dog Behaviour: "Environment has never made a man, animal or plant any better than the genes he or it inherited. What is often referred to as an ideal 'climate' can help any individual achieve his potential or nearly his potential. Poor environment can cripple the development of an individual until he can never achieve the potential he was born with, even if an ideal climate is later provided." To people reading this book in an effort to make up their minds whether this is the breed for them, I will do my best to describe this fascinating little dog, who — partly for his changing mood — has been referred to poetically by some as 'the fairy dog'.

In the past, in Tibet, the Shih Tzu was always kept as a member of the family and a holy dog who could do no wrong. He lived with the family and became very humanised. In China, in the Imperial Palace, he was treated as a great pet, with his own eunuchs to look after him, and he was taught a great deal.

This past history of the Shih Tzu has obviously played a large part in its character formation. He can learn by watching others, and then copies them. He learns quickly — sometimes the wrong things! Many have been very good at obedience training, as they love to show off and let you see how clever they are. It may not be easy to get them to do it the way you want, as they would rather do it their way. They love to demonstrate their accomplishments. Many have learned to retrieve with Labradors merely by observing and copying them.

Members of this breed need to be brought up as children of the family, and if there is a child for company, so much the better. The child should learn to have as much respect for the dog as the dog is expected to have for the child; it is cruel to allow a small baby to pull and poke a dog around, and even if the dog does put up with it, this is no excuse!

The Shih Tzu is capable of giving utter devotion and hours of fun and amusement, but he is not 'your servant the dog' and will expect you to respond in return; like many other dogs, he thinks he is your equal, if not your superior! If he does not get plenty of human companionship, he is quite incapable of developing his full character, and whereas this could be applied to many breeds, the Shih Tzu has considerably greater potential than some.

It is very difficult to give an adequate description of the Shih Tzu's character, for one really needs to be an owner to appreciate it fully. As James Mumford wrote in a delightful article in the American Shih Tzu News: 'No one knows how they (the eunuchs) added a dash of lion, several teaspoons of rabbit, a couple of ounces of domestic cat, one part court jester, a dash of ballerina, a pinch of old man (Chinese), a bit of beggar, a tablespoon of monkey, one part baby seal, a dash of teddy bear, and the rest, dogs of Tibetan and Chinese origin.'

This gives a wonderful picture of the Shih Tzu — its character is so very versatile!

There are very definite family characteristics which can be recognised, often as early as eight weeks old, and it is only by owning various bloodlines, and several generations of the same family, that you identify these traits. Shih Tzu do not breed like peas out of a pod. This is a happy little dog, full of fun, and seldom belligerent; he usually gets on well with other breeds, except when in a group, when they may revert to the natural mobbing instinct. Should a visiting dog arrive at the house, the Shih Tzu can be relied upon to meet it with courtesy, albeit treating human visitors with dignified aloofness, though some lines are much more friendly to strangers than others. He should not accept someone into the house without your approval.

Wilfulness and disobedience are faults of which he is accused. Wilful he is, but I cannot help wondering whether any disobedience could be the fault of those responsible for training him. Training must begin very early in his life, and to call him to 'come' at five weeks is not too soon. There are 'puppy parties' for training and socialising young puppies held in most places in the country — these are well worth attending.

Though I have stressed earlier that one of the great assets of the breed is its ease in whelping, I am doubtful that it is as good now as in earlier

Luxem B. Ch. Antoinette Zum Fledermausturmchen.
Owned by Linda Reinelt - Gebauer.

years. One hears of many cesarean sections being performed. A Shih Tzu bitch is usually an excellent mother, giving complete and untiring devotion to her puppies long after weaning. Their hearing is very keen, particularly when they are alert with a litter, and they are very sensitive to anything unusual going on either indoors or outside. They also have an acute awareness of atmosphere, and are extremely observant.

If you pick up a Shih Tzu, it may lie quite still, and even the puppies seldom wriggle. When put down, however, it comes to life, rushing round and round at top speed, dodging obstacles, chasing in and out, up and down, missing nothing, knocking nothing, until it finally drops exhausted — only to rise again and repeat the performance. Past masters at the game of tag, Shih Tzu are rightly labelled 'clowns of the dog world'. To watch them play can give endless enjoyment and amusement. It is not only sad but unnecessary when a dog is kept on its own and never allowed to play, just to preserve its coat for showing.

Shih Tzu often lie with their hind legs extended.

The Shih Tzu has a fascinating way of lying flat on the ground with legs outstretched; he will also sit patiently waiting, remaining so still that he looks like a small Buddha, his eyes gazing intently on your face, waiting for your next move. You can be sure he'll be beside you when you make it! Visitors are always impressed when they see six or more of my dogs in the room, all sitting motionless with expressive eyes gazing up at me. There was one exception, however — Eliza Doolittle, who always set her gaze (and herself if possible) on the visitor! Alas, she is now gone and sadly missed, for she had a wonderful personality. When the visitors get up to go, all those silent Buddhas come to life and bark ferociously at them. I have never quite found the reason for this — I feel it must be an inherent trait in many dogs, and something to do with the guarding instinct.

I said earlier in this chapter that the Shih Tzu is not naturally belligerent, but if attacked, he will stand his ground and usually come off worst, which can often lead to losing an eye. It is not in the nature of the breed to lose face, so he should not run away. A second dog will always go to the aid of a friend, and will rush in and out biting the legs or any other accessible part of the assailant's anatomy.

When this happens at home, particularly if one of them has 'told off' a puppy, another will fly to the rescue, then another will attack that one, and so on until they look remarkably like a rugby scrum. The trouble is that they forget who was the original troublemaker, and make it an excuse to have a good old free-for-all. The answer to this is to pick one up by the scruff of the neck to avoid getting bitten and remove it from the room, but you will find that instead of seizing just one, you have several others still hanging onto each other's tails. However, this sort of fighting is seldom serious.

Have you ever seen a dog smile? Shih Tzus do, and mine seem to do it mainly in anticipation of a tit-bit. The asparagus season brings them flocking to the table showing large expanses of teeth, and brussel sprouts are another great favourite. Of course, anything from our table tastes infinitely better than their own food!

This breed is very adaptable so long as it has been properly socialised, and will fit into both town and country environments, but must have human companionship. It is certainly not a dog to leave if you have to be out at work all day. Shih Tzus thoroughly enjoy a good country walk, and are quite capable of keeping up with most breeds; indeed, many of them go out exercising with horses. I recently heard of two who spent a wonderful holiday on the Yorkshire moors climbing, swimming and running, always keeping up with their companions — a German Shepherd dog and a Bull Terrier. On the other hand, a flat in town with walks in the park is quite adequate, and your dog will be perfectly happy with this life so long as you are around. By being around, I do not mean that it cannot be left for reasonable periods of time; this, like so many things, is largely a matter of early training, and something to which they can be accustomed from puppy days. To take a dog out shopping is not much fun for dog or owner.

The Shih Tzu is generally a robust little dog and if well cared for, should not require much veterinary attention. Both sexes are very affectionate; the dog in this breed is quite as affectionate as the bitch, often more so, so do not be misled into thinking that you must have a bitch rather than a dog for this reason.

Many Shih Tzu love swimming, but I do feel this should not be encouraged, since they are apt to jump into any dirty old pond and come out stinking. There is also the risk that they may rush into a fast-flowing stream, and be liable to get swept away with the current. Some are climbers and some are diggers — few are both, and many are neither. Most will jump if taught to do so, and they all learn tricks very easily. They have a strange habit of sitting on your chair as soon as you get up, because they do not like to sit on the ground. If there is a table by a window on which they can climb, they will most likely think it was put there especially for their benefit, and there they will sit, looking like models in the window.

The character I have tried to describe is obviously the general character of the breed; there are so many other fascinating little ways of behaviour peculiar to an individual or a family — things like dancing on the hind legs and welcoming you by stretching out the front paws as it dances, or welcoming you by picking up the hem of your garment (though mini-skirts have discouraged this) and bringing you presents. When overcome by excitement, it will snort and gurgle in its throat, or 'talk' instead. It has a fascinating habit of burying nothing, covering it with nothing, and then walking away contentedly. It may nose up its food dish and hide the food, although this is mostly observed with the brood bitch. It also has a special way of cleaning its face and whiskers. I could go on and on, but it is only by owning a Shih Tzu and having it as a constant companion that you can really get to know the breed.

Most Shih Tzu are quite content to stay around the home, but occasionally, you will find you have a wanderer; this can be of either sex, and it is most important you teach it some obedience, since the breed has little road sense. At least teach it the command 'stay'

Many people enquire whether these are sporty dogs. The answer is yes, and if given the chance, they will chase chickens, so they have to be trained not to do this. Neither should they be turned into 'toy' or 'lap' dogs, or kept in cages to grow their coats for show purposes, for this completely ruins their characters.

Most of the Shih Tzu I know of and have met have wonderful characters, and this is a great strength in the breed. I feel some breeders are not fully aware of the emotional upset which can be caused by uprooting a dog from the home kennel, where it has been perfectly happy, and transferring it to a new home at the wrong age, without its first being fully socialised. Much research is being devoted to the subject, and more knowledge in this respect would enable us to keep our breed strong in the correct character and temperament.

It is not surprising that the Buddhists classified the dog at the top of the ladder next to humans, for they were considered to be reincarnated humans who had erred during their lifetime. I only wish that as high a proportion of the human race possessed the same delightful characters as the Shih Tzu!

Training your new puppy
To know the character of the breed is one great help towards successful training. Training from puppyhood is important; everything has to be taught, except the lessons taught by the mother and his natural instincts. You will continue where the mother left off. The Shih Tzu is not by nature an obedient dog, nor does it look upon himself as your servant, but rather your friend and companion, and this is how you should treat him if you want to get the best out of him. He will regard you with utter devotion. Treated too severely or always kennelled and only permitted to run with other dogs and having little human companionship will not bring out its lively, intelligent nature. The Shih Tzu which shares your home and is treated as your companion will respond beyond anything you had hoped for in a dog, for it has great intelligence.

It is important that the Shih Tzu recognises you as his boss, otherwise he will take over and may become very demanding. All rules may have to be broken on special occasions, but it is good to make a rule and stick to it, just as you would with a child, so that the dog knows exactly here it stands. Spoiling a dog is one of the first and easiest faults to make, and there are many ways of doing this. Whether you are a breeder running puppies on or a pet owner, the procedure is the same.

A puppy's nervous system is developing between three and seven weeks of age, and by eight weeks, it has the capacity, if not the experience, of an adult. Early attention from humans, as well as the companionship of other dogs (i.e. litter mates), is most important. It is absolutely essential that puppies from three weeks old should have love and attention from the owner and the mother, if they are to end up really well-adjusted. A puppy will transfer its affection straight away to a new owner, for what it needs and wants is love, regardless of who gives it.

The method you use to transport your new puppy home is most important. Don't tuck him away all on his own in a box at the back of the car, this could frighten him. If possible, have a companion with you and let him be nursed, preferably by you, his new owner. If you are alone and driving, have a small box he can't get out of on the seat beside you, so you can touch him. To be frightened now in the car can mean fear of travel later.

Keep to the same diet and temperature conditions used in the home kennel. If the puppy has already been acclimatised to weather, and to sleeping in an unheated room, do not start to molly-coddle it. On the other hand, if it has not yet been outside (and this is difficult with winter puppies), care should be taken lest the nostrils tighten up and force it to breathe through its mouth. This tightening of the nostrils can happen very easily in a small puppy due to changes in temperature, so do be very careful not to transfer a pup from a heated atmosphere into the cold, or to allow him to stay outside longer than is absolutely necessary. Too much heat can be equally harmful.

For the first few nights, the puppy is bound to miss his companions, for he will have been accustomed to snuggling up to them (and probably his mother as well) for warmth. If you replace this warmth with a warm, not hot, bottle, wrapped in some woolly material, he will usually settle down very quickly. Leave some newspapers on the floor in case he wakes before you go into him in the morning, but at this stage, it is better for you to get up early and take him straight out to relieve himself, telling him how good he is when he has obliged. Always remember the word of praise, and make this exaggerated. Also remember the word of disapproval. Above all, be consistent, and do not permit one day something for which you admonish him the next. Try always to keep to a strictly routine timetable, especially with feeding.

A puppy, like a baby, needs plenty of undisturbed rest. He usually likes to sleep after a meal, so make a point of shutting him away from possible disturbances so he can do so in peace.

Holding the puppy
Do not make a practice of lifting a dog by the scruff of the neck, for there is far too much weight in the body, particularly as the dog gets older. Do not hold him by putting your hand under the elbows, against the side of the chest, for this is likely to push the elbows out and completely spoil the animal's front; even if you do not intend to show him, you want him to grow up correctly. Pick him up with the palm of your hand under the brisket, or under the tummy and chest, with your finger and thumb outside each elbow. As the puppy grows, your full hand will take the brisket. Your left hand should support the body by placing it under the tail and hindquarters.

Most Shih Tzu love to be picked up and cuddled, and will lie still for hours, but with an unfamiliar child, a puppy may wriggle and try to jump down, so if there is a small child holding the puppy, let them both be near the ground, then puppy and child can get used to each other in safety. If a puppy jumps from a height it may injure itself.

Beds
The puppy should be given a bed of his own, off the ground and out of draughts. If he has a wicker basket see that he does not chew it, and leave jagged ends, for these are dangerous to the eyes and can also catch in an adult's coat. Bind round any jagged ends for safety. It is risky to make do with a cardboard box, as those which have been recycled sometimes contain a poison. If the puppy chews it, sickness may result.

Basic commands, collar and lead training

I consider that basic training should have been accomplished before the puppy is eight weeks old, so he can learn his name and respond to the command 'come' as soon as he is on his feet. Recognising the breeder through this response can vary within the litter by as much as one to two weeks. Once taught, training must be continued; sound obedience training has averted many a catastrophe.

If your puppy has not yet been taught to 'come', don't waste time but begin to train him now. Once a name has already been given, and he has learned to respond to it, do not change this suddenly and completely even if you do not want him to keep it permanently. It is far better to continue using the original name, adding any new name after it; for example, if it has been called Fu and you want to rename it Ming, start with Fu Ming and then you can gradually drop the first part.

Each time the puppy comes to your call, make a great fuss of him, and sometimes give him a tit-bit. First of all, he must learn that it is fun to come to you — this will become a habit. When he comes, get him to follow you by calling his name, playing with him, clapping your hands and so on, anything to hold his interest and attract him to come after you.

The next step is putting on a collar, preferably a soft one at first and for gradually increasing periods. I use a cat collar. If you have bought a harness, get rid of it — it will only make him 'out at shoulder'. When he is accustomed to the collar — and he may scratch at first — attach a piece of string or a light nylon lead, but leave this dangling so that he gets used to the feel of it. Next, pick up the end of the lead and let the puppy lead you, which he will love to do. Never pull or force him, he must become accustomed to things at his own pace, and will do so quite quickly. The next stage is to lead him for a little way; if he pulls, let him lead you again, calling him along in the same way as when you have been training him to come. Lead him further, and gradually he will let you do the leading all the time. The time this will take varies, but most Shih Tzu are very easy to lead-train. Six weeks is really the best age to start, and it is ideal to undertake lead-training in a quiet area away from distractions.

By 12 weeks, the puppy will start to explore further away from the home; there will now be many more distractions, and a little more bribery may be required.

If you have a large garden, it is unwise to allow the young puppy to have the full run of it, for this is inviting trouble. Left to his own devices, he will gradually explore a little further each day, and will find everything very exciting. It is much wiser to wire off part of the garden. Never leave his run in the full sun — ensure you give him shade as well, and provide water for him. Give him some toys with which to play, or he will dig holes in your lawn if he gets bored. He is also likely to be a very good gardener, but does not recognise dead flower heads from those in bloom! He will also dig up the new plants you have just put in, and if you have manured the ground, keep him well away!

House training

A puppy is naturally clean; as soon as he is able to crawl from the nest, he will do so to relieve himself. Training is usually started on newspaper. A house-reared puppy will be far easier to train later than one left in a kennel or run without sufficient attention. You have got to keep him up to his high standard, which has been taught by the mother and nature. Puppies do not like soiling their own quarters, and yours needs to learn that his quarters extend to the full area of your house.

It is up to you to teach him just where to do his business. If you do not take the puppy out regularly to do the necessary, he can lapse. You will have to watch constantly when the puppy is tiny. He will last many hours at night, but during the day, he will spend numerous thimblefuls. It is a good idea to put him in a pen to start with; he will not want to soil it, so will cry to be taken out. The fault many people make is to put the puppy out on his own. You must stay with him until he has performed, always using the same word of command, i.e. 'business' or 'hurry-up', then praise him, give him a tit-bit for obeying the word, then have a quick game before bringing him back in. He should then, hopefully, be safe to run around the house. Eventually, he will understand, and as he grows older he will go out on his own to perform. However, some do not always bark to go out but just hang around the door.

Never hit a puppy or rub his nose in his little mistakes, but if you can catch him in the act, pick him up and say his name and 'out', 'business' or whatever the word you use. Any puddles on the carpet should be wiped up immediately, and soda water squirted on the spot will neutralise urine, or you can buy Shaws No Stain Carpet Cleaner and Spot Remover, which is very effective. You always know when a puppy wants to open his bowels, for he goes rushing around looking in various corners of the room, or to the door, trying to find the right place to go. Do as you did before — pick him up and say his name and 'out'.

Never leave puppies in their pen with excreta lying around, for this can start off the nasty habit of eating it and certainly does nothing towards house training.

At eight weeks old most puppies need to go out as soon as they wake up. They usually spend two pennies, then open their bowels. If they don't have their bowels open, you can bring them in for their morning feed, then put them out again after it; they will soon oblige. A cage or pen are useful for training a puppy. Do not leave excreta lying around in your own garden or out in the streets or parks; this gives dogs a bad name. It is revolting if you put your foot in a dog's mess, and even more so if a child falls over in the park and gets soiled. Mother is not pleased, and immediately suspects that her child will get worms; you then have another convert to the anti-dog brigade. It is useful to keep a plastic bag in your pocket. This is a good way of clearing up a mess, and more people should do so when walking their dog in public places. If they did, there would be fewer anti-dog protests. To use the device, put your hand inside the bag, pick up the mess, invert the bag and knot it, then find a disposal unit.

Inoculations and socialising
Refer to Chapter 6 - General Management.

Obedience
A word your puppy must learn right from the start is 'No', and this should be said in a very firm, authoritative tone, so he realises immediately that you disapprove. There is no need for smacking, which is far more likely to make a dog disobedient. Why should he want to come to a person who inflicts pain? Exaggerate the tones in your voice for both approval and disapproval; it is the actual tone to which the dog responds. When he does obey, give him a reward.

A Shih Tzu will be remarkably obedient until four months old. Try to train him before that age, for that is when he gets adventurous. Try to do a little obedience every day, especially teaching the sit and stay command as Shih Tzus are usually better at that than coming to you, but keep training to

73

'come' as well. A badly trained Shih Tzu cannot be let off the lead when out for walks. Never trust him near sheep or chickens unless you have him well-trained, for Shih Tzu are great chasers. As for chickens, they will catch them and pluck out the tail feathers.

The 'Flexi' extending leads are a great asset on walks. You can start taking him to obedience training classes as soon as he is over his inoculations; the Shih Tzu loves them. Or you can take him to the aforementioned 'puppy parties' which are the newest idea on puppy socialising and training. These are great fun and the puppy can attend them as soon as it is over its inoculations. It is a happy way of socialising.

Irish Ch. Rosella of Lyre.
Owners Gerry and Frances Hickey (Ireland.)

Caging

A cage is very useful for training a puppy as there are occasions when a dog needs to be shut away. You can use the cage in a car if you stay away at a hotel or in somebody else's house where a dog running around is not welcome; he will be quite happy if popped into his familiar cage.

If the dog has a comfortable bed, you should have no difficulty in training him to keep off the furniture. Mind you, he is sure to try it on, and you will no doubt come back from being out one day to find him sitting in your best chair! Say 'no, down' firmly, and pick him up and put him on the ground. I have never forgotten a story I heard many years ago. An owner left his retriever at home while he went out for the afternoon, and when he came back, the retriever was sitting on the couch. The dog was reprimanded. The next time the owner went out and left the dog, he told it not to sit on the couch. When he returned the dog was not on the couch, but the owner felt it and found it was warm, so the dog was reprimanded again. The next time he came home, the owner crept up to look through the window instead of going to the door, and found the dog blowing on the couch! The Shih Tzu wouldn't bother to blow! It would either stay there if it did not respect you as the pack leader, or if it feared you, it would rush away to its own bed as soon as it heard your car entering the drive. If it loves you, it will be at the door to greet you, barking joyfully.

Daily grooming

This will not take long, but is most important even in a puppy, for it facilitates his adult grooming. Use a brush with a fairly soft bristle, and do not use a wire brush on a puppy. If you hurt him at this age he will always resent grooming. Use a steel comb with both fine and wide teeth. It stimulates a puppy's coat to brush it in both directions. Either groom him on your lap or on the table; when adult, he is best groomed on the table. Although the puppy only needs a light brush and an occasional comb-through, he must be trained to lie on his back and his sides to have his tummy and the insides of his thighs groomed. This should be done gently by means of both brushing and occasional combing, especially the feet, as these are the parts of the body which mat most quickly and to which the animal is most sensitive. If the puppy resents lying on his back for brushing, get him used to it by stroking his tummy. If you talk or sing to him while grooming, he will find this soothing.

Follow the general technique suggested in Chapter 7, in the section dealing with the care of the coat. Be very careful how you use the comb, as this can pull out the coat. Some people feel you should never use a comb, but I think that both you and the dog will get in a frightful mess if you don't do so! Wash around your puppy's eyes and groom his whiskers gently every day, even if you have to miss the rest. A puppy who has been trained to grooming will look forward to this daily individual attention. You should by now have a fairly well-trained animal. Keep up the good work, and remember that you can always go to training classes when he is older. Do not imagine that you cannot train an older Shih Tzu. This can most certainly be accomplished so long as it has had love and human contact in its early life. A dog using his brain is a much happier dog, and far less likely to get into mischief than one who teaches himself or learns bad habits from others.

CHAPTER SIX

GENERAL MANAGEMENT

Inoculations

It is most important that your puppy should receive immunisation against distemper, hard pad, canine virus hepatitis, leptospiral jaundice and parvovirus. You can also vaccinate against some of the kennel cough viruses. If you are buying a new puppy, you must consult your vet as to the time to give inoculations.

If it is a puppy you have bred and are running on, you must take sensible precautions before inoculation. There is always an element of risk, and immunity has to be built up slowly. If you keep other dogs, there is inevitably some risk from them. Do not let the puppy run with dogs currently being shown and take all precautions when you return from a show, such as changing your shoes and wiping them over with a suitable disinfectant, such as Trigene (obtainable from your vet), which, if used at the correct strength, will kill many viruses and most bacteria. Wash your hands and change your clothes before going to your puppies. Diseases can be airborne and carried on your clothes. Should the vaccines be given while the puppy is already incubating a disease, they can have adverse results. So much depends on where you live. Dogs are more vulnerable to diseases in towns and dog-populated areas, although these places are so much easier for socialising. If you live in a town, you need to get the puppy immunised as soon as possible. In the country, with an adequate garden, it is sometimes better to leave it a little later, as immunity can be better for this. With the parvovirus vaccine, you must get current advice, as this is still changing frequently.

Do not walk your other dogs near the veterinary surgery, and if possible, not on common land where other dogs take their walks. You are taking a great risk if you exercise a nursing mother outside the home. I consider letting your puppy mix with your own dogs a risk you must take, for this helps them to adjust normally and not be aggressive with others. Most adult male Shih Tzu are ideal with puppies, but I'm not so happy about some of the old bitches. Do not let your friends bring along their dogs to mix with your uninoculated puppy.

Two weeks after the last inoculation, the puppy will be fully immunised and no time must be lost in fully socialising him.

Exercise

Never force a puppy under six months of age to go for long walks on the lead; short lead walks are alright for a little training, but most of the exercise should be taken free, in the garden, or, if out walking, allow him to stop and rest whenever he feels tired. Should the puppy be destined for a show career, it is unwise to allow too much romping around, but he should not be so restricted that he does not have the opportunity to extend his limbs and tighten his muscles. Remember that puppy bones are soft — never let a puppy stand up too much on his hind legs to watch what is going on, for he will tend to balance with his toes turned in and they may make him cow-hocked.

The adult Shih Tzu needs adequate exercise to keep him in a healthy, hard condition, and a show dog in particular should have regular road walking.

Shih Tzus are normally great walkers, and I hope this feature will remain with the breed. I have known many who exercise freely with the horses, as I have said, and they are certainly capable of exercise with the most active breeds such as gundogs, sheepdogs, whippets and Alsatians. They may be animated doormats at home, but can be veritable whirlwinds when out running, to the amazement of people who have stated that they would not be seen dead at the other end of a lead! It is amazing how much they will exercise themselves, indoors or out, by rushing around dodging obstacles.

I have only mentioned road walking as a necessity for the show dog, but the pet dog loves a country ramble; do not go in the heat of a summer's day, for their heavy coats will make them uncomfortably hot. However, the pet seldom carries the long, heavy coat of the show dog, as it either becomes rubbed off, combed out or cut down. Very long-coated dogs cannot be walked in rough country because the coat gathers too many twigs. Some people like to cut the coat back. If you do this, never trim it down to the skin, but leave on about two inches for warmth in winter and protection against sunburn in summer.

Wet weather

The Shih Tzu gets very dirty when out for a walk in the wet, and the easiest way to deal with this is to have a large bowl and cloth available on return and to wipe the undercarriage, wringing out the cloth in clean water and then removing the surplus moisture. Rinse each leg in turn in the water, gently pressing out the wet. If the dog is soaked, the use of newspapers or one of those new absorbent clothes for a preliminary mopping-up operation will save your towels. A male dog will benefit from being washed down in this way. Particularly when there are bitches in season around, he can get very smelly.

In summer

Do be very careful not to exercise dogs where there are grass seeds. Wild barley is the worst in this respect, for it works its way right through the coat and can lodge in the skin, particularly in such areas as the soft skin of the armpits, where if it gets under the surface, abscesses may result. Grass seeds can also get into the ears, up the nose and between the pads, and in all these places can be extremely troublesome to the dog.

In snow

The Shih Tzu loves to play in the snow, and is a very pretty sight to watch. However, he is not a pretty sight when he comes in from play. He will be freezing cold with snow 'balling' all over him, up his legs, under his tummy, just about everywhere. If he is a show dog, care must be exercised in removing the snow, because unless it is thawed off, the ends of the hair are likely to be broken. Stand him in a shallow bath of tepid water, and literally bathe the snow off. Better still, prevent it from happening in the first place by lightly smearing the vulnerable parts (e.g. feet, legs and stomach) with a thin, light oil, as snow will not stick to this.

By the sea

Sea water is not good for a dog's coat, especially since he will come straight out of the water and roll in the sand; this is liable to get into his eyes and irritate the skin, making him scratch sore places which can lead to eczema. Keep him under reasonable control on the beach; now, such is the anti-dog brigade that some beaches are forbidden to dogs. If he does get wet and sandy, rinse him thoroughly when you get home to get all the sand and salt from his coat.

Al Jarrau of Jenshu.

Be careful if you are near a fast-flowing river, for many Shih Tzu are great water dogs and will jump in. Also be very careful of swimming pools. Every year, I hear of Shih Tzus being drowned in these, usually when they have a cover — the dog does not realise it is not solid ground and jumps in, only to become completely enveloped. There is no escape and it drowns.

Bathing and grooming

This is dealt with fully in Chapter 15: Grooming and Coat Care. How often you bath depends entirely on your dog and you. Too much bathing is not considered good for the coat, yet others say they should be bathed weekly to get a good coat. It's your choice. Grooming usually keeps it clean. However, when the dog comes in wet and muddy, it is a good idea to shower down his undercarriage and feet. This is good for the coat as well as the carpet, as it will get rid of any gritty bits, sticks and leaves that may be adhering to it before they can do any damage and break the hair.

Internal parasites

Roundworms are the common internal parasites found in puppies. A puppy can be born with them, for the worm ova is passed to it in the bloodstream of the bitch. In this country, a young puppy seldom suffers from any other variety of worms. When acquiring your puppy, be sure to ascertain whether is has been wormed by the breeder. It should always be wormed before leaving the home kennel.

Roundworms vary in length and look like white garden worms; perhaps an even better description may be to say they look like pieces of spaghetti. If the puppy has not been wormed or is due for another dose, get tablets from your veterinary surgeon. Small puppies can be infected with worms without passing any visible signs or showing any of the symptoms, i.e. an indifferent or variable appetite, poor coat, general unthrifty appearance, a pot belly which feels tight and hard. Other symptoms may be running eyes and nose, a cough and a depraved appetite, (i.e. eating excreta, though this can occur without worms being the cause). There may be straining to pass a motion, which is frequently loose and contains mucus. If the worms get into the stomach, the puppy may vomit. It is not difficult to worm a dog; and modern worm tablets seldom have an adverse affect, so long as you follow the instructions. I prefer to get my worm tablets from my veterinary surgeon. Most worm medication desolves the worms so none are seen in the faeces.

Should there be a young child in the house, worming really is vital from all viewpoints, for a small child is liable to pick up a puppy's toy and stick it into his own mouth. See that their hands are washed after playing with the puppy, at least before they have their own meal.

Although I have emphasised the importance of worming, do not become over-preoccupied with this problem. There is a great deal of adverse publicity given to it and by no means are all the facts proven. Prevention is better than cure, and all adult dogs should be wormed three times a year for safety precautions. The healthy adult should become immune to this parasite, and throw out the ova before they have a chance to hatch. This in turn needs watching, however, for the adult will pass the ova in a stool, and it then lies around on the grass, so re-infestation can occur. Also, in public parks, children playing can become infected with the ova, hence the necessity to remove any stools. This is most important as it is the thoughtless owner who leaves dog's deposits around public places which eventually bars dogs from being allowed there.

Tapeworms are segmented, narrowing towards the head, and it is important that the head gets passed in a motion or the worm simply starts to grow again. This parasite requires an intermediate host, one example of which is the flea. An animal suffering from tapeworm frequently passes segments in a stool — flat and oval, resembling small pieces of dried rice. They can be seen sticking to the underpart of the tail. It is advisable to obtain suitable pills from your veterinary surgeon. Treatment is quite simple, and no longer has adverse effects as in former times. Many worm treatments will kill several types of worms.

External parasites

Fleas: The flea does not lay its eggs on the dog's body, but in nooks and crannies in articles such as bedding and in grass. The eggs develop into maggots and then into fleas which jump on the nearest living animal. Dog fleas do not as a rule remain on humans. This parasite is more likely to attack the young and old, the sick and unhealthy animals. Cats are frequently the cause of fleas being brought into the house and getting on dogs.

Flea allergy: Intense irritation will be caused by even one flea on a normally clean dog, if the dog has a flea allergy. Effects of just one bite can be very long lasting, ending up as dermatitis.

Treatment: There have been many outbreaks of fleas over recent years, but they have become resistant to various treatments. Other remedies which used to be successful have had their use restricted by the E.C. owing to the poisonous drugs they contain.

There are many preparations on the market — sprays, monthly pills and flea collars. Some products last over several weeks. Nuvan Top is one you can get from your vet, and Nuvan Staykil can be used in the home. This is something people forget to do — destroy the eggs laid around the dog's bedding and other corners of the house. I am very dubious about flea collars — many of them have been known to poison the animal, while others have proved allergic. I certainly would never use one unless it had been prescribed professionally. I prefer to bath the dogs with special shampoos which can be supplied by the vet, or you can get benzyl benzoate from the chemist. Use a teaspoonful to a pint of shampoo and bath as usual, but leave it in for a couple of minutes. Two shampoos may be sufficient to do the trick. Quellada and Tetmosol are others. If you want a special shampoo for dogs, you can get them from Vet Health and Pet Health. All Systems also does a good one for shows, where you feel there is a danger of your dog picking up parasites. Many germicidal shampoos do not kill fleas or lice, although they may act as a deterrent. Do not forget to treat all grooming tools and bedding.

Some remedies said to help keep fleas away: Vitamin B given in the form of brewers yeast tablets or in powder form is said to keep fleas from biting, as is garlic and apple cider vinegar — fleas are said to dislike the taste! A teaspoon of apple cider vinegar given daily will help stop the irritation. Another remedy for external use is a thinly sliced, unpeeled lemon soaked in a pint of water just off the boil. Leave it to soak overnight. Sponge all over the dog until the skin and hair are wet. Towel dry and leave to dry naturally. Another old method said to keep fleas away is to place lemon and orange peel around the beds — the oil they let off has an effect on fleas. I have not tried these remedies, but they may help to alleviate the situation while you are getting rid of the little creatures and their eggs.

Lice are very small and grey in colour, although they can be seen by the naked eye. They do not jump, but burrow their heads into the dog. They live their cycle on the host, and do not transfer to humans, but may transfer from one dog to another when there are several in close contact with each other. Therefore, all dogs in a group will need treating. The eggs are laid on the sides of the hairs and look like small particles of scurf, but unlike scurf, will not brush off and need to be removed with a special fine comb. The dog requires at least four regular weekly treatments to rid it of lice, the life cycle of the louse being two to four weeks. Nuvan Top can be used, but I think regular bathing with the above mentioned shampoos is more effective. EC regulations change so rapidly you may need to take advice.

Although it is a fairly easy matter to rid one or two dogs of these parasites, it is quite a different matter bathing a large number of dogs once a week for six to eight weeks as the eggs are insensitive to chemicals and are too firmly cemented on the hair to be easily removed by washing.

After treating your dogs, it is essential to prevent re-infestation by both fleas and lice. Burn all bedding, and dust over all beds with a suitable powder — your vet will advise on this. Be particularly careful to treat kennels, especially the corners and crevices — the easiest way to achieve this is to spray with a preparation which will kill parasites and their ova. Cromosal Ltd of Glasgow market is one such preparation which should be available from your pet store. Also, it is possible to hire appliances which can be wired into the nearest electric point to burn capsules to kill all such pests (e.g. Aerovap), but most of these are very expensive and more suitable for boarding kennels.

Ticks can be troublesome in warm weather. They are hidden in long grass and latch onto a dog as it brushes by. The tick buries its mouth part into the skin of the dog and sucks its blood, whereupon it swells up. If you are in a tick-infested areas (sheep-grazing areas can be bad), spray the dog with a flea spray before going out.

They must be killed before being removed or the head will be left in. It is most important that the whole head is removed, for if left behind in the skin, it will set up an irritation and may become infected. It is best to spray the tick with a flea spray, or you can soak a wad of cotton wool, in nail varnish, methylated spirit, dry cleaning fluid or chloraform, or even a lighted cigarette, and hold it to the tick. When the tick is dead, remove it with forceps. If your dog is troubled frequently, it is worth buying a pair of special tick-removal forceps.

Harvest mites are very small and difficult to see, except when in large numbers. They are a bright reddish orange colour, and inhabit chalky soil of woodlands, cornfields and grasslands, freshly baled straw and corn fields. The harvest mites usually attack the nose and face if the animal has been sniffing on the ground, but more commonly the belly in our low-slung dogs and between the cleft of the toes. They cause irritation. Seleen shampoo (most vets keep it) may be effective here as it is very good for stopping irritation.

Residual sprays and baths will kill larvae and prevent re-infestation. Keep your dog away from these areas if you have found them to be infested. Be very careful not to spray on vulnerable parts, such as the genitals and eyes. You can also try dipping the feet and undercarriage in a bath with citronella or eucalyptus added.

Cheyletiella are commonly called 'walking dandruff'. It is the scurf mite and does look like moving scurf — if you can see it. Many dogs can be infected without their owners realising until an owner is allergic to it and comes up in a rash. Animals can pass it on to each other, therefore all animals need to be treated with repetitive baths of special shampoos — Quallada is suitable for this. For a spray, Alucan is suitable, but not Nuvan Top. Take great care to see that every part of the dogs gets washed; particular care between the toes. Be very careful around the eyes, and do not use it in the ears — use Ouroto drops for the mites in the ears. Two bathings should be sufficient.

After treating your dogs for any parasites, it is essential to prevent re-infestation. Burn all bedding, and dust over all beds with a suitable powder. Be particularly careful to treat kennels, especially the corners and crevices.

Insurance
With veterinary fees being so high these days, it is well worth considering insurance. The Kennel Club now does insurance — you will get all the particulars when you register your puppy. There is also Pet Plan. Veterinary surgery has advanced so far in recent years that some very expensive operations can now be performed. On the other hand, owing to the high cost of vet fees, the cost of insurance has also risen. It does not cover such things as inoculations or cleaning teeth, and you have to pay the first £30 of any treatment. The Shih Tzu is a very robust little dog, but accidents can happen, and infection can take its toll. If you get an expensive illness, it is always nice to know your animal is covered. If you do not fully insure, it is important that you should have third-party cover — if your dog gets out on the road and causes an accident, you are liable by law and this could involve you in great expense with legal costs. The cost of third-party insurance is not high.

Kennels and runs
There is no doubt that the ideal way to keep the Shih Tzu is in the house as a companion, and this is usually quite practicable with small numbers. In this way, their characters are fully developed and they are best able to get all the attention they need.

From left Selco Tsu Yen (Bitch), Okima Foo Wun Kim (Dog), Okima Li Sien Lisi (Bitch)
Son & Daughters of Austch Tsampo Kwong Ho.

Now that the breed is so popular, more and more breeders are taking it up, either to start a new kennel or as a second string to an existing kennel. I feel some information and advice should therefore be given regarding the care of the Shih Tzu in kennels.

The breed can be kept in outside kennels perfectly happily so long as it is catered for correctly. It is an intensely curious and lively little creature, and to shut it away in a kennel while you go off to work is nothing short of mental cruelty. All kennel dogs should be given the opportunity to spend a certain amount of time in the home as well, especially bitches in whelp, who need extra love, and nursing mothers. Bring all your dogs into the home occasionally, even if they sleep outside; this will give them the chance to have the closer contact with the human family which they need, and which is indeed a hereditary right so far as the Shih Tzu is concerned.

Kennels should be situated near or beside the house, where the dogs can be both seen and heard and where they can hear your call and be aware of your presence. To have the kennels close by is to your advantage as well as theirs, for there are times when they may need attention at night. In the daytime, you can watch them in their runs, and it is a great help to be able to observe the progress of your young stock. There is also much pleasure to be gained in watching them play.

With this breed, there is great temptation to keep it too closely confined, with the aim of growing a coat and cutting down on the amount of work entailed when the dog leads a normal life. It is far better to have a larger-sized kennel, which can be sub-divided if necessary, than a tiny kennel which is not only difficult to clean out but quite inadequate for the dog when shut in. The heat in a small wooden kennel, for example, on a summer's day — and we do get them occasionally — can be quite over-powering. If it is necessary for the dog to be confined to its kennel, even for short periods, this should be insulated and should have shuttered windows which can be opened at floor level.

Several Shih Tzu can be kept together, although there will frequently be one very jealous dog or a stud dog who is 'kennel boss'. It is always wise to have more kennel accommodation available than you would normally require, enabling you to keep any trouble-makers or coat-chewers apart, or to separate them in cases of infection; ample accommodation also facilitates disinfection and annual treatment and repair of the kennels.

I prefer to keep my bitches in season well away from the stud dogs, which prevents the latter from becoming troublesome and losing weight. There is nothing like the proximity of bitches in season to cause fighting among stud dogs.

Providing several kennels with separate runs, plus one large exercising area, will keep the dogs more lively, for they can be moved from one to the other. This not only add a spice of interest to their lives, but is particularly beneficial if you are unable to take them out for daily walks, for without help daily, exercising is not always possible with a number of dogs.

The Shih Tzu can be kept alongside most other breeds, especially the gundogs and working breeds. This is the life the Shih Tzu likes, with the opportunity to go out with his active companions.

Never shut your Shih Tzu away in a cage and leave them to sit around for hours on end; they may end up with excellent coats but extremely poor bodies and action, quite apart from the fact that you will also cause much mental cruelty. You may fool some of the judges some of the time, but never all the judges all the time! The body underneath the coat and the action of the dog are of vital importance to this breed, and these can only be achieved by good kennelling and management. Coats which trail along the ground are quite unnecessary; they also impede the action of the dog. Always remember the dog should be 'lively, alert and active'.

Kennel runs

If you keep your dogs in the house and have an enclosed garden, you are indeed fortunate. However, if you have an open garden, as I have, looking out onto a busy main road, certain measures have to be taken, and if you have outside kennelling, you will also need runs. I think it is a mistake to run dogs solely on one type of surface, whether grass or concrete. If just grass is used, it means they must have a daily walk on a hard surface. Cement or concrete runs, favoured by most people because of the ease of cleaning, also have snags; they hold the water and can stay damp for some time, so in this case, benches or beds raised off the ground should be provided for the dogs to sit on. The imported H.U.B. bed is a good one, obtainable from H.U.B International, Butterflys, Peppard Farm, Peppard Common, near Henley-on-Thames, Oxfordshire RG9 5JU. Tel 0491 628897. There is no 'give' in concrete, and although it is a good — if rough — surface for bringing a dog up on its toes, to be on it all the time can weaken the pasterns.

Some makes of porous cement slabs are good, such as the Sussex Slab made by Thakeham; another is made by Garden Stone of Naphill, High Wycombe. However, others, particularly the pumice slabs, are too rough and tear the coat. These porous slabs should be laid loose on a sand base for drainage.

Shingle of a medium size — about 4in deep — is good for the feet; the dogs soon become accustomed to it, and will happily run around and play on it. Although cheaper than concrete, it does need constant replacement, for some will be removed with the faeces every time they are cleared up. Shingle drains well, but the dogs can dig in it and scatter pebbles in all directions.

Clinker runs are very good for the feet, but a dog should not be left in this type of run for too long; it is rough and breaks the coat. I do not think it is good for coated dogs. Shih Tzus are great diggers, using their mouths as well as their feet. They love to bury their toys and then, when thoroughly wet and dirty, dig them up again. When they dig, they very quickly break their whiskers.

The best answer I have come up with for runs is to have as many and varied types of surface as possible, which seems to work but does require more space. This is a help for the shows, as the puppy gets used to all surfaces and is not affected when changing from an indoor venue to outdoor grass.

Remember that grass runs must be limed once a year, and even this does not completely eradicate worm ova. Clear away all excreta, remembering that in wet weather, slugs attack the faeces. Slugs, in turn, bring lice.

Kennel cleaning

Kennels need cleaning out daily, although I find that most Shih Tzu are very clean in their kennels. Ample fresh water should always be available, and the containers must be washed out and refilled rather than merely topped up. Apart from daily cleaning, kennels should be scrubbed weekly, particular attention being paid to cracks and crevices. Use a disinfectant, but be careful that this is made up in the correct strength. The vet's 'Trigine' is better than bleach as it is kinder on the atmosphere. Too strong a disinfectant has been known to cause sterility. I put Vynol flooring down in all my kennels, which is easy to wash over, and I also spray all walls and floors monthly with a special disinfectant to minimise the risk of parasites.

Fencing

On the whole, fencing is not too difficult with the Shih Tzu, but if you have a naughty one or a persistent escapist, you need to take special precautions. I find 4ft chain-link fencing satisfactory in most cases. If you kennel bitches in season, you will need a 6ft fence, and if you have any straying Labradors around, it will need a guard rail on the top as well. I once had four bitches in season together inside their 6ft-high run, and on hearing a frightful noise, went to investigate, only to find a Labrador amongst them. From the reception he received, I think he was sorry he'd ever jumped in, but once inside, he found it difficult to jump out!

Plastic netting is not much use if you have a determined escapist, as he will chew through it and get away. The netting should be securely sunk into the ground. I have had some bitches who could get out of most things by chewing through wood or wire, digging under and climbing over, and these determinedly naughty ones invariably end up in the house. Just as with humans, it doesn't seem to pay to be good! We also get the persistent burrower, who will tunnel a way under any shed not on a fully cemented base.

Heating and lighting

It is a very great help to have electricity laid on in your kennels, and in the winter, lighting is virtually essential. Whether the kennels should be heated is a controversial point. I consider there should be some form of heating to keep the temperature above freezing point. The Vetbed, a type of thermal bedding, is very useful, not only for keeping them warm and comfortable, but also for allowing moisture to penetrate it while keeping the surface dry. If there is no heating, kennels should be lined and insulated.

This insulation is equally important in summer and winter since, as mentioned earlier, heat can become intense and too little notice gets taken of this. Any heating must be of a very safe nature; electricity is by far the best, although thermostatic-controlled electrically-heated oil radiators are quite acceptable. You can buy time switches, and room-controlled thermostatic plugs. Heated beds are also very good for kennel use in the cold weather. The Shih Tzu is better in a cool rather than very hot centrally-heated home.

Litter and bedding

Never, on any account, use sawdust on the floor. This gets into the coat, and when the Shih Tzu relieves himself he frequently scratches the ground with his back legs. What with this and shaking himself, sawdust ends up in the eyes — the next thing is an eye ulcer.

I would never recommend the use of wood wool for bedding for a Shih Tzu; this gets into the coat and tangles the hair. Small pieces can break off, bury themselves up to the skin and cause intense irritation. The same argument applies to straw. There are now various makes of polyester bedding on the market, the best and most expensive being Vetbed as supplied by the Animal Health Trust. Beds filled with polystyrene beads are comfortable and loved by the dogs. You need an outer cover which can be removed for washing. In wet weather, it is useful to use plenty of screwed-up newspaper which will absorb the worst of the moisture and can be burnt. It is both warm and absorbent. The main disadvantage is that the print rubs off onto the dogs' coats.

CHAPTER SEVEN

THE OLD DOG

Ch. Kareth Krishna age 12 years. Owned and bred by Mr Jim Peat.

The Shih Tzu is a long-lived dog; it has been known to live to 21 years, 13-15 being the average age. Generally speaking, the breed remains lively and youthful into old age, and the dog who has led an active and regular life, with sensible feeding, is likely to show the benefit when getting old. Ageing in the Shih Tzu does not start in any noticeable fashion until after ten years.

However, the old dog will naturally slow down, and it is necessary to keep his life well-regulated. He may become more set in his habits; food and sleep will become more important to him. If he does not continue to have some form of exercise, which for a dog adds both physical and mental stimulus, he is liable to sleep all day except when he can smell food around, and his joints will stiffen. The exercise may have to be given in a different form, for he will not walk so far and will go at a slower pace, though I have known of many who still lead very active lives.

It is very sad when an old dog has to stay in kennels, or indeed when any of his routine is upset. This is not so bad so long as he has his well-loved owner and possible dog companion with him, but if either leave him, he is liable to just pack up and die. I do not believe in trying to find new homes for very old dogs when their loved owner has died, or for some reason cannot keep them any longer. It is far kinder to have them put down by the veterinarian.

It is very important not to alter the old dog's routine, for however old they get, their internal clock seems to go on working, and they will wake up from their sleep at the routine times of feeding and exercise.

When any dog loses its constant companion, it is inclined to go into a decline. It is more difficult to know how to deal with this with the old one. People ask me if they should acquire a new puppy as a companion to it. There is no easy answer to this question, for it may or may not work. There are many things which have to be taken into account — age, general activeness and condition. It is no good bringing in a puppy if the old animal is in poor health, or is so old that it is sleeping all day, UNLESS you have facilities for keeping them apart. Again, if the old animal has always been used

to having a companion around it is more likely to appreciate another one. BUT, if it is a puppy, and many puppies are quite hyperactive, you must introduce them slowly and for very short intervals to gauge the reaction. It will be necessary to train the puppy to be shut away in a pen to allow the other old

Ch. Newroots Nankipoo of Snaefell owned by author, bred by Misses Fenner and Thomas. Showing colour changes from five months to 12 years.

animal its peace and quiet. It may love a puppy and mother or father it, but, enough is enough, and one thing they resent is being woken up by a young puppy who tries to rouse them into play.

Regular Grooming will keep the skin in condition. Otherwise, it is inclined to become scurfy and dry. Bathing him in Seleen shampoo may help and add a little extra corn oil to the food. These should help to combat dryness and a little light oil after a bath or added with grooming will help.

Many old dogs resent being groomed, especially round the head and face. If this is the case, it is far kinder to cut the hair back, especially round the eyes and beard. I have discussed this more fully in chapter 15, which deals with grooming and coat care.

Teeth: Many Shih Tzu loose their teeth early, as they do not have very deep roots. Have the teeth checked regularly; decaying ones should be removed, for they can poison the whole system. An anaesthetic will have to be given for this.

Body Odour: If older dogs are not regularly groomed, they are inclined to smell 'doggy'. Careful grooming will help considerably by cleaning the skin of its debris, and it is also helpful to rub over the coat with a chlorophyll cloth afterwards. I have never found any harm come to older dogs through bathing them, so long as care is taken to keep them warm until they are absolutely dry. In fact, they always seem to be very happy with themselves after the bath, and appreciate the extra attention they have had, even if they do not actually enjoy the bath!

The Senses

Sight is usually the first sense to fail with the Shih Tzu. The eyes of many old dogs will show a blueish haze; this is not necessarily a cataract, but may be ageing of the lens. Some old dogs develop 'dry eye' and these eyes need special attention as the tears are not functioning. You can use artificial teardrops which you can obtain from the chemist, but they do not do much good unless they are constantly put into the eye, meaning hourly. A new treatment of special lubricating drops has now been discovered. Refer to Chapter 17.

If the dog does go blind, he may still lead a happy life so long as he remains in familiar surroundings. It is surprising how well he manages to get around. Always be cautious when you approach a blind animal — speak its name and let it sniff the back of your hand before touching it.

If trouble is caused by discharge from the eyes, bathe them daily. It can also be helpful to cut away the hair around them, thus preventing the possibility of friction on the cornea. Make sure that as the hair grows it is not allowed to grow upwards into the eye, for that will cause friction again. It helps to soften the hair if you Vaseline round the eye daily after you bathe it.

Deafness: A deaf dog, even if it still has its eyesight, should always be approached gently, for any sudden movement can startle it and make it nervy. Never allow young children to worry old dogs, particularly when they are sleeping.

Diet

This is covered more fully in Chapter 8. Much depends on the dog's general condition. If he is in good health and showing no signs of failing digestion, such as vomiting or diarrhoea, bringing up wind or vomiting froth, you can more or less keep to the normal diet, but cut down on proteins and give extra vitamins and minerals, particularly vitamin E, or wheat germ.

If the dog brings up gasses and mucus, it might well help to give him a charcoal biscuit. Drinking extra water can be the start of many problems for a dog and it is best to get the animal checked straight away. A failing digestion or other symptoms may need veterinary advice, as this may be the first sign of some disease.

Some diseases of old age

Pyometra is pus in the uterus. It frequently occurs in veteran bitches, whether they have been bred from or not, particularly those who have suffered from false pregnancies. The very first signs of trouble usually occurs from 9-12 weeks after the season. An operation for the removal of the uterus and ovaries is the only cure at their age. The best way to prevent this happening is to have her spayed early. There is more on pyometra in chapter 17.

Lumps develop in many old dogs in various parts of the body. In bitches, these frequently appear on the mammary glands. These are often partly benign and partly cancerous. Some vets feel it is best to leave them alone unless they start to grow. Feed extra fresh foods, and keep the animal in as healthy an environment as possible. Physical and mental treatment works together, and many purists feel good feeding can delay the cancerous growth, and operating stirs it up. I would let your vet look at them and abide by his decision. If they are very bad, it maybe necessary for her to have a mammary strip.

Heart disease is another frequent cause for concern. The first obvious sign of this is usually a hard, dry cough, and veterinary advice should be sought immediately.

Diabetes may also affect old animals. Symptoms are excessive drinking, vomiting, possible loss of appetite and an enlarged abdomen, which gives the owner a misguided picture of fatness while the ribs and vertebrae are horribly prominent. Insulin injections can be given, but treatment by mouth is unsatisfactory. If the dog objects to the injection, it may be kinder to have it humanely destroyed.

Kidney Failure: Many old animals suffer from this, sometimes arising out of an earlier infection. The wear and tear on the kidneys can be very great over the years, particularly if the animal has been fed incorrectly or cheap proteins have been used in the diet. This will cause premature aging and death. Inflammation of the kidney can be brought on by damp, or if the dog gets chilled, older dogs being much more likely to suffer the effects than young ones. Make sure the dog is dry when he goes to bed. Excessive thirst and frequent passing of urine are early signs of trouble, and you should have your dog checked.

Bladder Weakness: Some old dogs may be affected, particularly if they have been castrated or spayed. They will need to be put out more frequently, or if they have to be left for any length of time, put newspaper by the door. Some may have incontinence at night and wet their beds. Use vet bed for their bedding as the urine will go through it and leave the surface dry.

Liver Failure: The symptoms can be similar to kidney failure, and the condition will need to be diagnosed by your veterinarian. A special low-protein diet will be needed. Both Petfoods and Hills now make one. These diets are only obtainable from your vet.

CHAPTER EIGHT

FEEDING

The feeding of dogs is big business. There are numerous manufacturers, most of whom have their own vets and dieticians working on their recipes. There are tinned foods, those which need a mixer meal and others which are complete. There are dried foods which are also complete, but require soaking or sufficient water in a bowl for the dog to drink. Then there are others in sealed long-life packets. Yet it can still be difficult to know which is best to use for your dog. Your dog, particularly a house dog, will have its own idea about diet — "You can take a horse to the water but you can't make him drink." It is most important to read the label as most of them have added vitamins and minerals, but not all sufficient in the ones your dog requires, and many experts are of the opinion that many of these vitamins are destroyed in the process of preparation. The manufacturers give their own instructions as to quantity to feed according to the size of the dog. All dogs vary in their appetite, and just like humans, some put on weight easily, others always stay thin whatever you feed. If your dog is doing well on the diet you are using, there should be no reason for you to change it.

Nutrition is one of the most important aspects of dog-rearing. New knowledge of dietetics and the consequent effects on the body are constantly coming to light. With the best of intentions, much harm can be done by adding too many extras to the diet and upsetting the balance as a result. The dog is a carnivorous animal, but this does not mean it only eats large amounts of red muscle meat (correctly speaking, it is an omnivore). In the wild, the dog firstly gorges itself on the vegetable protein substance of the stomach of a 'kill' before eating the entrails and offal. In this way, it obtains the vital vitamins and minerals. Therefore, to feed your dog entirely on red muscle meat because of its protein content is by no means sufficient as it does not cover all the nutriments, in spite of being a great body builder. It also lacks calcium.

We are often told that a dog does not require a change of diet; so long as it is on a good one, it should stay on it all the time. Now this is correct for many dogs, mostly kennel dogs. The majority of Shih Tzus are not kennel dogs, I am glad to say. Also, I do not believe any diet can be 100 per cent sufficient. Too much new knowledge keeps coming to light. Does anybody really know everything about food, especially when so many chemical sprays and drugs are used? I, like many other breeders, feel a varied balanced diet is more likely to provide the animals with all the essential vitamins, minerals and trace elements. The dog food manufactures will say it is impossible to make up a balanced diet at home. I say if you give sufficient variety, you will obtain all the necessary ingredients, and can add your own supplements.

What is a balanced diet? It usually means the NRC (National Research Council) recommendations of optimum quantities of nutriment, i.e. protein, fat and carbohydrates, the trace elements, amino-acids and vitamins. Unfortunately, these recommendations do not take into account any special conditions or performances of dogs, and from reading various authoritative books, I do not think everybody agrees with all their findings. However, their guidelines for the R.D.C. (recommended daily requirements) are very good. Different types of food will have different amounts and forms of minerals and trace elements; many manufactured foods have this added, but not all, so check. Personally, I like to play it safe and give the minimum requirement of balanced supplements daily. The danger to avoid is over-supplementation, which can be as bad or worse than giving nothing. This is why I think it best to use a complete supplement such as SA37, usually obtainable from vets and pet shops, or any other good one on the market (and there are plenty of them), rather than giving a bit of this and a bit of that. If something extra is required at a given time, it can be added. These supplements have been worked out by qualified people. The other safe way, if not using supplements all the time, is to boost the dog for a short period with whatever is required. Alternative supplements to give are bone meal or calcium, cod liver oil for Vitamin D and Vetzymes or brewers yeast tablets for the Vitamin B group. An American vet who believes in vitamin therapy advised extra Vitamin E 100iu and Vitamin C up to 1gm. Seaweed powder will give minerals and iodine. Garlic is used by many as it is a good internal disinfectant, and is said to be a worm deterrent, but this is doubtful. Vegetables and fruit which boost Vitamin C are enjoyed by many Shih Tzus.

Dogs can vary in their requirements just as much as people. You get the thin dog who is always bounding with energy, and the fat lazy dog. These dogs need some adjustments to their diet, both as pets and for show. Then again, there is the bitch in whelp and the stud dog who need extra care with their diets. There are also many minor ailments and allergies which can often be helped by changing and correcting the diet.

The daily diet for a normal dog

The normal dog requires only one feed a day. You can either feed it morning, afternoon or evening, but keep to the same routine daily, same time, same place and same dish. If the dog is on the small side, two meals a day may be better than one, but again, a routine time is important. The dog looks forward to feeding time.

Do not economise over food — always go for good quality. That does not mean the most expensive, as you are frequently told "a cheap cut of meat is quite as nutritious as an expensive one". Poor feeding is likely to lead to poor health, distress for the dog and vet's bills.

If you use tinned foods which requires a mixer meal, a normal, average-sized Shih Tzu should be fed half a large tin daily with an equal amount of biscuit meal — that is the manufacturer's instructions. The meal does not have to be fed with the meat, and it is no good telling the owner of that dog that it must. These dogs are better with two meals daily. Besides, there are those experts who tell you that meat and meal should not be fed together anyway. However, whichever you feed, the dog must have the carbohydrates in some form or other, and there really are many kinds to give. There is nothing wrong with an ordinary breakfast cereal, if you prefer to use that. A 'small' good-quality mixer meal is best for a Shih Tzu, or rice. They do require a larger biscuit to chew — this can be in the form of puppy rusks or even baby rusks such as Ovaltine. Do not use the very hard large biscuits put up for big dogs, as Shih Tzu teeth are not strong enough.

When feeding fresh foods, work on an average of 4-6oz of meat daily, depending on the size of your dog. Meat can be red muscle meat; lamb or beef are equally nutritious, though lamb contains more fat than lean beef. White meat such as chicken, turkey or rabbit are as high in protein as red meats, but remember, particularly when feeding puppies or bitches in whelp, that red meats are short in calcium. Fish is excellent, especially the oily fish like herrings, but go carefully — they are rich. Offals in the form of heart, kidney and liver are good to give two or three times a week. They are a good source of Vitamin B, but be careful that you do not overdo the liver as it is likely to make the dog loose — it is best cooked, but gently, so as not to destroy the vitamins. The other organ meats contain a lot of fibre and are not good fed on a regular basis. Tripe — the smelly raw green kind — is excellent for dogs. You can buy it frozen and minced from pet shops. I use 6-8oz per dog. I am against using knacker's meat, for too many drugs may have gone into the animal before it died, but I know many who use it with apparently no ill-effects. I hesitate to think what goes into some commercial dog foods when I read the Food Council's definitions of meat.

If you use the complete-meal dried foods, you should go by the manufacturer's instructions, but the quantity they give is often too much for one meal and best divided into two. Some are of a higher quality and more concentrated so you do not have to feed so much. There are now so many on the market from which to choose that it becomes quite confusing.

Buy small amounts to see which your dog gets on with best. The muesli type is used by many people with the addition of tripe. They are cheaper than some, though not necessarily the best for your purpose. They all vary a bit in their composition, so look at the analysis. Most manufacturers now make food for different ages and conditions. They vary a little in the content, mostly the protein. Puppies and active dogs require higher protein in their diets. Our Shih Tzus require a high fat content for their coats.

When you find one the dogs will eat well, keep a good check on their condition. Weigh them to start with and keep a regular check on weight. This will give you a quick indication of suitability for your animals. Most people like to add a small amount of meat to these dried complete foods, but be careful you do not upset the balance which has been carefully worked out by the manufacturers. You should not add more than 20 per cent meat. Whenever you use dried or semi-dried food, water must be left down at all times. If you do not do so, the dog may suffer from kidney problems. The semi-dried foods are expensive to feed in bulk, but quite acceptable to the dog.

Chopped vegetables and fruit are good things to add to the diet. French beans, spinach, chopped lettuce, brussels sprouts and tomatoes are very much appreciated. Carrots fed with the meal are best cooked as they are better digested that way, but give raw carrots to chew at other times, as they are good for the teeth as well as containing important vitamins. The dogs love their sweetness. Mine steal the ripening tomatoes off the window sill and chew holes in sacks of potatoes, taking them out and chewing them like bones. Beetroot are lovely, so long as you do not mind purple whiskers! Many Shih Tzus like fruit. They have been known to pick apples off the low branches of trees, and also rob strawberry beds — even oranges and bananas are enjoyed by some. Many of these vegetables and fruits will add some Vitamin C to the diet. It used to be said that dogs synthesised their own Vitamin C, but now it is known that many do not make sufficient, and certain illnesses have been helped and cured by giving it.

It is difficult to know what to say about bones. It is true that they are about the only thing which help to keep the tartar off the teeth, but they can also cause a lot of trouble when small bits are chewed off. The dog often vomits and you can see the splinters. Also, if you have several dogs, bones cause fights. If bones are given, they must be of the long variety, or rib bones, and never poultry, rabbit or chop bones. I do agree that something hard should be given to the dog to chew, and not all soft soggy food, but I prefer to give biscuits. You have to choose the right kind to suit your dog. Baked wholemeal bread is also good. Biscuits which are suitable to eat and can be obtained from pet shops are ovals, Vims and especially Biscrok, which can be bought in three varieties — wholemeal, calcium and mineral. Dogs have their preference — mine prefer the wholemeal. Laughing Dog (Roberts of Dunchurch) and Woffcol do some very good ones. Dog "chews" are also very useful. They are good for the teeth and stave off boredom, which can often lead to other problems such as coat chewing, excessive licking, scratching, etc. Don't use those which wind round and round as they have been known to be chewed until soft, then partially swallowed in a long string and stuck down the throat. The round or flat compressed ones are much better.

Make quite sure that all dried food and biscuits are fully expanded and do not swell when soaked. These are very dangerous if fed dry, as they expand in the dog's stomach. You can make a good stock of all left-over vegetable trimmings, cooked and ground down, in which to soak your biscuits.

Water should be left in a suitable bowl for the dog to drink throughout the day. Some nutritionists advise taking it up at meal times, but not if feeding dried or semi-dried foods. If your dog likes to have a drink of milk, give him one by all means, but it should never be given instead of water.

It may take several days for a dog to get used to a complete change of diet, and if possible, this should be done gradually. Add a little more to the old diet daily until the dog becomes used to it.

Shih Tzus do require extra fat in their diet for their coats. This should be in the form of a polyunsaturated vegetable fat — a teaspoonful daily added to their food is worthwhile, or you can give polyunsaturated margarine.

If your dog does not want his meal one day, pick it up after one hour and let him go without. Do not fuss him and give him something special or he will expect it every day.

The best way to know if your dog is getting enough, or too much food, is by his condition. A Shih Tzu should not be over-fat but nicely muscled. You should be able to feel its ribs without your fingers sticking into thick layers of fat, but at the same time, the ribs should not be prominent and bony. The body should feel hard and firm, not soft and flabby.

No matter how good the diet, the dog will not thrive without good husbandry. This involves regular feeds, exercises, love and attention. There are good feeders and bad feeders besides good and bad eaters. Dogs should be given their meal on separate dishes. Never feed a shy dog in company with a greedy one — put the shy one in a safe compartment. Several dogs eating together usually feed better than one on its own, but conversely this may cause them to bolt their food.

Puppy diet from eight weeks

If you have bought your puppy from a good breeder, I am sure you will have been given a diet sheet or, at the least, told how to feed it. You really should follow those instructions. The puppy is already under stress having just left its mother and siblings. If you make any change, do it gradually or the puppy will get diarrhoea.

Unfortunately, some people have not been told what to feed it, and others find the puppy will not eat the diet anyway. This frequently happens, for the new environment is very different, even the dish is different, and there is no competition to see who can eat their food first.

I will give some diets suitable for an eight-week-old puppy. I suggest four feeds daily, with a drink of milk last thing at night if you like. Some people give five feeds — it depends how well the puppy is eating.

Fresh Food Diet for an eight-week-old puppy

8am: A puppy may have been weaned on milk and Farex, and it is very good, but many of them do not like it and want to progress onto something else. Try milk and breakfast cereal, or milk and Farley Rusk, either soaked or dry. If the puppy tires of this — and many do — try a boiled egg custard — one egg to 1/2 pint of milk is sufficient for two meals for two puppies, and can be cooked easily in the microwave oven (see end of chapter on recipes). I give this as their last feed at night, and leave some milk for them to drink in the night or in the early morning, then give them a dry Farley Rusk to chew. They love it, and it is easy to eat. They might like scrambled egg — it is useful doing eggs this way as you can add milk which helps to give calcium.

Some will eat lightly boiled egg mashed up. If you give a raw egg beaten in milk, do not use the egg white. This should be cooked as it is indigestible raw and destroys the biotin, although an occasional one is unlikely to hurt.

12pm: 1 1/2 -2oz raw butcher's mince, or finely minced raw tripe, with crumbled biscuit meal or Allbran and a pinch of seaweed powder and supplements (SA37) unless this puts him off his food. If he eats it well, a little chopped vegetable can be added.

4pm: 1 1/2 -2oz of alternate meals, i.e. chicken, tripe, rabbit, or fish.
8pm   The same as the morning.

Always leave down a bowl of water for the puppy to drink.

If your puppy has been on this sort of diet, continue with it, increasing the amounts as the puppy grows older, giving 6oz meat at four months and 8oz by six months. You will have dropped one of the milk feeds early on around three months, but continue with the one milk feed, or just milk as long as the puppy will take it. Milk is good for supplying calcium.

A puppy needs some supplement to his diet, either in the form of bonemeal and cod liver oil for Vitamin D, or SA37 or Cal-D is useful for puppies if extra calcium is required. Do not overdose with either, and keep to the suggested quantities. It can do as much harm giving too much calcium and Vitamin D as giving none. Continue with these foods until 12 months, but stop grinding up the meal. Cut the meat into small pieces when he has some teeth, and let him have small biscuits like ovals, Biscrok, or rusks such as Farley to chew; but nothing that can be swallowed whole which could choke him.

A growing puppy requires more food than an adult dog. When the puppy is a year old, you can cut down the food to the adult diet. In all this feeding, you must bear in mind the size of your dog. If he is so small as to be below standard size, feed smaller feeds more often. If he is above standard size, give him the maximum amount of food. So long as the puppy is not getting too fat, permit him to eat all he wants.

Alternative diets

Dry complete foods: There are many on the market made specially for puppies, and so long as they are soaked completely, they can be used for weaning. When the puppy is older and has teeth, if you use unsoaked dried food, I cannot impress enough that you make sure the puppy drinks sufficient water. There are now so many makes of dried foods on the market, but you need to choose carefully, as some are too large for a Shih Tzu. Breeders who use them have their favourites.

Tinned foods: There are many complete diets in tinned foods specially made for puppies, and they contain all necessary nutriments so you do not have to worry about it getting the correct food or supplements. These do not need a mixer meal. Puppies can be weaned straight onto them, so long as they can manage to eat them. Petfood have brought out a very good and palatable new one. Denes also make one. Hills' Growth is highly recommended by vets. However, many Shih Tzus do not manage to eat it early on, so if they have not been introduced to it, keep your puppy on the breeder's recommended diet — even if the vet tells you it should be on Hills — you can slowly introduce it with its other food so long as the puppy can manage to pick it up and eat it. The flat face of the Shih Tzu makes it difficult to pick up, and it is likely to roll it round its mouth and spit it out.

If you are unsure whether your puppy is getting enough or too much to eat, go by his general body condition. The body should be nicely covered, not too bony and thin; neither should he be too fat and heavy. You can easily feel if there is a lot of excess fat on him. There are people who prefer a fat puppy and let it run the fat off as it gets to be an adult. I do not agree with this. A puppy's bones are still soft, the ends of the bones are still cartilagineous, and the excess weight on the puppy can so easily bend the legs and make him bowed. Puppies rush around more than adults, so you may have difficulty later on in getting rid of excess fat.

Most puppies go off food when cutting their teeth because their mouth is sore, so give nourishing but soft food. Let him chew beef rib bones for a short while each day, or play with a baby's circular teething ring to help his teeth. Eating should soon start again when the mouth gets less sore so long as food which hurts his mouth is not given. Be careful not to feed any large round foods which can get stuck in his throat if he swallows them whole. Poor eating is sometimes due to irritants in the stomach, such as hair balls which have not been passed, mucus which has become almost solid, and of course, worms and anything he may have picked up from the ground. He is just like a human baby at a certain age — everything goes into the mouth. This is why he should not have rubber toys if he chews them. The best way to be sure all these things get passed is by giving sufficient roughage in the diet.

If the puppy is having a bad time with his teeth to such an extent that he will not let you open his mouth, I would take him to your vet just in case there is any infection in the gums. There are some good homoeopathic remedies for teething. If he is just off his food, an injection of B12 might help.

If there are any tummy upsets, take the puppy off milk immediately.

Breeding

The stud dog

He should have been well-fed from puppy-hood, well-exercised and in lean hard condition. He requires a high-protein diet of 30 per cent dry weight. There are plenty of suitable foods on the market for the active dog, and if he is being used at stud frequently, one of these can be useful.

Bitches in whelp

The need for correct feeding in these cases is so important that all rules can be broken. The bitch needs to eat — if she does not, the necessary requirements for her puppies will come from her own body, and she will suffer first. She should have been on a thoroughly good diet long before she was mated. It is suggested that when she comes into heat, her maintenance diet should be increased by 10 per cent both before and after mating; this is thought to give the maximum number of puppies. After being mated, so long as she has been on a good well-balanced diet containing all essentials, including supplements, there is no need to alter her diet or give her anything extra until the sixth week. The last three weeks are the greatest time of growth of the foetus. There are good 'special' commercial diets, if she will eat them.

Raspberry leaf tablets, which can be bought from herb farms or health shops, are said to act as a tonic to the uterus and to facilitate whelping. Many of the extras beneficial to the bitch in whelp are contained in Easy Whelp, made by Pet-Tex The Animal Health Co, and contains most of the ingredients you need, such as calcium gluconate, probiotics, raspberry leaf and dextrose. This is given for ten days before whelping and ten days after.

Black treacle, $\frac{1}{4}$ teaspoon given from the first week after mating, increased to $\frac{1}{2}$ before the birth and continued until the puppies are weaned is said to be an excellent aid to pigment. Unfortunately, I've never managed to get mine to eat it.

At three weeks, nature dictates that she rests from food. This means she may starve herself for a day or so, often longer, then slowly come back on to her full diet. Do not worry over this, it is natural.

After one week of dieting, there is still no need to worry, but if she does not come back to eating, I tempt her with food and give a five-day course of Vitamin B12, Cytacon from Glaxo or Vet Health Iron and Vitamin B Tonic (this also contains B6). After all, humans get finicky over their diet when they are pregnant, and I don't see why the same can't happen to a bitch. She may suffer from nausea or just have fads for different food, so you must find out what she likes to eat and try everything. This can be expensive, but very necessary to producing a healthy litter of puppies. If you don't intend doing it well, it is far better not to do it at all. This is where you might have to break all your rules, like feeding her when you are having your meal; if she thinks it is your food she is more likely to eat it.

If the bitch is eating very little, then make sure the quality is of the best. Have her on a supplement (SA37 or VH Hypernutrient), to start with, giving the specified everyday dose, $\frac{1}{4}$ teaspoon, and increasing this from the sixth week. Always go by the directions on the bottle or tin — to give too much can do more harm than good. If she will not take the supplement with her food, which is quite likely, then you can give her Cal-D, but again, only in the recommended dose, and not in addition to the SA37. The best way to administer this is by syringe as it is a liquid, using one of those small throwaway syringes you can get from your chemist or vet. This is very easy as you just pop the nozzle into the side of her mouth and squirt it in, making sure it is swallowed. Do not overdo the calcium — you will get the puppies too large. If your bitch will drink milk, let her have it, but if she does not, then don't worry — you can put a teaspoon of dried milk granules on her food. She may drink the milk if you add a little glucose.

Try giving her small meals more often. You should do this anyway towards the end of the pregnancy. The pups take up a lot of room, so the stomach does not want to get too distended — it will give her indigestion and make her very uncomfortable. This alone could put her off her food, but she needs at least 30 per cent protein.

Does she fancy a little cheese or liver? You can grate these over the food and it may just start her eating. Frequently, a bitch prefers to have her food without any carbohydrates (biscuit meal, etc.). This can certainly be cut down, as a high-protein diet is essential now. Many prefer eating smelly foods, such as green tripe and liver or kidneys. Fish is good value, particularly if you can pressure-cook it so that all the bones are softened. These contain calcium and iodine which is lacking in the meat. Chicken and rabbit are good protein foods, and have as much food value as red meat. Also, the bitch will usually eat them. If she won't eat from her dish, drop a piece on the floor, as this often starts an animal eating again. Do this even if every bit has to be dropped. Also try spreading the food out a bit on a flat surface. Once you get her to start eating protein again, try introducing a little soaked biscuit or brown rice. It is important during those last three weeks to get her eating some carbohydrates. Eggs are very good food value. A couple of hard-boiled eggs for breakfast go down well with many bitches, or make an omelette or pancakes with them. Cottage cheese is excellent as it is high in protein and calcium. Spaghetti or macaroni is also enjoyed with some margarine melted on it. Give an Ovaltine rusk in milk at bedtime. Try all the other suggestions mentioned under *Finicky or Problem Eaters* p102.

Failing all this, if the situation becomes really critical, you can resort to feeding Complan by syringe.

Don't worry about the food value in the different meat, fish or poultry, as the protein in them is all much the same. Some do have more fat than others, and some are lacking in calcium and iodine, etc., but if you can vary the diet, most essentials are included. You should be covering the vitamin and trace elements requirements with your supplement. During the last three weeks of pregnancy, you should double the quantity of supplement, as it is really needed then.

If a bitch is heavily in whelp, divide her food into three meals a day, as she will digest this much better. A few days before she whelps, she may go off her food. It is certainly likely that she will refuse to eat at the onset of parturition, though I have known cases where this has not happened at all. On one occasion, the bitch ate her normal meal, then just turned around and produced a puppy without any warning!

Nursing the litter

It is most important that the puppies suck on the first day. They get colostrum from the bitch, and this contains antibodies which go into the bloodstream of the whelp. This is why it is so important that they should suck straight away as these antibodies give them immunity to disease.

Give the bitch a warm drink of milk and glucose as soon as she has settled after the litter is born; she usually appreciates it. Leave water nearby where she can reach it, as it is most important she has plenty of fluids. If she has not eaten for some time, nor eaten the placentas, which give her nourishment, she may be very hungry, so I give her a meal of chicken or fish. Some people go straight on to a full normal diet. I play it by ear, but rather favour the light diet with plenty of fluids, particularly if there is a small litter. What is the use of helping to bring in more milk than is required? Also, the bitch usually has a rise of temperature for three days, and does not feel like eating until it is down. In fact, most bitches are reluctant eaters for the first week. Drinking milk or water is most important — the milk will help to put in some calcium.

If the litter is a large one, naturally the bitch will need more food than if it is small. Mine are reluctant to drink milk after the first day, so I make some nice rabbit, chicken or liver stock to help get them started and to get the fluids in. The stock can be thickened with Farex and a tablespoon of dried milk can be added. After that, I go on to eggs, fish, white meats and cottage cheese, resuming normal and varied diet when the temperature has dropped. The diet should gradually be increased, depending on the litter size. By four weeks, the bitch should be having three to four times her normal diet, spread out in four meals daily. Of course, she should have access to water all the time. One cannot stress too strongly the vital importance of good and adequate feeding for the nursing mother. The addition of a small quantity of dried-milk granules on her food (Litterlac is good as it is made for dogs) is usually acceptable and adds vitamins and calcium if she is not drinking milk.

At first, she will expect you to feed her inside the whelping bed. If she is a good mother, she will not like leaving her pups to get food for herself.

Other foods I use are baked custard, 4 eggs to 1 pt of milk so that it is fairly stiff and can be cut when cold; porridge, again make it stiff, and rice pudding.

If you are unable to get in sufficient supplements, give Cal-D Oral. Give according to the instructions on the bottle — about 7ml for a 14lb (7 kilos) bitch.

If all does not go well, say, a rise of temperature for various reasons, i.e. mastitis, retained placenta, etc., and the bitch is put on antibiotics which again put her off her food and sometimes dry up the milk, one naturally gets worried about the whelps getting sufficient nourishment. You must keep them sucking, even if you are hand-feeding them, as the sucking helps to stimulate the milk to come back in. It is essential that you get fluids into the mother. When you feed the whelps, the mother gets worried and usually wants to try their food — this gives you the opportunity to get some nourishment into the her. I make up a solution of an egg yolk (do not use the white), $1/2$ pint milk, two teaspoonfuls of glucose, and about one tablespoon of evaporated milk. Beat them together and feed her with a Catac Foster Feeding Bottle standard size. I do not use the rubber teats for the mother, but drop the liquid into her mouth straight from the glass teat of the bottle.

Feeding the reluctant mother. See chapter 11: The First Three Weeks.

Once she has had the first drop, I have found no trouble in getting her to take more. She can stay on this until her appetite returns. You can increase the egg yolk and vary the liquids. Liver and rice balls often start her eating again.

The Thin Dog

A Shih Tzu should be fairly lean but muscular. You ought to be able to feel the ribs, but certainly not so that they stick out and feel bony. Unfortunately, many judges prefer show dogs who are too fat, and mistakenly call it "good body". You will often get away with an overweight dog, but seldom with one that is too thin. Vets have more problems with obese dogs than thin ones.

There can be many reasons for a dog being too thin. First, check for worms. This should be done at least three times a year as routine. If a dog is not in good health, this can cause thinness and is a veterinary problem. All we are discussing now is the healthy dog who is having difficulty in putting on weight.

I am presuming he is being given sufficient food. If he is not, you must increase the diet, and add fattening foods with more calories. Give two feeds a day, morning and evening. No doubt you are saying, "I try to get him to eat more, but he won't." You will find ways to help under *Finicky or Problem Eaters* (p102). Make sure what you give is fattening, high in calories, with ample carbo-hydrates and fats.

Make porridge with milk; make it thick so it can be cut and hand-held when cold. Most dogs love this. I find they need to be hand-fed or it sticks everywhere around the whiskers. You also need to watch it is not getting stuck round the inside of the mouth, so only hand out small portions at a time. Add a teaspoonful of suet to the meat diet, which is also good for the coat, or a little dried milk on the food. Spaghetti or macaroni with polyunsaturated margarine added, and some grated cheese, is usually much enjoyed. They like it fed warm as you would eat it. I usually cut it up — it's slightly less messy that way. Oily fish is excellent, if they will eat it — herrings, fresh or tinned in olive oil, sardines in oil or mackerel. Tuna fish is one of the favourites.

If your Shih Tzu likes milk, try goat's — it is best. Add a raw egg yolk, or a teaspoonful of Virol. You can even put brown bread in it if he is not good at eating dry biscuits, which are much better for him. I have even rubbed liver over the Biscroks to tempt them — it has usually worked.

A titbit of a slice of toast with Flora margarine at breakfast time will probably be enjoyed. Bad behaviour, I know, but they usually eat better if they think it is your food, and anyone trying to reduce their weight knows that eating between meals puts in on! However, make your titbits healthy ones, not a lot of sweet biscuits, though digestives are not so bad.

If you have a highly active dog, try to restrict his exercise a bit as he is burning up all the fat you are trying to get on him. However, if he is not a show dog, this does not matter — just give him the extra food to make up for his extra energy.

During the cold weather, particularly if the dogs are kennelled, extra food and vitamins need to be given as they are burning up their fat to help keep themselves warm. Give them a plate of brown rice with a little bit of tinned food added for additional flavour. Two feeds a day are important, and make sure the diet has sufficient fat. It is also beneficial to provide food warm.

Times when it is very difficult to keep male dogs in condition is when there are bitches in season. This puts most dogs off their food, as they fret to get to the bitches and very quickly lose weight. There is not much you can do about this except try to keep them well away from the bitches' scent. Put your bitches on Veterinary Amplex when you first see signs that their season is approaching. One sign is spending very frequent pennies when they are out for their walks, and the vulva begins to swell. Amplex given in time and kept up during the season is very helpful to these small dogs, but if you are intending breeding from the bitch, do not give Amplex, and if you are using other preparations sprayed on, you will have to stop them several days before the bitch is due for mating or you will put the dog off. Hills have a new product obtainable from your vet for sick and convalescing animals and those who are emaciated. A short period of this food might help. It is very concentrated and expensive, but the animals does not need to be on it for long.

The Fat Dog

It is not healthy for a dog to be too fat. Diabetes Mellitus and degenerate heart failure is more likely to affect the obese dog. I don't think this is on the whole such a problem in the Shih Tzu as in many breeds, but then the thick coat covers up the body so much that on looking, one cannot tell the difference between coat and excess flesh. Unfortunately, a dog often wins in the show ring on his "good body", whereas really he is just too fat for his own good. A too-thin dog never gets away with it! What you want to aim for is a well-covered body in good hard condition with plenty of muscle. When your fingers sink into soft flesh, you should begin to question whether your dog isn't putting on too much weight. You should be able to feel the ribs of a Shih Tzu, but not to play a tune on them, and he should have plenty of firm muscle on the thighs. This is what the standard asks for.

A spayed bitch can cause problems. I think the best way with her is to watch her weight as soon as she has been spayed and try to prevent her getting fat rather than trying to slim her down later. Prevention is undoubtedly easier than cure. You should note her weight regularly, keep her exercised, never give her titbits and keep her on a strict maintenance diet.

If your dog is really obese, it is safer to get the weight down by diet rather than sudden forced exercise. As the dog loses its fat, it will become more active, but forced exercise at that stage could be too much strain on the heart. The obese dog needs a vet's check-up and advice, and he may put it on to a commercial calorie-controlled diet. Some of these diets are only sold to vets, but they are very carefully worked out so that the calories are spread into ingredients which will not let the dog get overly hungry.

The majority of fat dogs are not in the previous category. If you really mean to get the weight down, you must co-operate even more than the dog, for he is not going to do it on his own. What is more he will make it as difficult as possible for you, by pleading and asking for food.

There should be no titbits. If you are too weak over this, see that it is a small piece of meat from his overall ration. The meal can be divided up into two or three (if there is enough of it) and spread out over the day. This may keep you and the dog happier.

The dog should be exercised an hour a day if possible, to see any result.

The dog's food must not contain fattening ingredients, and you can add non-fattening things like bran and vegetables to give bulk. You can try the following diet, which aims at giving bulk with less calories, so that the dog will feel replete. The rice can be cooked in a large quantity and kept in the fridge, where it will keep very well.

The following amount is for a dog around 20lb, which is above standard weight of a Shih Tzu (top standard weight of the Shih Tzu is 18lbs, but if the dog is oversized, it will weigh more without necessarily being too fat). For a 15lb dog, you would only give three quarters of the amount. You must check the dog's weight. If there is no weight loss at all after one week, reduce the amount.

> One 8oz cup of cooked brown rice
> $^1/_3$ of a cup of chopped lean meat
> $^2/_3$ of a cup of wheat bran
> Added supplement
> Chopped green vegetables and carrots may be added

I think the easiest way is to make up the quantity and divide it up for the amount you need. Put the rest in the fridge or freezer. It will keep.

If the dog doesn't think much of the diet and won't eat it, don't be tempted to give him something else instead. Let him go without; a little enforced dieting will help to get things started, and a few days' starvation will do no harm. Be sure there is always water down for him to drink.

The Old Dog

The older dog, from eight years upwards, should not be fed on a high-protein diet, except under special circumstances. High protein diets put too much strain on the liver and kidneys. The general condition and teeth must be taken into account. Any symptoms or diseases, i.e. diabetes, kidney or liver failure, must be treated with special diets as they arise. Your vet will give advice on these. There are many manufacturers who make special diets for the older dog. These mainly have less protein and calories.

A good idea if teeth are lacking is to substitute cooked brown rice for biscuit meal. If biscuit meal is given with the meat, it should be soaked. Some carbohydrate should be given; I find it better giving this as a separate meal from the meat. You can add some bran to the meat if no cereal is given. Many old dogs become very greedy for food, which frequently means they also become fat. For their health's sake, they need a controlled diet, but they will very much resent having their food cut down. The best way to get over this is to cut down on calories but keep the bulk. Give $^2/_3$ rice and $^1/_3$ bran instead of the biscuit.

The old dog does not require the energy food needed for the very young, but vitamin and mineral supplementation to diet is most important. Give the amount according to the labelled instructions, plus 250mg of Vitamin C and 200iu of Vitamin E extra. These should help to keep your dog more active and in better health for longer. I would also give seaweed powder, for this is a tonic.

If your dog is used to having tinned foods and they suit him, there is no reason why you should not continue as long as you are using good-quality ones, and if there is one made for the older dog, use that. Denes make a good tinned health food with added herbs. Tripe is very good and most dogs enjoy this. You can use bran-based breakfast cereals, or some wheatbran and add cooked brown rice. Eggs are another easily digested highly nourishing food, but not raw egg white, for this is indigestible and destroys certain vitamins. Eggs can be cooked in many ways to ring the changes. Finely chopped vegetables will do him good, but it is inadvisable to give bones, for these can cause too many problems if they get chewed, such as constipation and splintering.

Mainly give good-quality food. Liver is an excellent source of vitamins and 2oz per day added to the food is a great supplement. It contains many vitamins and trace elements, but not iodine. Give seaweed powder to supply this. It is also usually better to feed two meals than one large one — this way the animal does not overload its stomach and get indigestion.

I must conclude this by saying, eight years (this is the age most of the 'senior' diets suggest at which you start) is not 'old age' for most Shih Tzus, and if they are still very active, which many are, they will naturally need a higher calorie diet than the 12-year-old which is slowing up. You need to feed according to the condition of your dog, but the supplementation I have suggested is very important to keep them fit and youthful.

Finicky or Problem Eaters

You can have problems with eating at different ages and for many reasons, and though there are some hard and fast rules, they cannot all be solved in the same way. I am well aware that many people say, "If the dog doesn't eat, don't fuss it, take the food away and starve it until it will eat." My answer is that there are times to do this and times not to. There are times when you feel the dog simply has to get food into it, such as when in whelp and nursing puppies, or putting on weight for show purposes. However, it is important to fuss as little as possible and not to let the dog or puppy know you are fussing. Otherwise, they'll soon have you wrapped round their little toe and you will be buying special foods to satisfy their gourmet taste.

Environment plays a big part; it is nearly always the house pet who suffers this way, seldom is the kennel dog a poor feeder.

The causes for not eating can be many. Frequently, it starts from early bad habits. A new puppy is brought into the home and because of stress and having no competition, he refuses to eat. This is quite normal when you think of all the upset he is having. It is very bewildering for him to leave the home kennel, his litter mates and his mother, too. You fuss him, quite naturally, and give him special foods and tit-bits. You have broken rule one straight away — never let a dog know you are fussing over its feeding.

First, it will help to know why your dog does not eat. He may have been a poor "doer" from birth. Has he been wormed? Worms can cause a dog to be very greedy or finicky. Is he in good health? From where did you buy him? Was it a reliable place? Have a word with the breeder.

Try giving a course of Vitamin B12, which helps the appetite. This can be given as an injection by the vet, is most effective and often has rapid results. Or it can be given as a medicine — Cytacon for humans made by Glaxo — obtainable from the chemist. Give the minimum child dose, or you can give Vet Health Iron and Vitamin B Tonic with Sorbitol, obtainable from the Animal Care Centre, Little

Tey Road, Feering, Colchester. It may make the animal have a loose bowel, and if there is anything in the stomach that should not be there, it may be vomited. This is normal. There have been very good results from this and it is well worth trying.

There are various homoeopathic remedies which have been proved successful. H.G.Wolff suggests, for the chronic disorder one gets with poor eaters: "You may offer the dog whatever you like — he simply does not want it. It requires considerable guile to get him to take even a little. If you try and give him the same the next day, he'll turn his nose up at it. The dog has a capricious appetite, driving everybody to despair." This fits the picture of many dogs and Wolff suggests giving Chininum Arsenicosum 4x three times daily. Then there is the dog who, the moment he hears the rattle of his food bowl, comes running and appears very excited at the prospect of eating. Then when the bowl is put in front of him, he will just have a mouthful or two, then stop and go away. Appetite here is usually best in the evening. Wolff suggests this dog has a sub-clinical liver condition which does not show up in tests and he gives the remedy of Lycopodium 30x, either by injection or 10 granules placed on the tongue. He says just a single dose is often sufficient to bring about a change. With the dog who only eats when something has been put into his mouth, try giving China 6x three to four doses a day. The dog who will eat for some days then goes off his food for a few days, but seems perfectly well and happy wil be better for Ferrum Metallicum 5x, the cause being a problem in iron deficiency. For a dog who is just not doing too well, the following can help Abrotanum 3x and Ferrum Phosphoricum 6x each given three times daily. If you know a homoeopathic vet, it is well worth consulting him.

If your dog won't eat his meat mixed with biscuit meal, give it without, and get the biscuit into him in other ways. I have been desperate enough to buy packets of cheesy biscuits and feed these as titbits. This bad habit has never died and they all come running whenever we go to the tin. However, it started them eating dog biscuits.

You may need to bribe and break all the rules. Will he eat liver? It contains all the vitamins to help the appetite, but too much will make him loose. Try soaking meal in liver stock. Mix minced liver or a little grated cheese with the other food, or scatter it on top. I have got mine to eat their biscuits by wiping them over with liver. Warm the food as this brings up the smell and, if the dogs like it, it will get the salivary juices working. Dogs do have preferences for foods, and there are loads of commercial foods on the market to choose from. Have you tried any of the complete diets? They are too numerous to mention, and come in all types — biscuit, muesli and tinned. You need to try them out to see which your dog prefers. You can serve them dampened with a nice tasty stock or vegetable water (so long as it is not too salty) and rub in a little liver or something that the dog likes; or you can add a little tripe to make them more tempting, but not so much to spoil the balance.

The environment can play a big part. Some owners are bad feeders. I knew a bitch who was anorexic in her own home, but when she stayed with me, soon ate as well as any of my own dogs. When she returned home, she immediately became anorexic again. This was undoubtedly due to her environment; in desperation, she was given away to a sensible family with children, and they had no problems at all over her eating.

Competition certainly helps, but if you have only one dog, you have no competition. The food in the other dog's dish is always better than their own, and when they go to lick the other dish, I always put in just a little bit of food. If it is eaten, I add a little more.

Note how and where your dog likes to eat. I have had several silly ones. One liked to be fed away from all the others. She was a slow eater and a little timid, also she had to have her dish in the same place every day. Another liked to wait until all the others had eaten, so she could tell them off if they came near to eat hers. If she did not eat it, I took it up and gave it to her later. Another ate better in the morning than the evening. Yet another preferred it off a flat board so she could spread it out and pick up one piece at a time; every bit, including the biscuit, was eaten, just so long as she could pick it up separately! All those dogs ate well and I did not regard their idiosyncrasies as fussiness — it was just part of the routine.

Will he eat tit-bits from your table? A bad habit, I know, but if he thinks your food is better than his, it is a way of getting a little more into him. If he likes vegetables, cook a little extra for him and give him the leftovers. Always make him wait until you have finished, or he might start worrying and that is a habit not easily broken. You cannot always give him your food, but sometimes, you can get him to think it is your food. All these suggestions sound like forming bad habits. This may well be so, and he will always look forward to the tit-bit, but where is the harm so long as it is at the end of a meal and he is not worrying during the meal? Once he gets the hang of eating a decent meal, the titbits must get less. This awkward type of dog will seldom eat the same food two days running, and it must be fresh.

If you have been force-feeding or hand-feeding your dog, I would suggest giving it the maximum possible for two weeks, then stop all the fussing. By now, his stomach should be used to larger quantities and he will miss them. Put down a dish of good food twice daily, and pick it up if it is not eaten. A few days' starving will not hurt. Do not give any tit-bits while you are doing this.

All dogs eat less during hot weather, often as much as 25 per cent. He will go back to normal eating when the weather cools.

Dogs go off their food when there are bitches in heat around.

At all these times of eating less, be extra careful what you feed. Be sure it is of the highest quality, for if he is eating only a little, you want what he has to do him good. Don't mix supplements with his dinner at a time of not eating, as this just puts him off even more. He must have them, so mix them up in a spoonful of honey and push them into his mouth.

Here are a few rules to apply to all ages, but remember there can be exceptions to all rules, and to a certain extent feeding must be played by ear.

1. Never appear to be concerned.
2. Never leave food down more than one hour.
3. Always feed in the same place, that being where the dog likes to eat, i.e. shut away on his own, or with others. Puppies like you around when they eat.
4. If the meal isn't eaten, remove it and do not give something else instead. At the next feed, try to give something different that the dog likes.
5. Do not add supplements to the food of a dog being fussy. Let him enjoy eating his food first.
6. Prepare it as he likes it, i.e. cooked or uncooked, wet or dry, never straight from the fridge but always at room temperature.

7. Serve it as he likes it. I find some fussy eaters prefer to eat off a flat or large place mat, so the food can be spread and picked up bit by bit. Some flat faces do not like having to shove their nose into their food, neither do they like getting their whiskers in it. Tie them back with an elastic band. The ears too can be hooked back with a clothes peg, or cut the top off a nylon stocking and put that over the head to keep the ears back, that is, so long as it does not worry the dog. If the whiskers get in the mouth when they are eating, they will come out chewed and matted up thick with saliva.
8. No titbits between meals, and never during your meal.
9. Use the same dish. I find flat ones best for their short noses.

Allergy

Allergy may occur very suddenly and it may only take a minute amount to be ingested into the system for a reaction to occur. Frequently, the occurrence is after a sudden change of food or an excessive amount of it, even a food which the animal has been having for weeks, months or even years; then it is likely that the allergy will last for the rest of the animal's life. It is possible that a change in the method of preparing food, such as by cooking or feeding raw, can change the allergen.

Allergies are said to occur rarely. This may well be so, as the vets should know. Even so, with a simple change of diet a number of dogs I have known about have had their trouble cured. However, it may not have been due to an allergy — in many cases, the symptoms arose following repeated vet treatments, such as cortisone. This on its own is no cure.

Not all allergies are caused by food allergens. Respiratory reactions, such as a type of asthma, appear to have been caused in some cases I have known by grasses at certain times of the year, and in other cases by excessive excitement on returning home after being kennelled. The only way to avoid these frightening attacks is to try to discover the cause, then avoid it. A flea allergy is quite common; even one flea bite can cause trouble. It has been suggested that yeast or garlic tablets will stop fleas from biting. I have known a case where the yeast tablets worked. However, it is with food that I am concerned just now.

I remember a case where a dog could not tolerate eggs. This gave a very swift reaction and was discovered when the animal was just a weaning puppy. I frequently give scrambled eggs to puppies, as they usually enjoy them. The one who was allergic was always the one to eat it down greedily, then the poor little animal was sick until it had brought up every spot of egg.

The latest one I have heard about seems to be affected by something in the tap water. No one could find out what was the matter with her, and her owners knew she was far from her normal self. Many tests were done, and different treatments, to no avail, until it was suggested that she did not drink sufficient water. She loved her milk, and was taken off that and put on bottled water, with just a flavour of milk to help get her to drink more. This seems to be working. A lot of tap water contains impurities such as disease producing bacteria, fungi and harmful flora, as well as chloride, fluoride and various toxic matter added to reduce the infectious qualities.

If a dog is not well, give it a starvation day on distilled water and honey. This will remove much of the debris from the system, but if you use it for any period, you must be sure to add extra vitamins and minerals. After this, go on to bottled water.

It is difficult for me to say in other cases where the dog's trouble has been cured by a change of diet that it was a true allergy, but if symptoms can disappear by changing the food, it is a harmless way to cure your dog, call the condition whatever you like! Most of these have been skin troubles, causing excessive scratching. This can lead to sores which are then open to other infections, which might need antibiotics or other medication ordered by your vet. Excessive scratching is most disturbing to dog and owner. One case of excessive scratching was discovered by the veterinarian to be a meat allergy. When all red meats were stopped, the scratching went. Many things can cause scratching dogs besides food, and it is by no means a simple problem.

Always consult your vet, but I feel sure he will have no objection to a change of diet. When people ring me up in despair about their scratching dogs, or dogs who have weak stomachs and keep getting sick, the first thing I ask is, "On what are you feeding your dog?" So often it just takes a change of diet to put matters right, particularly when the diet has not been a well-balanced one. For instance, it is not wise to feed only such foods as organ meats, i.e. kidneys, heart etc. all the time. Liver is an exception; a little of that should be fed often, then it is only a matter of getting on to a suitable diet. First, give something very bland for a few days while the dog's system is being cleared out. Brown rice is my cure-all.

It is essential for the owner to fully co-operate to help the dog. It is no good being weak over this. I don't suppose the dog will eat the rice to start with — some will, some won't. If he won't eat it, let him go without. This will be a self-inflicted cure! Turn away when those pleading eyes look at you and be firm. If after two days he still won't eat, mix in a small amount of mutton, as this seldom causes allergy, or something bland like chicken or fish. On no account add biscuit meal, although strangely enough, the dogs who have benefited most from the rice instead of biscuit meal have tolerated Biscroks so long as they are given on their own. After this, go on to a full diet, but change to different food from what you fed previously. It can be expensive feeding your dog, but to have a healthy dog is cheaper in the end than continual visits to your vet. You may find one of the complete foods suit your dog, but of course it is important that it should be palatable as well as nourishing. Keep off the biscuit meal; give the brown rice instead. Try mixing it with green tripe, bought frozen and cut up from your pet suppliers. You may not like it, and it stinks, but most dogs do like it, and it is one of the cheapest and best foods for dogs.

The common foods to cause allergies are beef, wheat (gluten) and milk (casein).

If you suspect that your dog is suffering from an a food allergy, change his diet completely. You could use lamb and cottage cheese, for the protein, barley or brown rice instead of mixer meal and bottled water instead of tap water. Try this for two weeks. After five days, if it is doing any good, symptoms should start to disappear, and you know it is a food allergy. Slowly introduce one other food to the diet at the time, trying it out for two weeks. As soon as you see any adverse reaction to one of the added foods, take him off it. After a couple of weeks, try the food which upset once again, just to make sure it was that. If you get a reaction again, you may be sure you have found the cause. Always write down the foods you are giving, so you can refer back to it. It is safer than one's memory.

Recipes

To cook brown rice

1 tbs corn oil

A measured quantity of brown rice and twice the quantity of water, vegetable water or preferably some tasty flavoured stock.The rice does not need to be long grain if it is brown, as this does not stick together. You can buy broken basmati rice in large bags from Asian grocers at a reduced price, and this can be used for the family as well.

Put the oil in a pan with a lid and warm it. Stir in the rice until it is covered with oil, and add the water, hot or cold. Bring to the boil. Simmer covered on the lowest temperature for about 20 minutes. Do not stir it until it is done. You can add a pinch of salt, and liver or other tit-bits, and cook them with the rice.

If more rice than is needed is cooked, it will keep well in the refrigerator.

June's meat loaf

2 kilos minced meat or chopped ox cheek
1 large packet of mixed vegetables
1 cup of bran
1 cup of wheat germ
$1/4$ cup of Kelp or seaweed powder
Enough water to make the mixture sloppy
50g packet of gelatine
Put all the ingredients except the gelatine into a pan. Bring to the boil, and simmer until cooked, stirring occasionally. Add more water if necessary.
When the mixture is cooked, make up, as directed, the gelatine, and add this to the pan. Stir well. Pour into ice-cream containers or margarine containers and place in the refrigerator to cool and set. Cut into slices to serve. This will keep in the freezer.

Anne Pickburn's salad

Chopped rabbit or chicken meat
A small portion of chopped lettuce, tomato, onion, carrot
Grated cheese
Half a hard-boiled egg
Apple sliced into small pieces
Melon may be included, chopped finely
If your Shih Tzu likes fruit, give a fruit salad as an extra meal. Small portions of apple, orange, banana, pear and grapes with the pips removed. (It's worth being a dog in that household!)

Jean Squire's dog biscuits

1lb Allinson's wholemeal flour
4oz Flora margarine or corn oil
$^{1}/_{2}$ pt of milk
1 egg
1 tbs of black treacle in the milk
You may add extras such as bran, cheese, stress or seaweed powder, Oxo cubes etc.
Rub the fat into the flour, or add the oil and mix. Add all the dry ingredients and work into a dough with the milk. Roll out fairly thinly to fit a greased and floured baking tray. Mark into fingers about 1" by 2" and bake in a moderate oven for $^{3}/_{4}$ hour. This quantity can manageably be trebled.

Liver cake

(There are many different recipes for liver cake, which is for the dog, not you!)
8oz of liver
Wheatgerm
Bran
Flour
Oil
Clove of garlic
1 egg
Carrot.
Grind them all down together and bake in a shallow dish in the oven for 30 minutes at 175 degrees Celsius (350 Degrees Fahrenheit, Gas Mark 5).

Microwave boiled egg custard

1 egg beaten
$^{1}/_{2}$ pint of milk. Add to beaten egg and beat.
Grease a dish. Pour in the mixture. Microwave on high for one and a half minutes then low (defrost) for 10 minutes. It helps to stir between times.

Baked Custard

As above, but use two eggs.

For You and Your Dog

For those of you who may live alone with just your pet dog, it is often a help to make food that will suit you both, and cheaper, too.

If you cook spaghetti or macaroni, use the wholemeal type and don't forget to add polyunsaturated margarine when it is cooked. This is very good for the animals and their coats.

Microwave Souffle

A simple way with eggs, and great for in-whelp bitches and puppies.
2 eggs
2oz milk
pinch of salt or sugar

Beat the ingredients together. Add to a greased 1lb basin. Place in microwave on high for two minutes. The souffle will rise high in the centre when fully cooked. Turn out on to a dish and break with a fork. Leave to cool.

Casseroles

Most casserole dishes you make for yourself are very suitable for your pet as well. Just add a little extra, such as:

> Casserole chicken with onions, carrot, tomatoes, green beans or any chopped vegetables.
> Liver, bacon and sausage casserole.
> Toad in the hole, a very old-fashioned dish.
> Spaghetti bolognese and many other pasta dishes.
> Lamb stew with barley and mixed vegetables. Give your dog more of the barley and less gravy.
> Little meat balls in tomato sauce.
> Fish pie.

Marika Hanbury Tenison's Recipe for Cauliflower and Meat Pie

Marika — who sadly died of cancer very young — owned Shih Tzus. Her 21st birthday present from her husband was a Shih Tzu he bought from me.

Ingredients: 1 large onion. 2 rashers of streaky bacon. 2 tbs of olive oil. 12 oz minced beef. 14 oz of tinned tomatoes. 1 tsp tomato puree. 1 pt chicken stock. salt & pepper. 1tsp ground cumin. 1 large cauliflower. 1 $\frac{1}{2}$ oz of butter. 1tbs of flour. $\frac{1}{4}$ pt milk. 2 oz grated parmesan cheese. 2 eggs. Pinch of nutmeg.

Method: Finely chop the onion. Mince the bacon. Grate the carrots. Finely chop the celery. Heat the oil in a pan and add the onions, bacon and meat. Cook on high, stirring till slightly brown. Add the carrots, celery, tomatoes, tomato puree and the chicken stock. Season and mix in the cumin. Bring to the boil. Simmer gently uncovered for 45 min. Mix well to break up the tomatoes. Break the cauliflower into florets and steam until tender. Layer the cauliflower and meat sauce in a lightly buttered casserole dish. Melt the butter, add the flour and mix well. Gradually blend in the milk, stirring until thick. Add half the grated cheese and season the sauce with salt and pepper and a pinch of ground nutmeg. Beat the eggs and add to the sauce, beating well to blend smoothly. Pour the sauce over the casserole, sprinkle with the remaining cheese and bake in a moderately hot oven (190C, 375 F) for 30 minutes. This meal goes a long way and the leftovers are loved by dogs!

CHAPTER NINE

THE STUD DOG AND BROOD BITCH

The Shih Tzu should be an easy whelping breed. Unfortunately, there are more Caesareans performed today, though many of these do not seem to be due to anatomical deformities. I wonder how much this is due to modern feeding and environmental conditions, such as lack of exercise, for one seldom hears of the single pet bitch having any trouble. A bitch who is anatomically unsound should not be bred from as she is likely to pass this on to her offspring.

In the little Chinese booklet on The Lhasa Lion Dog by Madame Lu Zee Yuen Nee, the chapter on disease points out that 'bitches have great difficulty in the delivery of puppies. Because of the long coat, flat mouth and short legs, the bitches cannot lick the organs at the time of delivery, and the bitches are not active in exercise during pregnancy. The weakness of the pups also makes labour difficult, often causing the death of both the pups and the bitch.'

This is quite contrary to our early imported Shih Tzus, who were renowned for their easy whelping. Let our dogs benefit from the lesson which Madam Lu has unintentionally given. Do not breed too low on the leg, or too short in the back, so that a heavily in-whelp bitch is unable to turn round and lick herself. Exercise your in-whelp bitches to keep up their muscle tone. Cut or tie their coats back during whelping. There are other references to the difficulty of breeding the Shih Tzu in the Imperial

Saroshim K'o chin with daughter Sarosim Liang Chin and grandson Saroshim Chin Hu.
Owned by Pauline Brook

Palace. I cannot go along with the idea that this was purely due to the eunuchs' inexperience, because they were experienced dog breeders, and the majority of our early breeders, who had no whelping troubles, were not. Never let us sacrifice our easy whelping breed for the sake of whims and fancies. I quote from a letter written by Lady Brownrigg to the Kennel Club:

"In the years we were in China, the dogs we saw were mostly bigger than those we brought home — ours were 12lb 2oz, 13lb 10oz and 14lb 9oz. One of the great virtues of the breed has been their facility in whelping. The only tragedy I had was a very small bitch which we acquired later in China who died whelping."

Never breed purely because you have been told that 'one litter will do her good'. One litter will not prevent pyometra later in life, although at one time this was thought to be so. The safest way to avoid that is to have her spayed. It is doubtful whether breeding prevents false pregnancies. It is normal for all bitches to have a greater or lesser degree of false pregnacy due to the hormones. This can be most distressing, I deal with this subject later under pregnancy.

Many breeders start by owning a pet, falling in love with the breed, and deciding to go in for showing and breeding. This is fine, so long as your adored pet is healthy and well-bred, with a good temperament. She must be a good representative of her breed, and you must have the time to look after her and money to buy the good food she and her litter need, not to mention the vet's fees if she requires medical attention. You should seek advice from an experienced breeder as to her suitability.

Having ascertained your bitch is of the necessary quality (for to breed from a poor specimen can very soon help to destroy the breed you love), you must carefully consider all the other snags. It is two months before the puppies arrive, and another two months before they are old enough to leave the home. A great deal of your time will be taken up — you may not be able to sell them to suitable homes straight away, and growing puppies need space and time to train, for you will have to give them some training while they are in your charge. You may still have them when their inoculations are due. The cost of rearing a litter correctly is considerable, and the bitch requires three times her normal food intake while nursing. You will be most fortunate if you do not have to meet any vet bills, as these can run into several hundred pounds (whelping bitches so often need help out of surgery hours). Stud fees are also quite a heavy item.

Looking on the black side, you could be unfortunate enough to lose the whole litter after paying most of the expenses. If the puppies become ill, you will have to work night and day looking after them, and suffer heartache if they die.

If you decide to go ahead now, at least I have made you aware of some of the difficulties. The greatest one of all, which I have not yet mentioned, can be having to part with those lovely little balls of fluff. You will have come to love them dearly, and they in return will love and trust you (indeed, if this is not so, you should not be breeding!). It may not seem difficult now, but I can assure you from experience that it is. I have kept several animals because I could not bear to part with them, because I thought the prospective buyer unsuitable, or because the puppy did not settle well in its new home and I took it back. Not all homes are good. A high price does not ensure a good home. Some homes which you would never suspect have treated their dogs badly. I have known of dogs shut away in coal sheds, with coats so matted they could not walk, and their trousers soiled with excreta, causing abscesses and sores round the anus through the poor animal trying to pass faeces.

Feet bound up with hair, nails grown so long that they pierce the pads, hair neglected on the face so the eyes were bunged up and the dog completely blind, ears just solid lumps, completely closed up with wax, dirt and hair — don't let this happen to one of your babies.

The stud dog

The advisability of keeping your own stud dog is debatable. It is certainly not a good idea to keep a stud dog with the fixed idea that you will never use anyone else's. Neither is it really sensible to commence with one; gain some knowledge and experience first. You may have chosen the dog carefully, but you can never be quite sure what hidden genes he — or the bitch — has, or how they will combine with each other. You might be lucky, but then again you might not. Every breeder has a responsibility to work with the sole aim of improving the breed; this is not only true where showing is in mind but also where pets are concerned. It is a matter for regret when breeders disregard anatomical or structural points, as this can eventually lead to disaster for the breed. Whatever your reasons for breeding, your aims and object should be for overall physical and anatomical improvement, while retaining the good health and temperament of the breed.

One should never use 'the dog down the road' purely because it is convenient. Always try to choose the most suitable dog for your bitch, and seek advice from the breed clubs if this is needed. One of their main functions is to give help and advice with the prime objective of doing everything possible to improve the breed.

Do not keep dogs and bitches together unless you have facilities for separating them when the bitch comes into season. She should not be bred from on each season. A dog can get so used to running in close proximity with in-season bitches that he may not mate; in time, he can lose the desire.

In this breed, the best age to start training a stud dog is about ten months. A dog not used at stud often loses all desire to mate after he is two years old, and sometimes has no idea which end is which! Having used your dog around 10 months old, it is best not to use him again until he is 12 months and has reached maturity. For his first time, try to use him on a placid or flirtatious matron, not on a maiden bitch or a grumpy one who turns on him every time he mounts her, for this will only put him off. Moreover, most stud dogs of quality and keenness are also show dogs and too much stud work at an early age can ruin their top line and front.

Always keep your stud dog in top condition, well exercised and well-fed. Give him extra protein if he is in frequent use, but do not allow him to become too fat. Diet is important for fertility, and a varied and balanced diet will ensure he has the necessary vitamins. Though it is advisable to add an all-in-one supplement, yeast tablets will provide Vitamin B, which is lacking in many diets. A total of 100-200 iu of Vitamin E, or wheatgerm, and 500-1000 mg of Vitamin C can be given (reduce the amount according to what the supplement contains). Green vegetables are also a help. On the morning of a mating, it is a good idea to give the dog a raw egg. He should not have a heavy meal just before a mating — he is likely to vomit.

As the owner of the stud dog, always ask to see an unknown bitch's pedigree and make quite sure she is registered with the Kennel Club. If she is not, the puppies cannot be registered. It is just possible that the bitch may be cross-bred (this has happened) or that the breeder never gave a pedigree because the bitch was not to be used for breeding. Although the dog is only 50 per cent responsible for the puppies, he invariably gets the blame or credit for their quality!

State the dog's stud fee, remembering that if he is unproved, it is usual to give a free service. If he is a very good young dog, you might consider suggesting that a small stud fee should be paid if the mating results in a litter. It is to your advantage to have your dog used on a good and well-bred bitch. Sometimes a breeder is prepared to take a puppy in lieu of a fee.

The stud fee is normally payable immediately after the service, and it is paid in consideration of the work done by the dog. If there are no puppies, it is unfortunate, but you do not return the fee. Most stud dog owners are just as anxious for the bitch to produce a litter as her owner, and will usually offer a free mating next time with the same dog. A copy of the dog's pedigree and form for registering the puppies, duly signed, should be handed over to the owner of the bitch on receipt of payment.

If it should be required for the bitch to stay it is the responsibility of the stud dog's owner to see that she is carefully looked after. Some bitches get very upset when away from home. It is most important that the bitch is not distressed more than necessary.

I cannot stress strongly enough that should any special terms be made regarding the stud or puppies they should be put down in writing. It can save a lot of argument and unpleasantness later.

Of course, it should go without saying that your stud dog must be clean and free from parasites and all infection. Also make sure that the long hair on his sheath is cut, as this can get in the way.

Some people are worried about using a dog who has not served a bitch over a long period, thinking his sperm will be stale or sterile. This is not so — fresh sperm is manufactured all the time, with the stale sperm passing out with the urine.

The service

Two services are advisable if there is any doubt about the correct day, or if the first service was on a maiden bitch who was not relaxed. Provided both parties feel satisfied that the bitch was ready and the mating has been satisfactory, there is no need for a second attempt. If a second mating is being given for other reasons than the above, then this should be done 48 hours later. The sperm has been known to live up to 11 days, though from 48 hours to seven days is more normal. The ova take 72 hours to mature after coming down.

It is best to use a small room where the dogs, if free, cannot move too far. With the small size of the Shih Tzu and its long hair, it is far easier to use a table for the mating as one can see or feel what is happening. Before the mating, make sure both dog and bitch have had a chance to relieve themselves.

Never throw a dog and bitch together and leave them to get on with it. The stud dog may get injured, and the bitch may become very frightened and snap at him, the end result being a useless stud dog, a bitch who is always difficult to mate, and no puppies at that. The stud owner has an important part to play in this operation, and if the dog is to be any good at regular stud work, he needs help in learning his job.

Whether you use the floor or a table, a non-slippery surface is essential. A table should be steady, and not so big that you cannot hold the animals without stretching right over. Disparity in the heights

Ch. Meggy's Promise For Lharing. Owned by Mrs Freda Harvie.

of the animals may have to be compensated for by placing a pad under one or the other.

If you are completely inexperienced at matings, it is advisable to seek the help of an experienced breeder. Things do not always work out as simply as nature intended, and it is best to have an assistant who can help by holding the bitch. Do not have any other spectators, as this will only worry the dogs. The assistant — who may be the bitch's owner — must be ready to hold her in front and prevent her snapping. The stud-dog owner should be ready to help the dog by seeing that the bitch's tail and trouser hair are not in the way, (these can be tied back with an elastic band) and to assist in any other way required. Some bitches completely collapse on the table, and need to be supported.

The dog will mount the bitch (a smear of Vaseline beforehand will facilitate matters) and once he has penetrated, it is most important to see that the bitch does not move suddenly, else he will slip out before the tie is made. The tie is peculiar to the dog and no other animal. After a few seconds, the bulb at the body end of the dog's penis will swell, and at this point a maiden bitch may cry out and try to extract herself from the dog, but she must be held still and calmed. Sometimes the dog does not tie inside the bitch, in which case it is necessary to hold him in position. This is the important time during which the sperm are actually being ejaculated by the dog, and the first 60 seconds are absolutely vital. A long tie does not necessarily mean a good mating, only that the seminal fluids will help to protect the sperm and enable them to live longer.

The dog, still attached to the bitch, may turn himself, or you can help him to turn so they are standing tail to tail. You should then keep hold of the tails in case one or other tries to pull apart. The tie will last until the bitch relaxes the muscle and lets the dog go. If the bitch is particularly small and the channel tight, the tie can be worryingly lengthy. Ties can last up to an hour or more, though 10-20 minutes is more likely. I admit to getting worried once with a small tight bitch, who would not let the dog free — he was getting very restless. After one hour, I rang the vet in desperation. He said Shih Tzus were notorious for long ties, and to leave it a little longer. If they were not separated then, I should ring him again. I am not quite certain what he intended doing, but I assume he would have given them something to relax the muscles. All was well, and they separated normally. I have read on good authority, but never tried it, that the best way to deal with that predicament is to turn the dog again so that he is on the bitch in the mating position, and press him into the bitch, to increase depth of penetration. This should relieve the constricting effect of the vaginal ring so the dogs can slide apart.

Some bitches can be so difficult to mate that they need tranquillising. It is important not to give too much so that they go to sleep at the critical time.

After it is all over, the dog will lick himself. Make sure that the sheath of the penis is back in position; if it is not, you may have to gently roll it back. Put him on his own for a while — certainly not with another dog or there might be a fight. Take the bitch somewhere where she can be quiet, and do not allow her to pass urine for at least an hour.

If the dogs cannot mate together and it is important, an artificial insemination can be performed, but as the Kennel Club frown on this, you should get their permission first. However, with the advancement of frozen semen, it might be a thing of the future.

Choice of sire

It is up to the bitch owner to pick a suitable sire, though it is sensible to ask the advice of the bitch's breeder. You should recognise the faults in your own animal first, and try to choose a dog who neither carries the faults himself nor has parents or grandparents with them. It is the first three generations of the pedigree which carry the greatest influence.

Study the pedigrees, the dogs at the Championship Shows, their puppies and the dams of their offspring I would prefer to go to the sire rather than his unproven prodigy, for they may not be such good producers. There are several methods of breeding. You should read about them in other books written on that subject.

There is in-breeding, line-breeding and out-crossing. There are good reasons for all. Whatever method you choose, pedigrees are most important, not just the look of the prospective sire, or that the pedigree is full of Champions. This will not necessarily make him the suitable sire for your bitch, for unless he is a very dominant dog, he may not be able to throw his good points.

In-breeding is very close breeding, such as father to daughter, mother to son, brother to sister. This way you may stamp in both the very best and the very worst. It should not be undertaken by the novice, as you really need to know about the other animals in the pedigree or you could go very wrong. In-breeding for too many generations can bring down the size considerably, and if continued, can weaken the stock. There is a limit to how much can be done safely. If you do not know what is behind the lines, a test mating by close in-breeding can be useful. This is the best way to show up the recessive genes.

Line-breeding is breeding to one animal who comes in the pedigree several times. It is slower, but you get there in the end! You must be sure the animal to which you are line-breeding has what you want; it needs to be a rather special animal for one reason or another.

Out-crossing is done for many special reasons. One is to strengthen stock and bring in fresh blood.

I have out-crossed a bitch line to an out-cross sire, and vice versa. Both have been successful, and I have not done sufficient breeding to advise which is best. But I do like either my line or the out-cross to be fairly closely bred. I prefer 'like to like', at least in the points I hope to retain. I like my out-cross to carry the same good points as in my own line with the addition of something I feel I need to improve. Size does not worry me. It is also important to know that the out-cross line has produced good progeny.

You must not expect to improve everything in one generation. Pick the puppy in the litter who has taken the points for which you were breeding, then breed her back into line.

The season

The age of starting season varies from six months to ten months, and I have known it to be both earlier and later than this. Never breed from your bitch too young. The third season is best, preferably before she is three years old. Too young a bitch has not completed her own growth and should not be expected to put all that is needed into her puppies while she is still developing herself.

A bitch normally has two seasons a year, but some are awkward and have only one. Others have three, but one of these is usually a 'false' season when no ova comes down and conception cannot take place. Some confining is necessary. Do not let her run loose in your garden unless it is secure. If there is no garden available and she has to be taken out for walks, carry her away from your front gate and if possible, take her to an open secluded space by car. It is better to let any stray canine Casanova come sniffing at somebody else's front gate rather than your own, for he won't stay there very long if there is no bitch around. It is not only the odour of her discharge which attracts the dogs, but her urine as well. The attraction from the urine commences before she actually comes into season, and you may notice she 'spends more small pennies' than usual. I find veterinary Amplex tablets are excellent. If you start them at the very beginning of the season, you should not have much trouble.

The season comes in three stages and normally last for 21 days, sometimes less, frequently more. An abnormally long season in an old bitch may well be the first sign of impending trouble.

Ch. Mort of Bellakerne at Lharing. Owned by Mrs Freda Harvie.

Firstly, there is a straw-coloured discharge which in a few days becomes darker and more blood-coloured. The vulva is swollen but hard at this time. The colour weakens to straw colour again, and the vulva softens. Lastly, the vulva then subsides to normal, the discharge gradually decreases and the bitch will probably be over her season after the third week. She must be kept away from dogs all this time except for the mating; if she is to be mated, do not give her Amplex or any other 'keep-away' preparation. Even after the mating, she must still be isolated from other dogs, as it is possible to have a dual conception, in which case the names of both dogs have to go down on the pedigree of the puppies. It is now possible to have a DNA test to confirm the correct sire.

Should an accident occur, and the bitch becomes mated by the wrong dog, ask your vet to give her an injection to prevent the unwanted conception rather than let her have the unplanned puppies . This must be given as soon as possible within 48 hours. Her season will recommence and you must be careful to see she does not get mated again.

It is not unusual for a bitch to go off her food during her season, but do not worry — she'll come back on when she is ready. Some bitches show very little 'colour' when in season. Others are so clean that they lick themselves a lot and you see no signs of blood. Others 'swell' very little. There can also be a white season when a bitch shows no colour; these are quite normal but very difficult to tell when the bitch is 'ready' and she needs to be mated every other day while she will stand.

The day of 'readiness' can vary from season to season. The normal criterion is the 10th to 14th days.

Signs when a bitch is ready

Take careful note of the first day of the season, although it is easy enough to miss it. Start looking at her vulva if the season is due and she has started spending frequent 'pennies'. Note when the red discharge changes to straw colour, her vulva has softened and she is 'tailing', i.e. swinging her tail to one side when you rub her back at the tail end, and standing for a dog. It is easier to tell when you have a dog of your own around. Forty-eight hours after this, she is likely to be ready. I have had them ready from 3rd-21st days. Some are ready when they are still showing colour. Some flirt and stand for a bitch long before they will stand for a dog, and long after! Some, particularly maidens, will not stand for a dog without being held. To be sure you have the right day, it is worth getting your vet to test her.

Never force a mating on a bitch unless you are quite sure she is ready. It is ideal when the bitch 'stands' voluntarily for the dog. If you insert a Vaselined gloved finger into the bitch's vagina, you can tell if it is soft. You will then meet a hard round ring — this is a muscle which the bitch will relax for the dog. You should never force your finger in it or you could damage the bitch.

If you do not wish your bitch to have a season, there are preparations for this and you should consult your vet well ahead. There are hormone injections which can be given, but from what I have heard from people whose bitches have had them, I would definitely want to know more about the long-term side-effects. Also it is advisable to let her have a full season before the one when you intend mating her, otherwise she may not conceive.

It is often possible to arrange to give the stud owner a pick of the litter in lieu of paying a stud fee, but this arrangement does have a number of snags. Firstly, any such agreement should always be in writing, thus avoiding argument, for memories cannot be relied on where arrangements are purely verbal. This can be advantageous if you do not want to keep any puppies yourself. A further advantage is that you can save an expensive stud fee, especially if your bitch does not conceive. Against this, the stud fee is often only half the value of a puppy, and if you want to keep one from the litter you will be losing the best one, unless of course the agreement is for the second pick. Should you decide to come to such an arrangement, I suggest you register the puppy under your own affix, provided that you have one, otherwise you will not be recognised as the breeder on the pedigree in subsequent generations.

Always be prepared to leave or bring your bitch for a second mating if necessary. You may have the wrong day, or the dog may not oblige. After the bitch has been mated, there are two very important 'don'ts'. Don't let her relieve herself for at least an hour. Don't let her get with any other dogs, because she is still vulnerable, dual conceptions are possible.

If you have a pet dog who is over-sexed, you are sure to be told by well-wishing friends to find him a wife! This is not good advice. Having one stud will make him keener, and unless he is a show dog, and you are known in the breed, you will find it difficult to get other studs for him. Better to consider having him castrated — this will not alter his character. Many young puppies start by being a bit too sexy but very soon grow out of it.

No puppies
This is always most disappointing for both the bitch and dog owner. So long as the dog is fertile, the trouble is most likely to be with the bitch.

Was she too early or too late? Try extra matings at different times with an interval of 48 hours between the matings.

Long journeys can upset a bitch, so allow her time to settle after the journey. Stress of any sort is bad. Always allow time for love-play with the dog, though I know only too well that some bitches will not respond this way and there is nothing for it but to hold them. If a bitch is fat, she may not get into whelp, as the sperm will have difficulty swimming up the narrow passage which has become even narrower due to excess fat. The same applies to the over-fat dog. A stud dog should be in lean, hard condition.

There may be infection, so speak to your vet before she has her next season; he may take a swab to check for infection when she comes into season again. A swab will only go into the vagina, not the uterus, and there is nearly always some sort of bacteria there, and most bitches are not affected by them. There has been trouble in recent years with pasteurelle and pseudomonia; these will certainly need treating with the correct antibiotics. I think all bitches and stud dogs should be receiving their dose of Vitamin E and C.

If there are several bitches not conceiving to the stud dog, it is advisable to have him checked. There may be a reason for it, like infection in the sheath of the penis, though this is unusual as it is usually washed out with the urine; or a low sperm count. A test of the latter is not always satisfactory, as the sperm die very quickly.

Sterility and impotence

If sterile, the dog is unable to produce offspring. If impotent, the dog lacks the desire to mate.

Sterility is hard to understand in a normal healthy young animal. It can be brought about by disease or infection or even stress. This has been known to happen when dogs have been imported, or exported. It is recommended that the dog should have his diet changed to raw meat, and be given plenty of exercise so that he is in a thoroughly hard condition. Sometimes a complete change of environment helps. It is certainly worth trying him on several bitches (of your own!) Often, he will eventually become fertile.

Impotence can usually be overcome as it is frequently psychological. Kindness, gentleness and patience are required to get the dog over it. If he is housed with a very dominant companion, this may be the cause. A young dog is frequently difficult to get going, and should never be put to a reluctant maiden bitch or one likely to snap at him. Preferably let him have a bitch who will flirt and encourage him. He may be dominated by his older kennel mate, in which case pecking order does not permit him to serve the bitch.

Spaying and castrating

The most frequent question is, 'If I have my dog castrated, will it alter his character?'. The answer is, 'Only for the better.' He should be less sexy and not quite such a dominant character. However, this does not stop him from mating a bitch, though he is unable to sire puppies.

A dog can sire puppies well into old age. How long to continue breeding from a bitch depends on many factors — primarily her health, how many litters she has had, how important it is to breed. I usually stop at six years and certainly think eight is quite long enough. The Kennel Club has a ruling — they will not register any puppies from a bitch who has had over six litters and is eight years and over.

CHAPTER TEN

WHELPING

During pregnancy

Your bitch should have been wormed prior to mating, then again within the last 14 days prior to whelping, but never during the first 35 days of pregnancy. There are many preparations on the market; you should take advice from your vet on the matter. My vet's advice was to worm again during the last three weeks of pregnancy and again one to two weeks after the puppies are born. This does not ensure your puppies will be free from worms. You will still need to worm them.

Take your vet's advice regarding inoculations. Some like the bitch to have them during her seventh week of pregnancy, while others prefer to give the yearly booster when it is due, and leave it at that, because they feel the puppies get too much immunity from their mothers, which affects the later injection of parvo.

So long as the bitch is on a good diet, there is no need to change it until the sixth week when the puppies are growing really fast. She should then have a good quality high-protein diet. She should have adequate vitamins and minerals which include calcium and Vitamin D. An all-in-one vitamin mineral supplement is best, such as SA37. In addition to this, Dr Linus Pauling, a great believer in vitamins for many purposes, recommends a small dog should get 1,500 mg. of Vitamin C and 100 iu of vitamin E when pregnant and lactating. The amount of these vitamins already in the supplement should be subtracted. It was found by a Peke breeder, Mrs Yvonne Bentick, that the vitamins of the B group, particularly Riboflavin, B2, help to prevent cleft palate and hair lip, and if there has been an occurrence of that in the line it is advisable to ensure your bitch is having an adequate supply, though hair lip and cleft palate can be recessive hereditary faults. B6 and B12 do help the appetite and are worth giving when the bitch refuses to come back to eating normally after her fast at three weeks. For further information, refer to chapter 8.

It is hoped the bitch will not get ill and require antibiotics early on, for these have been known to affect growth and development of the foetus. Tetracyclines and Kannamycin can stain the unborn puppies' teeth yellow and should never be given. If given early in the pregnancy, they affect the first teeth; if given late, they affect the second teeth.

A bitch in whelp normally remains active and should have gentle exercise daily, until she becomes heavy, to keep her muscles well toned. At the later stages, when she is heavy, allow her to walk at her own pace — do not force exercise on her, but permit her a free run. When you pick her up, support her abdomen. A fat, flabby bitch is likely to be a bad whelper. The bitch having a false pregnancy usually lies around a lot.

There may be a change in her temperament. Some bitches become very loving; they all need affection at this time.

I wonder if the suggestion put forward in 1983 by vet Mr Cruickshank has ever been followed up? It was this: if there had been prior history of fading puppies or eclampsia, he considered that the stress symptoms of each were similar. He treated possible eclampsia cases by giving 1 ml of lipiodal, which is an iodine in oil for injection to show up certain X-rays, any time three weeks before whelping.

Introduce your bitch to her whelping quarters two weeks or more before she is due to whelp. If she is used to them and approves of them, you will have less trouble with her settling down afterwards. She will have her own ideas about whelping quarters which do not, as a rule, coincide with yours. She may well investigate unsuitable places, such as under the garden shed or in a cupboard — mine have a fancy to get under the garden water butt as it is cool there. You must discourage such activities because they usually involve squashing a very fat tummy through a very small hole, and this could harm the unborn puppies.

Choose a place removed from other animals, as she will need to be quiet, but equally, it should be where it is possible for you to have a quick look from time to time to see that all is well. If you must have her in the same room as another animal, see that she has a quiet secluded corner, preferably with a run round the box, so that she knows she is quite safe from prying eyes. A second bitch in the room may try to take over her puppies, and if she objects to this, there will be a fight and the puppies will get injured. There are exceptions to this, and some people own wonderful maternal grandmothers who will foster any puppy and are always permitted to do so by their grand-daughters.

At five weeks, a teaspoonful of olive oil given twice a week facilitates the birth, but beware, the whelps will be slippery. Some people like to give raspberry-leaf tablets as a birth aid, but don't overdose or she may drop her puppies early. Tablets can be bought from herbalists. Two who specialise in dog products are Dorwest and Denes. Pet-Tex sell a supplement called Easy Whelp, to be given ten days before whelping and afterwards. It contains some very useful ingredients, including raspberry leaf and probiotics.

Make sure she is having her supplements now. If she will not take them, you can give liquid Cal D, according to the directions on the bottle. or you can use bonemeal and Vitamin D. Although calcium and Vitamin D are most necessary, it is very unwise to give too much. You will get the puppies much too large and the bitch may have trouble whelping. In fact, this additional calcium is controversial. Consult your vet.

Signs of pregnancy

Pregnancy lasts from 56 to 66 days, though we normally count 63 days from the first mating (See Appendix D: Whelping Chart.) It is difficult to tell whether a bitch is in whelp during the first few weeks. There may be signs such as a change in temperament, and she may become matronly and have some sickness.

Between the third and fourth week, or 21st to 28th day, it is possible to palpate for signs of puppies. These appear as pea-sized nodules along each side of the abdomen. If you want to know if she is in whelp, it is best to ask your veterinary surgeon at what age he or she would like to check for this. After the 28th day, these nodules cannot be felt as the horns of the uterus become filled with fluid. Puppies may be able to be felt again after the 50th day.

Unfortunately, although puppies can be felt at that early age of three to four weeks, there is no guarantee that they will all be born, as some of them may die and get re-absorbed. This palpating does no harm and will not dislodge the nodules.

The blood and urine tests which can be done on other animals do not work on the bitch. The ultrasonic scan is now frequently used, but not until after the fourth week. Even this is not always accurate, as again puppies can die after the scan, or may have been high up and out of range, but it does have great use in showing up any disease in the uterus.

At three weeks, the bitch usually goes off her food if she is in whelp — this is normal. Allow her a few days' starvation if she wants it. It does become a worry, however, if she fails to regain her appetite after a week. This is by no means unusual — many do not regain their appetite until around the seventh week — but try tempting her with food. Like humans, she has her fads and nausea. If this goes on too long, I have given Vitamin B6 and B12 in the form of Cytogon, obtainable from the chemist or in other forms from Vet Health — nearly always obtainable at championship dog shows. This frequently helps. I also give liquid Cal D during the non-eating period. You may need to break all the rules in the book to get her to eat, like feeding her when you have your meal, and letting her think it is your food. When she has commenced eating again, I return to the general vitamin and mineral supplement I gave her earlier. This lack of eating does not seem to affect the whelps, but it must weaken the bitch. Try feeding her little and often (see Chapter 8).

Another sign of pregnancy is the nipples turning pinker and standing out more firmly from around the fourth week. Later, they become a darker colour before the breasts enlarge, and nearer to the birth, a milky substance can be squeezed out of them.

There should be a colourless discharge from the vagina from around the 32nd day, then ceases a few days before whelping. If this discharge does not start until after the 42nd day, it is more likely to be a false pregnancy. If any other discharge occurs, take her to your vet and have her checked.

Some bitches suffer from irritation of the flanks and persistently scratch them. It has been suggested that Epsom salts will help. I have not tried it!

Do not let your pregnant bitch run up and down stairs after the fifth week, nor jump off chairs or from any other height. See that she does not become drawn into a fight; other bitches can be very jealous and may seek a scrap with her if they see you are giving her the extra attention she now needs. By the sixth week, there should be a thickening and hardening of the body at the sides of the abdomen, but sometimes it is difficult to tell if the bitch is in whelp, for she may be carrying one or two of her pups high up under the rib cage.

Prior to whelping

If the coat is very long, it is advisable to cut it shorter. The tummy hair must be cleared very carefully; see that it is cleared all round the nipples. Long hair left round the nipples can stranglehold them or form a mat across the nipple so that the whelp cannot get to it to suck. Mastitis may then start.

Make sure her coat is clean; it won't hurt her to have a bath a week before she is due to whelp. Remove as much undercoat as possible, as this will help with her grooming. Some bitches can't or won't wash themselves behind, and get urine sticking to them which makes them stink. Wash them.

Plait the long hair on the tail so there are no loose long pieces; these can get twisted round a whelp's neck. All these things have occurred to one person or another and notice should be taken of them.

It is worth trying to preserve the tail hair if you have a show bitch. Most lose their coat after whelping, but is is the tail and trousers which take the longest time to grow again. The best way to ensure no coat loss is to feed the bitch extremely well when she is nursing besides giving daily attention to her coat. She should have three times her normal diet by the time the puppies are three weeks old, but she will need more than that to save the coat — five times the normal amount is not too much if she has a big litter. In fact, you really should feed the bitch all she will eat.

For the actual whelping, I prefer a large wicker basket, kept solely for this purpose. To ensure it is quite clean, scrub it round with a disinfectant such as Trigene (one the vets use) before and after whelpings. I choose a basket of this type because it gives the bitch a rough surface which she can grip and push her back against during the actual whelping. Also, the low sides make it far easier to attend to her than if she is in a high-sided box. Line this well with newspapers, to give her material for her bed-making.

After the whelping, when I think she has quite settled down, I put her in the whelping box with her puppies. The size of this rather depends on the size of the bitch. For a large bitch, it needs to be 2ft square by 18 in high, as it must be big enough for her to lie out fully. My box has a six-inch hinged flap in front to keep the puppies in when they are small. This can be let down when they get up on their feet, for it is then they like to crawl out of the nest to relieve themselves rather than soil their beds. Above this is a door so that the bitch can be shut in, if necessary. I prefer a door which can be completely removed rather than a hinged one. Do not shut the mother in the box all the time; Shih Tzus are very good mothers and she will like to get out of the box at times and sit beside it, just watching. There is also a lid to my box. I also prefer this to be removable rather than hinged. Some of these are made with wire mess peep holes, or a glass window. Inside the box is a moveable rail

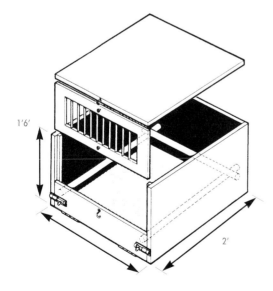
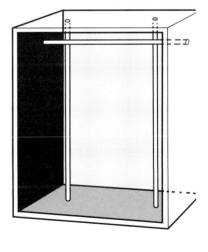

1'6'

2'

Figure 1   whelping box.

123

about two inches away from the sides and one and a half inches from the floor. This ensures that the bitch cannot lie on puppies which get behind her. As her back is not forced against the sides, it also gives the whelps room to wriggle around.

Even if you do not think your bitch is in whelp following a mating, take all the usual precautions. Vets have been known to be wrong and it is not always possible to be certain, though many vets now have a scanner, and others X-ray prior to whelping. Many a puppy has been lost because a 'singleton' has been well tucked up high under the rib cage, and an unsuspecting owner has found her poor bitch with one dead puppy.

Once parturition is only about a week away, I make a practice of never leaving my bitches for long periods. I once made the mistake of leaving a bitch five days beforehand; all seemed perfectly well, there were no signs whatever of imminent whelping, she had a normal temperature and was eating her food. Alas, I think the poor thing panicked and brought on her whelping prematurely, for I came home to find three dead puppies tucked under the cushions of the chairs. I learned my lesson then, and pass on my sad experience in the hope that it will save someone else from making the same mistake.

Get your bitch accustomed to her whelping box if you can, and take her up to your bedroom when you go to bed. Not all bitches follow the same pattern; one may show signs 72 hours before whelping and another only 2 hours previously. I do not think that Shih Tzus whelp as easily now as they did when I first came into the breed. A maiden bitch does not always have her natural instincts about her. She may not know what to do next with this 'thing' that has caused her so much pain and discomfort; and may have no idea what to do next; especially with her first and probably most difficult whelp, when she is feeling exhausted. Also, a maiden bitch seldom knows what is required of her until she hears the puppy cry, and if it is in the membranous sac or amnion, it cannot cry out. The sac must be removed immediately or the puppy will drown, but there is more about this later in the chapter. With the short muzzle of this breed, it can be difficult for the bitch to tear off the sac and bite the cord. I have known bitches who have injured their pups when doing this.

Signs of imminent whelping

If your vet practises on his own, it is wise to warn him that your bitch is near whelping so he will be on the ready should you require his assistance, or he will let you know where to call the duty officer. Since there is only sufficient space in this book to deal with a normal and comparatively straightforward whelping, I recommend that more detail can be found in The Mating and Whelping of Dogs by Captain R Portman-Graham. (Popular Dogs)

Remember — always be observant, but don't fuss. See that your whelping tray is ready to hand; you will require the following articles clean, disinfected and sterilised:

Whelping tray.

    Bowl of disinfectant;
    Trigene surgical hand scrub.
    Lint or cotton wool — this is used to grip the puppy if necessary in a breech presentation.
    Vaseline — if the whelps get stuck, as can happen in a posterior presentation. It is often sufficient just to ease a greased finger round the vulva.
    Blunt-ended curved scissors, preferably not too sharp. Blunt ones cause less bleeding.

A pair of artery forceps, to grip and hold the placenta when the cord is cut.
Sterilised thread — this is only required if the cut cord bleeds. Paper, pen and watch.
Towel, kitchen roll or tissues.
Brandy and smelling salts.
Surgical glove or finger stalls.

When whelping commences, you will also require to have handy:
Spare newspapers.
A clean box with a blanket or towel well wrapped round a warm bottle — don't forget that puppies burn more easily than babies.

Unless you have a warm radiator, have a towel wrapped round a second bottle, in case you should need to rub down the newborn whelp. The mother may be too busy with one to deal with the next arrival straight away, and she is also apt to lick them until they are soaking and then leave them to get cold. If this happens, I take the whelp away, dry it with the warm towel and pop it into the warm box until the mother is ready.

Whelping room temperature should be 75 deg F. (24 deg C). Have a warm, even temperature in the room, and keep the lid off the box as much as possible to allow the air to circulate.

Some bitches start intermittent bed-making several days before they whelp, while some never bed-make. Once the bitch has commenced the whelping cycle, try not to move her around as this can stop the proceedings.

Normally, she will refuse her meal if labour is starting. She will become very anxious and not want to be left. Other signs of the first stage of labour are restlessness, panting and shivering and usually more bed-making. You do not see abdominal contractions at this stage, but if the bitch is lying out, you may see rippling of the flanks. The normal time for this first stage to last is 6 -20 hours, and these signs should become more vigorous and progressive during this stage. If they do not, it can be a first hint of inertia. There have been cases when none of these signs has shown at all and the bitch has just dropped a puppy.

There is a temperature drop to around 99 deg F (37 deg C) during the last week. It rises again then drops to 97-98 deg F (36-36.7 deg C). First stage of labour should commence within 24 hours of this drop. If it doesn't, you should notify your vet as it will alert suspicions of uterine inertia. Some people take the temperature twice daily for the full week before, so as to be sure of not missing the drop. During all this time, she will frequently ask to go out to relieve herself, but do not let her out unaccompanied in case she finds a place in which to hide.

You will know when parturition is getting close as she will lie quietly waiting, with her head between her front outstretched paws, and then she will frequently turn her head towards her tail and lick her vulva. Attacks of shivering will occur, the vulva becomes swollen and softens, and there is a clear mucous discharge.

It is most important that you should be with your bitch while she is whelping. She should be in the house, never on any account left to whelp all alone in a kennel; this is not only cruel to her, but you may well end up with some dead puppies.

Although I emphasise that you should be with your bitch, remember that you are there as an observer and to give her encouragement and confidence. On no account must you fuss unduly — if she thinks you can take over, she will probably have inertia.

When the labour goes into the second stage, the cervix should be dilated, and she will give visible severe strains. It is important that you note the time of the first strong strain. The strains, which may begin at 15-minute intervals, now become more frequent and more severe, and the bitch presses her rear back against the basket. The first whelp may arrive quite soon, or not for another hour and a half. Do not leave her to strain longer than this. If no puppy has appeared an hour after the start of the first strain, inform your vet; all may be well, but your vet may not be free just then, and no harm is done if the puppy turns up in the meantime. With regard to puppy mortality, in the first born it is frequently due to panic on the part of the attendant who tries to effect a delivery before the cervix, vagina and uterus have reached a state of readiness.

The birth

The short-bodied bitch, heavy with pup, or distended with fluid, consequently unable to turn around and lick her vulva, seems to have more trouble than the long-bodied bitch who is able to lick herself.

It is estimated that 40 per cent of bitches are born posterior presentation. This is not a breech, but considered quite normal, though it can be a more difficult birth. Each puppy is normally born inside a membranous sac attached to the afterbirth or placenta. This sac contains fluid, and the first sign of the birth is usually a bubble appearing from the vulva, followed shortly afterwards by a strong strain

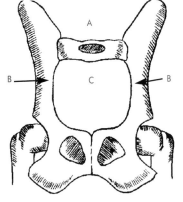

Figure 2   The Pelvis.

1) shows normal pelvic girdle with normal pelvic orifice.

A: Pelvic
B: Ilium
C: Orifice

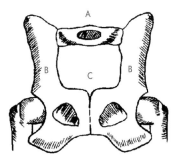

(2) shows pelvic girdle of achondroplastic breeds with the shortened ilium shafts causing the pelvic opening to become narrow.

A: Pelvic
B: Ilium
C: Orifice

when the puppy normally shoots out head first, still in the sac which has cushioned it as it journeyed through the cervix and vagina. Some bitches do tear off the sac and attend to everything themselves, but don't necessarily expect yours to do so, especially if she is a maiden. Remove the sac from the puppy's head first of all, to enable it to breathe, then wipe and clear its air passages. The bitch may want to take over at this point, so allow her to lick the puppy. I am always apprehensive of an excitable bitch who tries to do everything much too quickly. A good bitch licks the puppy all over, and patiently waits for the placenta to come away. Sometimes this comes with the puppy, but if not she will keep on licking; do watch to see if she eats the placenta. As soon as the puppy is free, she will lick it well and thoroughly 'rough-house' it all round the bed; this is quite normal, and is her way of getting the lungs working. Do not rush to cut the cord, for it will certainly bleed if you do. The puppy is coming to no harm attached to the mother, unless of course it needs to be revived, or the mother drags it round the bed, in which case it is best to separate them.

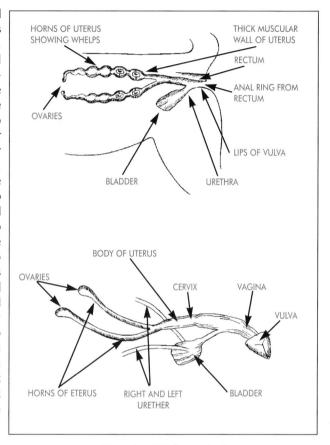

Figure 3   Bitch's reproductive organs.

Severing the cord

I prefer to break rather than cut the cord, unless the puppy is so short-corded that one cannot get hold of enough of it. Pinch the cord between the thumb and finger of the left hand, about half an inch away from the puppy's abdomen. Having grasped the cord, pinch it tightly to stop the flow of blood, squeezing it towards the puppy. Grip the cord with the artery forceps (the bitch's side of your thumb and finger) to prevent it from slipping back into the bitch, and tear. This is more satisfactory than cutting as it is simulating the bitch's biting and usually prevents bleeding but, if there is bleeding, tie the cord with the sterilized thread. Watch that the bitch does not tear if off again and in so doing shorten the cord too much. You can leave the artery forceps on the end of the cord until the placenta comes away on its own (though you have to be careful that they do not get in the way and stick into the bitch) or, after waiting 15 minutes, you can gently but firmly pull the placenta out. You must wait for a good 15 minutes before doing this, otherwise you may cause a haemorrhage. The retained placenta, if left behind, usually comes away with the next puppy, leaving the second placenta inside.

The next puppy may follow immediately, or not for another 1-3 hours. This varies with different bitches, which is one reason for keeping a record, so you will know what to expect next time.

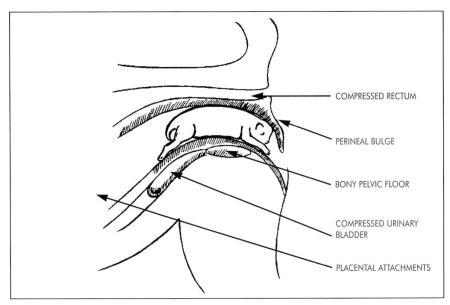

Figure 4 : Whelping Diagrams (a) Normal presentation. Head first.

If the bitch does not attend to the puppy herself, it is up to you. While it is still attached, rub it over with your warm towel, and if it needs reviving, cut it clear of the bitch as mentioned earlier. Hold it downwards to drain the fluid from the nose and mouth, and rub its chest briskly but gently. It should then cry, and you can put it to the bitch to suck or in your warm box. If possible, put puppies to suck as soon as they are cleaned up.

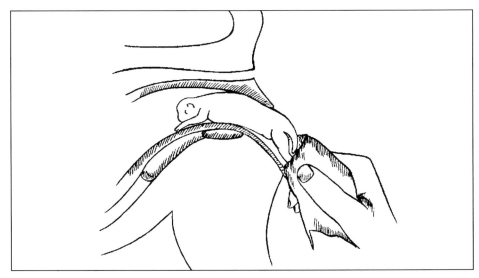

(b) Posterior presentation. Feet first. If assisted, the whelp should be pulled outwards and downwards at 45 degrees. Both these presentations are quite normal.

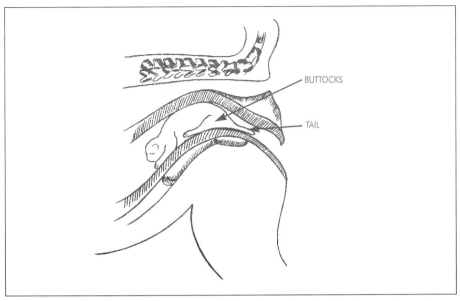

(c) Breech presentation. The back legs are tucked under the buttocks. Veterinary assistance is required.

Resuscitation of the lifeless whelp

Rub the whelp briskly but gently on its back and chest with a warm, rough towel. The rubbing and warmth frequently bring life into the pup, but if this is not effective, hold its head downwards, making sure that the tongue is well forward, to enable any fluid to come away from the air passages. Taking it in both hands, with your thumbs behind its head to support it, swing it forward and down in an arch so that its head is swung downwards and then back again. This forces out fluid and allows air to be forced in.

Another method devised by Joan S. O'Brien, D.V.M. and given in the Shih Tzu news of America, is: after the preliminaries of wiping the fluids from the mouth and rubbing the puppy, tilt the puppy down. Hold the puppy with both hands, one hand over the shoulders and the other over the hindquarters. The method of holding the puppy is all-important. To explain further, I hold the fore-quarters in my right hand with the hand arched over the withers. The thumb on the shoulders and upper arm, on one side, the index finger supporting the head and the middle finger holding the shoulder and upper arm on the other side. The hindquarters are held in the left hand with the hand arched over the rump. The thumb holding the thigh, the index finger curled down over the anal area and supporting the floor of the pelvis, and the middle finger firmly holding the other thigh.

Pretend the puppy is an accordion. The hands on the fore-and hindquarters are holding the handles. Stretch the puppy to its full length. Wait two or three seconds for the lungs to fill with air. Push the puppy together to its shortest possible length. The air should be heard leaving the lungs, and often fluid is seen coming out of the mouth and/or nose. Be sure to keep the puppy at the 55 deg angle with the head down. Repeat the stretching-wait-push sequence about 12 to 14 times per minute. The movements should be gentle but strong enough that the puppy is visibly lengthened in the stretch portion and visibly compressed and the ribs rounded up in the push portion. I have not tried the American method as I have had success with the first one.

Work on the pups for at least 10 minutes to get them going.

Direct mouth-to-mouth resuscitation in a tiny whelp can be dangerous as you may perforate the lungs. It is safer to do this through a small bore tube. It can be done with a biro pen which has the ink tube, the metal tip and plastic cap removed, thus leaving a small hole through which you can blow gently at intervals of two to three seconds, allowing the puppy's chest to deflate and inflate in the correct time. A drop of neat brandy on the tongue, or the use of smelling salts, may make it gasp and start to breathe. When you get it breathing, place it on the warm bottle.

As each puppy is born, merely give it a cursory examination, as it will upset the bitch to see you handling her pups more than necessary. When the newspapers become wet, just put fresh ones on top to disturb the bitch as little as possible.

I have given a detailed description of what may need to be done, but I must stress as before that your job is to observe without unnecessary fussing. Give confidence by your presence, and occasional encouragement by your voice, doing no more than is necessary; if you are over-anxious, you will impart this to the bitch. Many bitches have their puppies so easily that one or two have been born before you realise anything has happened, but not all.

Puppies are normally born head-first, but many puppies come feet first, incorrectly called 'breech'. This happens so often it is considered quite normal — 40 per cent are said to have them this way. The bitch seldom has any trouble in delivering such puppies, but if the first one is large, the head can get stuck. In this case, you should hold the slippery legs of the pup firmly with the lint or cotton wool, and on the next strain, ease it out. Do not pull on the puppy except when the bitch strains, and this must be done gently and firmly in a downward direction. If you insert your finger into the vagina, be sure to wear a sterilised vaselined glove, or scrub your hands in the bowel of antiseptic; you may be able to ease round the head. In a breech presentation, the hind limbs are tucked up under the body and the tail and buttocks are presenting.

There is some divergence of opinion as to whether the bitch should be allowed to eat her placentas, which are said to stimulate the uterus and sustain her for the next 24 hours. They certainly make her bowels very loose, which in the long-coated Shih Tzu can mean washing and drying her trousers, during which time she is fretting to get back to her puppies. I allow my bitches to eat one or two placentas; if too many are eaten, they are usually vomited. The important thing is to note carefully if all the placentas have come away, and if you are at all unsure about this, get your vet to examine her. He may give her an injection which will cause the uterus to contract and evacuate its contents. In some bitches, the uterus is always slow to contract after parturition, in which case the bitch requires an antibiotic as well. In any case, it is a wise precaution to get your vet to examine the bitch after her whelping, particularly if you are inexperienced.

Care after parturition
Once whelping is complete, the bitch usually settles down contentedly with her puppies. Give her a drink of warm milk and glucose, take her out to relieve herself (unless it is wet or cold, in which case allow her to use newspapers), and clean up her bed. I use newspapers for the bed for the first two weeks; the puppies cannot get lost in them, and I think the smooth surface is a help to them when they gyrate around. The bitch sometimes finds vet bed too warm for her. It is always a bit of a problem to know what to do for the best. Each bitch is different.

If the bitch has had a difficult whelping or a ceasarean section, it will help the bruising if she is given the homoeopathic remedy of Arnica 6 x four times daily for a few days.

If you have not yet weighed your puppies, or examined them for sex and any abnormalities, now is the time to do so. Note any distinguishing markings; if you can distinguish one pup from another, it is so much easier to make sure that each one is sucking. In the case of any obvious abnormalities, ask the vet to put them to sleep when he examines the bitch. It is usual, by the way, for masks and noses to be pink at birth, though some are born with a black nose.

Your vet may ask you to bring your bitch and her puppies to the surgery for examination, though it is preferable if they call to your home as it is less disturbing and stressful for the mother — the last thing she wants is added stress at this time. This is not always practical as some vets do not like doing house calls, and the charge could be very great. If she is not checked, keep a vigilant watch on her.

For emergency use, you should have:
> **A milk substitute:** One I have found good is Welpi. You can make up your own milk formula if it is needed. The one I have given in the next chapter with evaporated milk has been very successfully used by many breeders.
> **Cal D:** a liquid vitamin D with calcium.
> **An electrolyte solution** such as Dyoralite, which you can buy from the chemist in sterile packets. If you have no electrolyte, in an emergency you can make up a solution of a pint of water to a teaspoon of glucose or sugar and a pinch of salt.
> **A blunt-ended or digital thermometer:** the latter is by far the easiest to read and well worth the extra cost.

When to call in your veterinary surgeon

It is correct to have green discharge immediately following the birth. Joan Joshua (FRCVS) says some bitches have a light green mucoid discharge 24-48 hours before labour commences. I have never seen this.

Be ready to call your veterinary surgeon in the following circumstances:
> *If nothing is happening for 12 hours after the final temperature drop down to 97-98 F (36-36.7 C), she may have primary inertia.
> *If the first stage of labour is slow and long (it can take anything up to 36-48 hours) it is advisable to report to your vet after 24 hours from the start. (The problem is to know when it starts.)
> *If she is straining hard for more than an hour and no puppy appears, report to your vet. Although up to two hours should cause no anxiety, it is always better to report early than too late.
> *If three hours elapse between puppies and nothing happens, but you feel sure she has not finished whelping, she may have secondary inertia.
> *If a puppy is showing and has got stuck, do not wait more than ten minutes.
> *If the bitch shows signs of packing up, and the strains are getting weaker, she may have inertia.
> *If two water bags are appearing together, there may be two puppies presenting together.

Inertia

Primary inertia is when the bitch really never gets going at all. It is quite devastating to see no signs that parturition has started. By the time you realise, the puppies placentas have probably separated and they have died. This can mean a ceasarean and dead puppies. This is one reason for taking the bitch's temperature twice daily the week before whelping is due, and when you get the fall, you will have been alerted.

Secondary inertia occurs after a bitch has already passed one or more puppies and after straining for some time, her muscles have become weak and she is exhausted, so she just gives up and her strains become weaker. It is important to call your vet.

Caesarean section

Should it be necessary for your bitch to have a caesarean, you may experience difficulty in getting her to accept her puppies, or even to get them to suck, for the stimuli of the normal vaginal delivery is missing. If this is not her first litter, there is less likely to be trouble. If one or more puppies have been born before the operation, there is less likely to be trouble.

If it is a first litter and no puppies have been born normally, it can be difficult to arouse the bitch's maternal instincts. You must persevere, as those puppies need to suck as soon as possible and get the valuable colostrum from the teats. This comes in before the milk and contains antibodies, but only lasts six hours. The milk may not have come in yet and sucking will stimulate this.

As soon as the bitch is round from the anaesthetic, you must encourage her to nurse the puppies. She may respond to their crying but most likely will not want to know them. The best thing for getting her instincts working is to get her to lick them. Once she has done this, she is likely to start to nurse them and let them feed. If she will not do it when you hand them to her, try smearing their bodies with her vaginal discharge; this usually gets her going. If it does not, there is something else you can try. Stimulate the flow of urine from the puppies on to one of them, and give it to her to lick. This is said to resemble the amniotic fluid and a bitch nearly always licks it. Once she has started, she should keep on, but you will have to keep a watch on her; she has after all just had a major operation and has stitches in her.

If there is no milk, you may have to start feeding them with glucose water. Do not let them become dehydrated. The vet will give your bitch a shot of Oxytoxin to bring the milk in. The homoeopathic treatment for bringing in milk is said to be urtica urens 30x just one dose. You must give this higher dosage. A low one of 6x helps to diminish the over supply of milk. I have not tried it as my bitches have always had the milk in.

No bitch who has had a caesarean through an anatomical defect should be bred from a second time as the offspring may inherit this.

Pseudo-pregnancy

These can vary, but the condition usually starts about 40 days after heat ends. The bitch will go through various changes and may come into milk, which can be quite copious and may be prolonged through self-sucking. Sometimes, she collects objects which she regards as her puppies, and will guard them. The best way to treat the condition is to try to get her mind off it and take her for walks.

Do not encourage her to nurse her 'puppies', as this will only prolong the false pregnancy. If she has milk, this will be helped by giving a little Epsom salts — this helps to draw fluids from the body. The vet may suggest giving her a hormone injection. There is homoeopathic treatment which many people have found to work well, and which is far better and safer than the hormone treatment. Also, it is meant to lessen the severity of the false pregnancy each time until they stop.

The treatment is this: Pulsatilla 30x three times a day for seven days, after which symptoms should have cleared.

Phantom pregnancies

In this condition, the bitch does conceive, but the foetus dies early and is re-absorbed into the system. The body still goes through the various changes, however, but when no puppies appear, the bitch returns to normal.

Abortion

It is more frequent for bitches to re-absorb their puppies than to abort them, but it can happen especially late in the pregnancy. If a bitch is found to be bleeding when she is pregnant, you should contact your vet immediately. She may lose one or two puppies, but seldom all of them. Do not give parsley to an in-whelp bitch — this has been known to cause abortion; it contains apiol which is similar in character to quinine, which contains ergot.

CHAPTER ELEVEN

THE FIRST THREE WEEKS

You must monitor your bitch and her puppies very carefully. Success depends on your observations. The first week, especially the first three days, are of vital importance. This is the greatest time for puppy loss.

The whelping box should be placed in a quiet corner, away from all disturbances and draughts, so the bitch can settle down with her puppies. In the first three days, she is unlikely to want to leave them. It is important you do not interfere too much and distract her attention from the job in hand, but equally important to watch out for anything unusual. You will have to take her out to relieve herself, but see that the puppies are left warm, or they will cry and she will be frantic. A bitch may prefer to have newspaper in the box for bedding at least to start with; other than that, the best bedding to use is Vetbed.

So long as the bitch is happy with her quarters, all should be well. This is why you should introduce her to them well before the whelping. Otherwise, she is likely to move the puppies to some other place she prefers, like in or under your bed — the wardrobe is another favourite place, nice and dark and snug. She is looking for a safe quiet corner where there will be no interference or disturbances. Unfortunately, her choice seldom leaves enough access for you to give her attention when needed, and you must be able to observe that all is progressing as it should. Family pet bitches may not settle until they are allowed back with the family, as some do not appreciate being shut away on their own. One of my bitches was a nightmare. Two or three times every night, she would go round the room scratching up everything and eating the paint off the wainscotting. She really had me worried. My vet could give no explanations. I never did discover why she did it. The vet did suggest giving her five drops of brandy in a teaspoonful of water to settle her. It helped a bit, although I think the other way round would have had more effect! I gave her extra doses of Cal D. In my early days, I had one bitch with a large litter who, at three weeks of nursing, ate the mortar from the bricks of the house. The reason for her doing this should have been obvious to me, but I regret that it was not. Her calcium metabolism was breaking down and shortly afterwards she went down with calcium drainage, and had a temperature of 108 degF before an injection could be given. I was lucky not to lose her.

After whelping, some bitches do not settle well. Her temperature is likely to be raised — the extra heat of the whelping room and box add to this rise of temperature. She is likely to pant. If the panting becomes very intense, there is always the possibility of sub-clinical eclampsia (some vets will not recognise this). Give her a dose of Cal D. I would give her this regularly now she is feeding puppies.

This conditions of sub-clinical eclampsia does not lead to clinical eclampsia, but the same treatment and dose works — an intravenous injection of calcium, or just a tranquiliser, may be sufficient in this case.

It is vital that the puppies are kept warm. The room temperature should be up to 75 deg F (24 deg C). You can lower it a little the next week and again the next week, naturally so long as all is going well. Warmth from the room temperature is not sufficient — the puppies need contact heat from the mother and. If she is nursing them properly, they will get sufficient heat from her. The danger lies when they stray away, or she moves around the bed and leaves one stranded. To overcome this, you can use additional heat in the bed, except in the heat of summer when it may not be needed. I like to use an electric heat pad, either a human or special dog one. It should be only just warm. Some people recommend using overhead heat, such as an infra-red lamp. I am against this. The heat given out can be much too drying for the Shih Tzu and if not placed carefully, it is much too much for the bitch. Never use one.

You can also buy electrically heated dog beds — lovely for kennel dogs in the winter, but not for a bitch with puppies. I have tried one and found it very useful for orphaned puppies. I also tried it for a singleton, but it was too much heat for the mother, and instead of nursing the puppy, she sat away at the ends of the bed where the heat was slightly less or just outside the bed watching. Puppies certainly remain very content, but good nursing should be instilled by the mother into the whelps. If you use these beds, be sure to have a non-slip surface. If the whelps are on a shiny surface, they will not be able to move around well, their muscles will be weak and they will end up like "swimmers". If the mother nurses her puppies properly, she throws out sufficient heat so long as they are in contact with her tummy.

I prefer the use of an electric pad, as I mentioned earlier, or else a hot-water bottle which is well covered and just gives a gentle warmth. This is placed to one side of the whelping box away from the mother. There is one danger to guard against though — a puppy who has crawled or been pushed away from the dam may become too contented on the warm pad; in this case, it will not cry or make any attempt to return, and the busy mother's instinct may not be aroused unless she hears its cries. If left for too long it will become weak from lack of food and have difficulty in pushing its way in to suck; even though it appears to suck it cannot ingest the milk, and if not attended to will fade. Supplement its diet until it has gained strength.

Many bitches are given antibiotics after they have whelped. If there has been any internal interference or a caesarean, then it is important that they have them. To give them as routine is very questionable; I certainly do not like my bitches to have them. The disadvantage of antibiotics is that they do harm as well as good. They are passed on in the mother's milk to the pups, they destroy the good bacteria in the intestines, they can cause a gradual build-up of bacteria which are resistant to the antibiotic which is being administered. One important bacteria which is destroyed is Lactobacillus acidophilus and without this the staphylococci will increase. The puppies can then become ill, sometimes with severe diarrhoea, and fading puppy syndrome with their little tummies becoming swollen and hard, and then the crying starts, and goes on and on until they die. It is important to get the Lactobacillus acidophilus into these puppies, and the mother too. This is contained in live yoghurt, and should be administered to the puppies before each feed; just let them lick a little off your finger. If fed this bacillus in yoghurt, or even a different bacteria, the puppies will have a good chance of survival. Use the natural live yoghurt, it is best obtained form a health shop. Make sure it contains the bacteria you want. Or you can buy cultures and make your own. By no means all puppies whose mothers have had antibiotics will suffer in this way, but I would not wait to see; start them all off on the yoghurt before there is any trouble. Give it during the full course of the antibiotics and for two days after. The addition of Vitamin B1 is also of considerable importance when antibiotics are given, for a deficiency of this can also cause the destruction of normal intestinal bacteria.

It is wise, if you are not already sleeping in the same room with her, to look in on her three times during the night for the first three nights, just to make sure that all is well. Bitches vary in their behaviour at this time. Some are a bit clumsy and find it difficult when moving around the bed and lie on a puppy and smother it. If they are very placid you have little to worry about, but If they are excitable and trying to move their puppies around and getting frantic whenever they cry, you will need to keep a closer watch. She should be nursing her puppies close to her, to keep them warm.

You must weigh the puppies daily. They mostly gain $1/2$ oz a day. This is the surest check to know if they are getting sufficient nourishment. They may be sucking but not ingesting the milk. If they do not gain, there is a reason for it. Either the bitch has no milk, the other puppies are pushing this one out, or it is ill and weak. Give the puppy some glucose water. Never start by giving milk substitute. You must be sure that the puppy will swallow, and the glucose is very important.

Look carefully at the bitch's teats. Sometimes the puppies are unable to get a firm grip on them. They may be inverted or very small, or so full of milk that they have become hard. If inverted, you will need to draw them out until the puppy can suck. Try gripping one with your thumb and finger and putting the puppy on to suck. Or you can try warming a bottle, placing it over the teat closely (don't have it hot to burn the bitch). As the bottle cools, it may draw out the teat. When a teat is overly full of milk, the puppy needs to be held to the teat and the milk gently squeezed into its mouth, until it grips for itself. It's easier to write about than do! If there is one already sucking strongly, put it to the teat first to start the milk flowing, then take it off and put the weaker puppy on.

Care of the dam and post-natal complications

Check the bitch's temperature morning and evening. It is likely to be up to 102 or 103 deg F (around 38 deg C), but should drop by the third day. If it is still raised, suspect trouble and inform your vet. There could be infection from a retained placenta or a dead puppy. She may need antibiotics. I have told you how I feel about antibiotics but when they are needed, there is no question but that they must be given. It is possible for the milk to be infected. If this is so, the puppies may need to be taken off the bitch and hand-reared. If the bitch's teats are congested, they may need to be bathed to soften them and then some milk drawn off.

The bitch will usually drink a bowl of milk after she has whelped, or if she has not eaten for a very long time, she will be hungry and enjoy a light meal of fish or chicken. Drinking is very important and you should see she has access to drinking water. Common sense will tell you not to stand a bowl of water within her whelping bed as this will get upset; it should be hooked on or else outside where she can get at it. Having said that, most bitches sit tight and expect you to hand the drink to them.

The bitch is often difficult over her diet during the first week. She will need to be tempted, and all food should be of the highest quality you can manage. Many pet food firms do make up dried or tinned special foods for bitches and rearing puppies. These are high in protein and have all vitamins and minerals added. I don't doubt they are very good. Mine would not touch such food at this time, and anyway, I prefer to give a varied diet of fresh foods and add my own supplements. The mother's job is to look after the puppies, yours is to look after her, and she will expect to have her food handed to her in her box. See that all is well and only interfere when necessary. (See picture on page 143.)

The bitch should be taken out three times a day to relieve herself. She may not want to leave her puppies, so ensure they are warm and contented, for she will come running back if she hears them cry. Even if they are fast asleep and contented, she will probably disturb them by washing them all over to get the smell off them if they have been handled.

Bitches seldom have their bowels open before the third day, and then, if they have eaten the placentas, it is usual for them to pass a very loose black stool. After this, she may need to be washed down. Always see she is thoroughly dried before being put back with her puppies. Some people prefer to let her use newspaper, which can be very useful in bad weather, but she badly needs to get a breath of fresh air into her lungs and stretch her limbs. Do not take her for a walk, however, as she may pick up some infection and carry this back to the litter.

Immediately after whelping, there will be some bright green discharge from the placentas; after this, a bitch has a dark bloodstained discharge which gradually lessens. If it persists after four weeks, or is offensive, brown, dark green or thick yellow in colour, inform the vet. She should be washed under her tail and around her teats, and the latter should also be inspected daily for any signs of congestion (which can lead to mastitis) or sores. After the first three days, you can give her a thorough groom before putting her back with her puppies. She will feel all the better for it, and it will enable you to prevent mats from forming; you should remove the dead hair which otherwise gets swallowed by the mother when she is cleaning herself and can form hair balls in her stomach.

The mother should keep the puppies clean; she will lick their tummies to stimulate the urine flow, and this licking is also an aid to digestion after feeding. She will also lick the anus to stimulate the bowel action, and clean up their excreta. The young puppy cannot manage to pass anything without this extra stimulus. If the bitch does not attend to this, you must do it, for it will get ill and die if it does not pass anything. Take a warm wet cotton wool swab and gently pass it back and forth over the two openings until the puppy obliges by passing urine and faeces. You are simulating the bitch's tongue. A blocked anus in a puppy can cause death. You must keep the bed clean, changing it if it gets damp, and make sure the dam is doing all she should.

Feeding.
You will find this in Chapter 8.

Mastitis
Watch the teats. Sometimes the breasts fill up so hard the puppies are not able to get hold of the nipple. You should put the strongest puppy on and let him draw the milk off to soften it, and keep a watch or you will have trouble with mastitis, which can lead to a breast abscess.

In acute mastitis, the mother will have a temperature, be very listless, refuse food, and be in severe pain. She may have half an aspirin tablet to reduce the pain. The puppies should not suck from the infected teat as the milk will be impure.

Treatment: Early on, bathe the offending breast with hot and cold water at least four times a day, and when it is slightly softened, massage gently with oil and put the biggest pup on to draw off some milk, so long as its ph is only 6.0-6.5. and the milk is not yellow and thick. Give $^3/_4$ teaspoon of magnesium sulphate (Epsom salts) daily, as this draws away fluids from the body. Aspirin ($\frac{1}{2}$ tablet) may be given to help relieve the pain. If the milk is infected, the ph is 7.0 and the milk will be thick and yellow. The pups must not suck this. Bathe the breasts as before, expressing milk 2-3 times daily until it becomes clear and binding off the nipple to prevent the puppies from sucking. The bitch's temperature should be raised. Antibiotics are required.

Repeat this treatment for five days, when the milk should be cleared up and the puppies can suck, unless they are three weeks old, when it would be wiser to wean them.

Breast abscess

If the breasts start to become blue, a breast abscess is likely to be forming. This will come to a head and burst. Bathe it frequently. It will leave a big hole. Antibiotics may be needed. If it drains well, it will soon heal up, but keep the puppies off it by bandaging round the breast.

Eclampsia

This is due to a breakdown in the calcium mechanism. The most usual time for it to start is around the third week of nursing, when there is a great drain on the milk supply, but it can happen much sooner, even before whelping although this is unusual. The first signs are restlessness, panting, rapid breathing, whining and a rapid rise of temperature. These symptoms get worse rapidly. The bitch walks around stiff-legged; if left, she will eventually fall down in a fit. Death occurs within hours of the first symptoms. This is an emergency.

Treatment: Notify your vet immediately, for this is an emergency. An intravenous calcium injection is needed. It is best to take the puppies off the dam and wean them, unless they are very young. In this case, you will have to bind the body round the teats with a crepe bandage or put her in a 'baby grow' to prevent the puppies from sucking. If the puppies are permitted to go back to be nursed by the mother, she must be watched carefully for any repetition. The dose of Cal D may need to be increased, but be advised by your vet.

Acute Metritis.

This is an infection which can follow parturition. The infection travels up the birth canal to the lining of the uterus. It may be after a retained placenta or a dead puppy or of course from any interference during the birth of unsterilised hands or instruments. This is one important reason for taking the bitch's temperature daily after the birth. If it has not dropped by the third day, act promptly and take her to your vet — she will need antibiotics.

Retained placenta

It is most important to try to account for the full number of placentas, (one for each puppy) Incidentally, it is possible to have twins, but you would see that they are attached to one placenta. If you cannot account for them all, sometimes it is very difficult to know whether one has come and she has eaten it. Play it safe and get your vet to inspect her after the birth. He will properly give her an injection to help expel the contents of the uterus. To have a placenta retained can lead to an infection of the uterus.

The puppies

You must watch your puppies very carefully. Their lives can depend on your observations.

Puppies are not able to shiver until they are six days old, so to compensate, they jerk in their sleep. Watch for this. If a puppy just lies quite still and does not jerk at all, it is likely to be a very sick puppy within 24 hours.

You must weigh your puppies — at birth and daily for the first two weeks. It is not sufficient to say, as I have heard, "I do not need to weigh them as I can see if they are not gaining". Sure you can see, but not soon enough. Their weights at birth are variable, usually between 4-8oz. These will catch up and overtake each other as they grow. Sometimes they are as small as 2oz. These are likely to end up at the bottom of the standard weight scale. Others are 10oz. I would expect these to end up at the top of the weight scale.

A tiny puppy is not necessarily a runt. A runt is a weakling with possible internal deformities which will not show up until later. It may be very blue, which can show a heart condition. Work on it by all means for a few days to see if it pulls round. If it does not, and it still shows signs of weakness, it is kindest and most wise to have it put down. Many of the smallest puppies are strong — they will wriggle their way to the milk bar, and end up bossing all the others around.

The experts say puppies should gain a gram per pound of adult weight per day. I like them to gain at least $1/2$ oz per day and double their birth weight in a week to ten days.

When a puppy is first born, its temperature is the same as the mother's, but it rapidly falls to 94 degF (34.7 C) and then slowly rises when close to the mother being nursed.

A healthy puppy is firm to hold and feels warm. It will go immediately to the teats when woken up. A weak puppy is flabby and limp and may well be blue and cold. It is likely to cry a lot. If it is just born, rub it gently with a warm towel and place it away in a warm box. If it shows improvement, try giving it a little glucose water before putting it to suck the mother. There are preparations now available on the market which would be useful for such occasions. Nutri-drops are obtainable from Net-Tex Agricultural Ltd. Priestwood, Harvel, nr Meopham, Kent, DA13 0DA. Tel 0474 813999. They also supply Col-Late Puppy Colostrum.

It is important that the puppies suck during the first hours to get the colostrum from the mother. This contains vital antibodies and gives the puppies some immunity. It comes in before the milk and only lasts four to six hours.

Dew claws

Removal of these is optional. They can cause a great deal of trouble, pain and distress later on by growing into the pads of the foot if their owners neglect to cut them, especially on the back feet. It is best that they are removed when the whelps are three to five days old.

Eyes

The eyes should start to open between ten and 14 days; when puppies are kept in the dark, they open sooner than when they are in the light. If the eye is slightly sticky, bathe it with warm weak tea or some eye lotion such as Optrex. It is possible for the eye to open partially and then close; it can become infected inside and is very painful. As there is no opening for the discharge, the eye bulges and is very painful. The whelp wails pitifully. Antibiotic ointment smeared on the eye, after bathing, maybe sufficient. You should let your vet look at it straight away.

When the eyes first open, they are a misty blue, but they will clear and darken later. Keep the puppies away from bright light.

Ears
The ears, which up to now have been sealed, will unseal around ten days when the eyes open and the puppy will be able to hear.

Troubles in the nest

Fading puppies and early deaths
This is a term used to describe puppies which apparently start off strong and vigorous, then gradually stop sucking and cry plaintively. Their tummies usually become hard and distended, and they get weaker until they just fade away and die. It can affect all the litter, and an autopsy seldom shows anything. Fading is a very loose term which covers all puppies which die early without any reason.

As I mentioned earlier, many puppies are affected when the bitch is given antibiotics, this being due to the lack of the good flora and fauna in the intestines which are killed off by the antibiotics. I have the answer to this one. Give yoghurt and Vitamin B1 (Thiamine).

There are many other causes, mostly unknown. It can be stress or infection and, as soon as trouble is suspected, remove the puppy from the mother and place it away in a warm box and hand-feed it, but remember to start with glucose and water. If the cause of the trouble is known, it can then be treated.

Many an early death goes undiagnosed. There may be internal imperfections; some whelps are without orifices and these may live for only three days. "Drowning'" occurs when the puppy has taken an overly long time to be born, the lungs do not expand properly, and it has been drowned in the fluid surrounding it. The lungs in the puppy are the last thing to develop. If they are born too early (more than a week), this is likely to have been the problem. The lungs do not become fully functional at the first gasp — it takes 24 hours. It is a good thing to give the puppy glucose and water. NEVER GIVE A NEW PUPPY MILK FEEDS TO START.

Cleft palate and hare lip
The cleft palate is when the centre line of the palate is not joined. It is more common than the hare lip, when the top lip is not joined below the nose either on one side or both. This can be congenital or hereditary — the cause is uncertain. There are several theories. It can be inherited through a recessive gene, or it can be due to a virus, excessive use of cortisone drugs or lack of Ryboflavin (B2). The following treatment has been practised with success. Vitamin B2 is given to bitches who have previously produced clefts. It is given when the bitch is mated to a week before whelping is due. Bitches treated this way have had no further trouble.

Chilling or hypothermia

This is very serious. There is a very great danger for a tiny puppy to become parted from the warmth of the dam (this is why we like to put a warm pad on one side of the whelping box). The body temperature falls very rapidly, even when the room temperature is quite high. The puppy's temperature will drop to 94 deg F (34 C) within half an hour. It is possible that the dam has discarded this puppy because it has a congenital defect; all puppies who are ill have a 'sick' smell to the bitch. The symptoms may be similar to those of a fading puppy, or it may just lie still and feel limp and cold to your touch. If put it to the teat, it may appear to suck while not actually having the strength to draw the milk. The condition of chilling can go on unobserved while the puppy becomes weaker.

When the puppy's temperature gets as low as 94 deg F (34 deg C), hypothermia is setting in and it must be treated straight away if it is to be saved.

Treatment: The puppy will take two or three hours to warm up and this must be done very slowly. The best way is to tuck it inside your clothes against your body, and jog it around a bit. Do not give it any milk mixtures, for it is unable to digest them. Give a glucose and water solution, or honey if you have no glucose: $1/2$ ml per ounce of body weight. Give this every hour until it is warmed up and moving normally. It can then be put back to the mother to suck.

Hyperthermia

The opposite from hypothermia, this is a condition where the puppy becomes too hot and the temperature rises too high, this can end in death, just as heat stroke. If a bitch is nursing her puppies close to her, they receive adequate heat, and overhead lamps and heated pads — unless the bed is very large — may not be required.

Nostril trouble

There is a condition, which thank goodness seems to be becoming quite rare, which may prove my theory that no animals who have suffered from it should be used for breeding.

This condition usually attacks at 10 to 21 days of age. Some puppies are born with a tight nostril. This is curved inwards, with a very tiny opening, and is undesirable, but not the condition to which I am referring. These puppies are usually born with wide nostrils and they do not tighten until the trouble starts.

The cause is uncertain, but is sometimes hereditary. It can be bred out if affected puppies are not used for breeding. It can also arise from an infection, possibly due to a blow causing collapsed cartilage in the nose, or because of a variable growth rate in the puppy. Originally, penicillin would cure this complaint if it was caused by infection, but now it does not respond to this. Lincocin Aquadrops (Upjohn) given in the strength of $1/4$ ml (five drops) twice daily for five days has brought about a cure in some cases.

The symptoms are not dissimilar to those of the fading puppy. The pup crawls around the bed, refusing to suck even when in the proximity of the teats. It's mucous membranes are swollen, as with a catarrhal condition, and it cannot smell, so does not find the teats. At the next stage, it cannot breathe through its nose, it wails continuously with its head up and mouth open, and if left, it will eventually become weaker and die.

It is important to notice the symptoms early. The puppy must be hand-fed, and frequently put back to the bitch to see if it will suck; occasionally it will do so, but then relapses. It must, of course, be kept warm. Hand-feed small quantities of a puppy-rearing formula hourly, adding a teaspoon of brandy to one teacup of feed. It will be reluctant to take the food and great care is needed to make sure that it swallows and the fluid does not go down into the lungs. The duration of this condition is from one to about 14 days.

If a young whelp becomes a bit snuffly and has a runny nostril, give it the same treatment of Lincomycim — $1/4$ ml twice daily for five days. You should see results within three days. Amoxil suspension (Paediatric) is also suitable — 4 ml twice daily for seven days. This is quite different from the case of the puppy who becomes snuffly when teething, which is dealt with under rearing.

Diarrhoea

If this is not serious diarrhoea, but just a too loose bowel (though it is difficult to see when the mother is cleaning them up all the time), it usually shows up by staining on the bed. I would give the mother a probiotic. These are obtainable from various animal drug firms such as Vydex Animal Health limited and Pet-Tex The Animal Health Company. After three weeks, it could be fed direct to the puppies

On the other hand, diarrhoea can be very serious in puppies; the loss of fluid will cause them to dehydrate very quickly. It is safest to inform your vet as diarrhoea can be the start of parvovirus and other infectious conditions. In this case, the stools will be most offensive. This is not to be confused with the very new whelp who is suffering due to the mother's antibiotic. As soon as you see the puppy has severe diarrhoea, take it off the bitch, treat her with probiotics, give the puppy electrolyte solution to combat any dehydration and check with your veterinary surgeon.

Bloating

This can be due to various things such as intestinal infection, toxic milk, over-feeding, and not having the bowels open, or even worms. The puppy's stomach will be like a drum and it will be screaming in pain.

In the Nest.

Treatment: Some mothers neglect their duty to lick the puppies' tummies and anus after feeding to make them urinate and pass stools. It is most important that this is done. If the mother is not attending to it, you must take appropriate action if you suspect it is due to this, try to get the puppy to pass a stool. Give $1/2$ teaspoonful of milk of magnesia — this can be given every three hours. Insert a Vaselined, blunt-ended thermometer into the rectum to stimulate and ease the passage if the puppy is constipated. It can also be due to a build-up of gasses in the stomach. This is serious, rather like the adult 'bloat'. It can be due to the mother's milk being too acid or infected. No ordinary remedies for wind such as Dinnefords or Aselone (for humans) are any help.

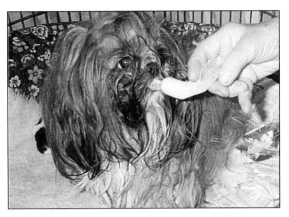

You need the vet, who will pass a tube and draw off the gasses, but the condition can re-occur, and it is as well to get tuition from your vet as to how to pass the tube correctly. If there has been an occurrence of this, the homoeopathic remedy of Lycopodium six, three times a day for a week, may well help to keep it from recurring.

Acid milk

Some puppies, just like babies, cry a great deal, and it is difficult to find a cause as they seem to be thriving as they should. One suspects the mother's milk is too acid for them.

Feeding a Reluctant Mother.
(See page 136)

Treatment: It is worth putting a pinch of soda bicarbonate into the mother's water bowel, this can help counter the acidity of the milk.

The flat puppy and the swimmer   *(see pictures on next page)*

These are two different conditions. The flat puppy syndrome is skeletal and the swimmer is muscular. The flat puppy is physically flat; triangular in shape with the legs pointing outwards. It has more difficulty in moving round than the normal puppy, though it gyrates remarkably well. You will have to give it help to get it up on its legs. The swimmer, on the other hand, is flat-chested from lying on its stomach and not using the legs. Lying on a slippery surface can cause this.

Treatment: You need to encourage the legs to come under the puppy, and to do this, mould the puppy with your hands every time you pick it up. Place your hands over the top of the puppy's back, around the rib cage, gently moulding it round into shape. The bones are soft and amenable to this.

If must be done regularly and as often as you can. See that it is on a rough, non-slip surface in the whelping bed, as this all helps it to use its muscles. As soon as it is able to get its legs under it sufficiently — this will not be before the three weeks when puppies get up on their feet — put a hobble between the front legs so they cannot splay outwards, and a bandage under its tummy, so that you can give it support, and encourage it to walk like this. The swimmer will not need the moulding. You must do everything to help it strengthen the muscles.

Hobbling a flat puppy's legs to aid walking.

Hernias

There are umbilical hernias, which are very frequently seen in this breed. These are a protrusion of gut at the sight of the umbilical cord. Sometimes they are very tiny, and no more than a small lump of fatty tissue, and are not serious. It is the degree of the hernia that is important. If it is reducible by being pushed back inside, it is not serious and may get smaller and close with age. If it is large, an

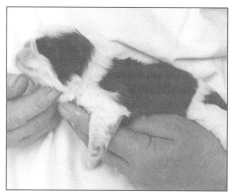

Flat Puppy at one week. (see previous page)

Flat Puppy at 6 weeks, after treatment.

Normal Puppy at 10 days.

operation may be advised. It is a help to gently massage round the site of the cord in a new puppy. Once it has dried off, this can stimulate it to close up. These hernias do not show up fully unless they are really bad, until the puppy gets up on its feet and the weight of the stomach pushes it out.

The inguinal hernia situated in the groin is serious. These hernias should always be operated on and the animal never used for breeding.

There are various theories about the cause of hernias. Mostly, they are considered to be hereditary though it has not been proved. I regret that umbilical hernias are very common in the Shih Tzu. It can be caused through tying and cutting the cord too close or by there having been too much pull on the cord at birth. This can happen easily in the Shih Tzu as so many births are short-corded.

Infection of the cord

The stump of the cord can become infected. It will look red and swollen and may drain pus. It is important that this is treated as it may lead to septicaemia. Sometimes iodine is applied to the stump at birth to reduce the risks.

Treatment: Clean the navel with a dilute solution of hydrogen peroxide and apply an antibiotic ointment. Panalog is good. If it does not clear up, consult your vet.

Puppy rash

This maybe due to a milk or urine rash on the tummy. Treatment: It can be treated after gently washing, with castor oil and zinc ointment, and will soon clear up.

Parvovirus

The first indications that your puppies have parvovirus infection will be very offensive diarrhoea. This is dealt with in chapter 17: Health.

Supplementary feeding and hand rearing

If the litter is large, supplementary feeding may be necessary in order to relieve the dam and/or to assist any individual puppy who shows signs of under-feeding. On the other hand, unnecessary or premature hand-feeding may cause the dam to lose interest.

For the first two days, one auxiliary feed may be enough, then give a second. Use the same formula as for hand-rearing, and give the supplementary before the puppies are allowed to feed from the dam. Do not neglect to weigh daily.

If the whole litter has to be hand-reared to save it because the dam has died or become ill, the best solution is to get a foster mother if this is at all possible. She should be a bitch whose puppies are around the same age, or who has lost her own puppies — though not of course from any infection. Precautions will have to be taken when transferring these orphans to her. The best way is to remove her from her own brood for a short time while you introduce the new puppies, mingle them with her own and rub them around among the others to transfer their smell.

The only time I have ever experience the situation of introducing a foster mother who had lost her own puppies to another bitch's litter was to console the foster mother. She already knew and loved the puppy who was three weeks old. She took to it well enough but nature told her it was only just born, and she was most perturbed when it got up and walked! Each time, she would lead it back to the nest by walking backwards so that it followed her mouth (at this age the mother often regurgitates food for the puppy). I would not do this again. To introduce in the normal way, it would be best if the bitch is first encouraged to lick the puppies thoroughly rather than straight away putting them to suck, as the bitch will most likely resent this. To get the bitch to lick the puppies, smear them over with milky food, or preferably with the bitch's own milk

If you cannot get a foster mother, you may have to undertake the job yourself. Two people are better than one for this job, for it involves night and day feeding and attention. Follow the instructions below for weak puppies.

Milk formulas

Breeders usually have their own pet formula. You must see which suits you and your puppies best.

1) Several firms now make a substitute bitch's milk. I have used Welpi with success, and Vetzyme also make a puppy milk. Lactol I do not like, but some people do. Your vet usually keeps these in stock, or your chemist will get them for you, or

2) For emergency use and also good for the mother.
   1 pint of cow's milk
   1 tablespoon of cream
   1 teaspoon of glucose
   1 egg yolk, or:

3) 4 fl oz Carnation evaporated milk
   4 fl oz boiled water which has been cooled.
   1 level teaspoonful of glucose
   1 small egg yolk, size no 4 (no white at all)

s. Ch. Santosha chocolate Orange. (red/gold and white) d. Bosster of Bellakerne.

s. Bellakerne Rory Do (black/white) d. Dusky rose of Bellakerne (solid Black)

Two of the litter at three weeks.

Gold/white litter at three weeks.

Always strain these mixtures twice through a nylon strainer, and keep them in an airtight jar in the fridge shaking well before use.

If it is a case of feeding a weak or sick puppy, do not give these milk feeds to start. Always start with a glucose solution of one level teaspoon of glucose to one fluid ounce of boiled water. or five level teaspoons to a quarter of a pint of water. This should not normally be fed by itself for more than 12 hours. Then use your electrolyte solution obtained from your vet or the chemist. This can be fed by itself for up to 48 hours. Then go on to alternate feeds of milk formulae and eletrolyte.

If the puppies lose their mother at birth, you must keep them warm and not allow them to become dehydrated (which can happen overnight) or they will die. If you cannot get fluid into them by mouth, then glucose saline may be administered by the vet, or you can tube feed.

To hand feed

Have the puppy on your knee, resting on a warm bottle protected by a towel wrapped around it. Use a puppy feeding bottle or even a kitten feeding bottle. I like the Catac bottle best. The Belcroy baby premature feeding bottles are also recommended. It is always difficult to get the correct size hole in the teat, so see that you have several teats available. Nick a tiny one with sharp scissors. You have it correct when a drop comes out when you hold the bottle down.

With your thumb and forefinger, gently squeeze the corners of the mouth which will cause the mouth to open. Pop in the teat, then check that the tongue is under the teat and not in the roof of the mouth.

If the puppy will not suck, gently stroke the throat to encourage sucking or the muzzle on either side of the nose. Give approximately a teaspoon per feed every two hours day and night for the first two weeks. Gradually increase the amount of feed and time between feeds as the puppy grows. Once a day give Paediatric multi-vitamin drops such as Adexolin — just one drop the first week, then two the second, but not if you are using a milk substitute which contains vitamins.

At three weeks, you can slowly start to wean.

Puppies which have been hand-fed from birth will accept you as their mother and become very humanised; it is often very difficult to get them into whelp later on.

Tube feeding

Tube feeding is becoming more widely used. This has many advantages, especially if the puppy is weak and unable to suck. You should not attempt to do it unless you have been carefully instructed. Care is needed and the correct equipment or you will damage the delicate tissues of the new puppy.

You will need:
    10ml syringe
    A feeding tube. A Rhyles stomach tube for premature human babies is best if obtainable.
    For new born puppies, use catheters size 3FG to 6FG.

You need to know the correct length to pass the tube. Lay the tube alongside the puppy, and measure to three quarters length to the last rib, then measure carefully to the mouth. This is the length you will pass the tube. Mark the position on the tube. Carefully pass the tube over the back of the tongue and down the throat as far as your mark on the tube. If there is any resistance, withdraw the tube. When you are quite sure that the tube is in the stomach, you can attach your syringe with the warmed-to-blood-heat feed, being careful your syringe does not contain any air. Slowly and smoothly depress your plunger. This should take about one and a half minutes.

All your equipment must be kept as clean and sterilised as for a human baby. Use Milton.

If your feeding is correct, the puppy will gain in weight and strength. The stools are a good guide. If they are very loose and green, you are likely to be over-feeding, or the formula does not suit the puppy. Cut back the amount and give 1ml of milk of magnesia every three hours with the feed. If the stools become grey or like curdled milk, the puppy is not digesting any nourishment and is liable to become dehydrated. Give water between the milk feeds. If it does not improve, give the electrolyte solution.

CHAPTER TWELVE

REARING THE LITTER

Progress after the first three weeks
You now breathe a sigh of relief and satisfaction — your bitch and puppies have come through the most critical time, and all is well.

The bitch should now be getting at the very least three times her normal ration of food. This should have plenty of top quality protein in it. Poorer second grade vegetable protein is not what she needs. If she will eat and enjoy Hills Growth Diet, it is recommended as a convenience food. I still maintain that a good variety diet with added supplements is best, and this is what I like to use. Cooked lamb tongues, raw heart, raw beef or lamb, chicken, a little cooked liver — careful, as liver can cause looseness — eggs and milk, fish (an excellent food and high in calcium) are all good, whereas meats and poultry are low.

If it is a large litter, you should be thinking of weaning the puppies, as your bitch will have had enough if she has fed them well. You must take note of her milk glands and see that they do not become congested, as the puppies will take less milk from her.

If it is a small litter, there is no rush to wean. I would not start until four weeks, and then take it slowly. You usually find it is far more difficult to wean a small litter than a large one, as there is such a plentiful supply of milk, and the little ones prefer that to anything you give them.

Puppies at play. Owner Jean Luc Lambert (France.)
Photo: Jean Luc Lambert

150

General progress of the puppies

By the third week, the puppies start getting up on their legs and there is frequently one who is more forward than the rest. At this stage, they like to be able to crawl out of their nest to pass urine as their natural instinct is not to soil their beds. Let down the front flap of your whelping box and put a sheet of newspaper in the front of it. This is the start of house training.

By the fourth week, their tails are up and they will wag them when they see or hear you.

Gentle grooming can now be started,

Snaefells Oswald 12 weeks.

brushing the coat in both directions with a soft baby bristle brush. Hold each puppy on your lap and get it used to having its tummy attended to. Or you can lay it on a soft rug and do it that way, as this will be good training for adult grooming. If the mother has stopped washing their faces, you must wipe round the eyes and mouth daily and, as they get older, follow the instructions in the chapter on grooming.

It is most important that you give the puppies plenty of love from the third week onwards. It is claimed that the vital time for puppies to become really well-adjusted to people is between the third and 14th weeks of life, and that between the third and seventh week is the best time of all for establishing social contact. Once this has been established, their affection can easily be transferred to others. Those animals which are regularly fondled and groomed during this critical period are reputed to learn faster, show more initiative and be generally brighter and healthier because they are more resistant to stress.

A litter of puppies eating. Owner Jean Luc Lambert (France.)
Photo: Jean Luc Lambert

151

It is said that the effect of handling is not only psychological, but that puppies so treated develop heavier adrenal glands — the organs which produce cortisone and other protective secretions. I cannot answer for this personally as I would not dream of trying the converse by NOT giving my puppies plenty of affection; though people who have a lot of puppies at the same time might not be able to, especially the poor little puppies reared in puppy farms. The little boy who, when asked what he fed his dog on, said "kisses and cuddles" knew the answer better than many an adult. (I do hope it had other food as well!)

At three weeks, some mothers decide they have had enough of cleaning up the puppies and their bed. I have noticed the mother frequently gets a bit sick around this time, but it's nothing to worry about as a rule. Also, when they have other foods, she does not clean them up any more. You must see that the area around the anus is clean; when the mother stops her stimulating licking, they may have difficulty in passing their motions, and become constipated. This is when you must help them or they may get a prolapsed anus. The abdomen will become distended and hard and the puppy will cry and be distressed. It may help if you insert a vaselined blunt ended thermometer into the anus, but be very careful and do not attempt to force it; then withdraw it and simulate the mother's licking by using a warm swab. One teaspoonful of milk of magnesia can be given. If everything fails, an enema will be needed.

Prolapsed anus
This can occur in young puppies while straining to pass hard faeces.

Treatment: The protruding rectum should be gently pushed back inside with a vaselined finger. Olive oil or liquid paraffin should be given to the puppy to prevent a re-occurrence.

Living area
Now that the puppies are not getting cleaned up by the mother, their run and bed is likely to become soiled. Clean up straight away — do not give them the chance to develop the revolting habit of coprophagy (eating excreta).

The puppy run should have a non-slip surface — never use sawdust, as this can get into the eyes and cause ulcers.

At five weeks, the mother usually stops sleeping with the puppies, and should be given a night bed away from them.

By six weeks of age, the puppies need a sufficiently large area to enable them to run around and develop their limbs. They will still spend a large part of the day sleeping.

Nails
Cut the nails as soon as they become long and sharp, for they will scratch the mother's tender tummy and can cause her pain and sores. You can do this with a pair of ordinary nail scissors as their nails are very soft.

Naming

Give each puppy a pet name at an early age, which they will recognise and to which they will respond. You may in any case prefer to choose their registration names later on as they develop their characters. Papers for registration are obtainable from the Kennel Club. The whole litter should be registered together as it costs a great deal more if just one is registered at a later date, though some people prefer not to register puppies they are selling purely as pets. Make this situation quite clear to the new owner or you may have problems.

Now that your puppies have pet names, they can learn to come when used to it. This is all part of early obedience training, for the Shih Tzu can be very stubborn. If the new owner wishes to give their puppy a different name from the one you have chosen, suggest adding the new name after the old one until the puppy becomes accustomed to it. Then the old name can safely be dropped. Otherwise, the good you have done with your early training maybe undone.

Early car travel

If you can possibly manage to do so, take the puppies out in the car early; this should prevent car sickness at a later date, as it is so often caused by fear and stress. A puppy going to a new home for the first time in a car may well feel stressed.

Worming

It is most important that your puppies are wormed before they go to a new home.

I find vets do not all agree as to the time for worming. My old vet used to say at three weeks. My present vet says four weeks. Another vet and the literature on some worm pills says two weeks. You would be wise to check this with your own vet.

I usually worm mine at the end of three weeks or beginning of four weeks, and have never had any problems. No doubt if you suspect that your puppies are affected by worms, you should do it earlier. There are many different worm tablets on the market — just make sure the one you give is for puppies, not adults.

Even when the bitch has been wormed before whelping, and during the latter weeks of pregnancy, the puppy can still be troubled by worms, usually roundworms. The worm ova can be passed from the dam, via the placenta, before the puppy is born.

Signs of infestation are variable appetite and pot-bellied appearance, particularly after meals. There may possibly be runny eyes and a cough, and a generally unthrifty look. Worms can be passed in the faeces or vomited. Because the puppies show no symptoms it does not mean that they are quite free of worms. It is the responsibility of the breeder to make sure that worming is completed before the pups go to their new homes. Puppies can pass worms to small children who allow them to lick their faces, or who put a puppy's toy into their mouth. If worms should get behind the eye, blindness may ensue, and while this is very rare indeed, don't let it happen through any neglect on your part. Routine worming should be carried out up to the age of six months to prevent worms from becoming established.

Weaning

As I mentioned earlier, there are no hard and fast rules about when to wean. If it is a large litter, you start early; a small litter and you can start later. It also depends on the condition of the dam. If she is looking worn out, thin and in poor condition, help her out early. You may have been supplementing the litter already. At least try getting them to lap early on.

Feed the puppies in front of the mother so that she can see just what is happening (she usually likes to finish up their feed) and seems quite happy to know just what her babies are being given. Start with a milk feed — one of the formulas would be alright — or you can use goat's milk, which is rich, or even sheep or cow's milk. Do not thicken the feed at this

Gold black masked puppies at 10 weeks.
Owner Jim Peat

stage. Their digestion must get used to things slowly and added carbohydrates are difficult to digest. I find the best way to get them to start lapping milk is by lowering their heads into a shallow dish so they get milk onto their muzzle and lick it off. Then they usually put their heads down for another taste. You can do it by holding a spoonful to their mouth and just tipping a little for them to get them to lick your finger first. After a few days when they have learnt to lap, you can start to thicken the milk with Farex — just a little to start.

At four or five weeks, begin to give small quantities of scraped, lean raw meat twice daily. Increase the amount slowly to one teaspoon in two days, or the puppies will get diarrhoea, and you can get them used to soaked puppy meal. Increase the amount of meat slowly, and by six weeks, 2oz can be given if it is not upsetting them. It may now be minced and should not be fatty. Continue with the milk and Farex twice a day. Also use the ABEDEX drops, and a little Cal D. If the puppies do not lap up the Farex at first, let them lick it off your fingers or pop it into their mouths. Eating is a habit, and if they eat well now, they should continue to do so.

Puppies at 8 weeks, with author

When they are weaned, the puppies should be having four to five meals daily — two of milk and two of meat.

I suggest the above diet, which has been well tried over many years, but there are so many good convenience 'complete' puppy diets on the market now, you might prefer to try one of them. They are suitable for weaning.

When you are weaning in earnest, you must remove the mother from the puppies for longer intervals each day. Do not take her away altogether, because she loves her puppies and will play with them and teach them to fend for themselves. Between four and five weeks, as they are getting on to solid food, the mother frequently disgorges her own food for them. This is a normal reflex action, but make sure it is suitable food for the puppies. The mother's food should be cut back to her normal diet, unless she is out of condition, in which case you must feed her up. Make sure her milk is drying up and her breasts are going back to normal. Refer to *Puppy diet from eight weeks* in chapter 8: Feeding

Lead training

I know that lead training at this age will seem very early to some people, and it is just about impossible outdoors if they do not have a suitable garden or weather. It must not be done outside your premises until the puppy has had all his inoculations. You may be able to manage in a room in your house, though it is not so easy. However, if you manage, it is well worth it.

Puppies at 10 weeks. Owner Wendy Hughs-Keast

Prior to the training, if the weather has been suitable, I like to get my puppies outdoors and play with them on the lawn. I call them to me and they soon come running. After this, it is an easy step to get them to follow wherever I go. The training must be carried out with each puppy individually, away from all distractions. For full instructions, see *Basic commands, collar and lead training* in chapter 5.

Teeth

Teeth can be quite a problem. Shih Tzus are often late in cutting their teeth. The eye teeth appear first at around six weeks and you can feel and count the central incisors in the gums. There should be six of these in both upper and lower jaw. Teeth can be a problem in brachycephalic breeds because of the shortening of the jaw. The jaw should be wide, in which case there is more space for the teeth to fit in. Many only have four incisors. In some countries, this would not be acceptable for breeding or show. In England, it is usually accepted if all else is good, though it is not liked..

At eight weeks, one cannot be sure that the bite will end up correct, though a good breeder usually has an idea how their own line develops. Even if the puppy you are selling does not have its teeth quite through, it is nice to be able to feel six in the gum. The addition of Cal D in the correct dosage can help.

Snuffly puppies

During teething time, many puppies become very snuffly, and are inclined to breathe through their nose with their mouth open. It is a worrying time as they really should not be sold like this, although it can be explained to the new owner that the puppy will most likely get over it when it has finished teething. Their vet is just as likely — not knowing Shih Tzus — to tell the new owner to take it back to the breeder and demand their money back, so it is better to hold the puppy back until it is better, if you can.

Treatment: Not much has affect. Antibiotics can be given. Give the puppy suitable bones or biscuits to chew on to try to get the teeth through. Make sure it is having its vitamin drops — I have known the addition of vitamin A to help. One breeder gave a snuffly puppy Vitamin A for three weeks, and while several trips to the vet had no effect, the snuffles vanished. Worth a try.

Puppy head gland. (juvenile pyoderma)

This is a rare condition which can affect a puppy, usually around eight weeks. Very little is understood about it. It can be slight and respond to treament quickly, or it can develop badly, with the animal needing to be put down. The early signs are spots around the head and mouth. Many have started in the anal area.

Treatment: Antibiotics. Usually starting with Lincomycin. The antibiotics need to be kept on for some time. Many I have heard about have been cured within a month.

DO NOT ON ANY ACCOUNT LET YOUR VET GIVE THE PUPPY INOCULATION WHILE IT IS SUFFERING. If it does have its inoculations, you are likely to have your puppy suffer with T-cell immunity, in which case it will be on antibiotics all its life.

Bathing

It is not too young at this age to give your puppy a bath, and it is nice to do this first bath at home rather than let a stranger — and perhaps one unfamiliar to bathing puppies — do it.

You must be careful not to frighten a puppy for this first bath. It is better to use a sink or baby bath and pour water over from a jug, rather than to use a shower, as showers often frighten puppies. Place a non-slip mat at the bottom of the bath, and hold the puppy firmly. Use a baby shampoo, and a 'no tears' shampoo for the head is a must. Dry it thoroughly and carefully, do not use too hot a hair dryer. Make sure it is kept in a warm place after the bath and let it have a sleep.

Selling your puppies

All too soon, the time comes to part with your puppies. Do not condemn them to an unhappy life by selling unwisely. The breed is very popular both abroad and at home, and there are many dealers from unsuitable countries trying to buy in stock for their pet trade. Do try to make quite sure that your puppies are going to be loved as family pets, whether for showing or not. Love and affection is essential to this delightful breed. Do not sell whole litters to one buyer, or even a pet owner. Two from a litter is company, but no more. If a dog and a bitch go together, make absolutely certain either the dog is castrated or the bitch spayed, (the best time to have a bitch spayed is mid-way between seasons, when the oestrogen levels are at their lowest.). Do not sell your puppies under eight weeks of age, for up to at least seven weeks, the puppies should still have some contact with their dam. The best age is eight to 12 weeks.

Age of inoculation is usually eight weeks. Never have your puppy inoculated unless it is in perfect health. If it is snuffly or spotty, wait until it is better.

Always provide a diet sheet with your puppy so it continues with the same food and will not get an upset tummy. Give full advice on feeding and grooming, so the owners know they can come to you for help.

If the puppy has any defect such as a hernia, always tell the new owner — do not let them find out about it first from the vet. Some vets who do not realise the a small umbilical hernia is very common in the breed make a big thing of it.

Suggest that the new owner joins a breed club. If you do not have a membership form, give them the address of one of the secretaries whom they can contact. This will give them contact with other owners and more knowledgeable people who are always ready to give help and advice if required.

CHAPTER THIRTEEN

THE PUPPY

Growth, Development and Problems of Management

Up to this point, I have written mainly on the physical care of the Shih Tzu, but this is only half of what goes to make it the unique dog so many people consider it to be.

It is no good having a physically beautiful animal with an unsatisfactory temperament and unpleasant personality. I will try to give a little help by telling you what some experts say regarding socialising and having a well-adjusted animal.

Do we pay enough attention to the first 19 weeks of our puppies' lives? A great deal of research has gone into early behaviour of the dog, and it is up to us to give our dogs the chance to benefit from it.

Puppy to champion.
Ch. Snaefells Limited Edition 4 weeks
Owned by Author.

Most good breeders realise that love and good food are essential if they want their puppies to develop into loving, friendly, well-adjusted animals. At certain critical ages, love is not sufficient in itself. I have heard of puppies being exported from well-known kennels, who I know take the greatest care of them, only to arrive at their new home so hysterical that they have been quite useless for show. I have made my own mistakes, too. Despite giving all the love I could to the puppy, it has shown emotional upset in its new home. It is up to you and me to try to prevent this happening.

If we understand more about the 'critical periods' in a puppy's life, it helps considerably towards avoiding mistakes.

Genes play a great part in the mental as well as the physical make-up of the animal, and good environment without the right genes is no good either. If one starts by breeding from stock known to lack a bold temperament, and this does not necessarily mean nervousness, it is all the more important to socialise the puppies with extra care.

Ch. Snaefells Limited Edition 12 weeks.

Ch. Snaefells Limited Edition 10 months.

Dr Scott has done a great deal of research on rearing methods, and basic behaviour at the Jackson laboratories in the United States. He used five different breeds for his experiments, but not the Shih Tzu. There were some differences in certain behaviour patterns of the breeds, but the critical periods were all the same.

I will touch lightly over the critical periods as given by Dr Scott. The first three weeks, or average 19 $\frac{1}{2}$ to 21 days of the puppy's life, it is completely unafffected by its environment. All it requires is the food, warmth and massage of the mother. Alright, so the mother looks after it, and you do not keep interfering, and letting the children or friends pick the puppies up. Though it is unaffected by its environment, you need to keep a pretty close eye to watch that all is going on well, and if the mother is not treated correctly, the puppies will certainly suffer.

Puppies should be in the home where you can see what is happening, not tucked away in an old garden shed where you cannot see them without making a special visit. This can get tedious in the pouring rain, and the next critical period requires that you give them more attention.

The second critical period lasts for the next four weeks, or until the puppy is seven weeks old. The puppy can now hear, see and smell, and his brain and nervous system are developing. At the age of seven weeks, it is developed to the capacity of an adult, but lacking the experience. During these four weeks, the puppy needs to learn to mix with people and dogs. It has frequently been found that the hand-reared puppy who has not mixed with dogs up to the seventh week is the one who picks fights when an adult.

From three weeks, start handling and gently grooming your puppies. I find Shih Tzu develop very differently at this age. All should be getting up on their feet at three to four weeks. Some start to wag tails and bark, while others in the litter may not do this for some time. At this age, they will play with their litter mates and may have fighting games. The hand-reared puppy who has lost his mother misses this, and does not have the chance to get used to other dogs, or have his mother to keep him in order.

By seven weeks, the order of dominance is setting in. This is usually very noticeable with the Shih Tzu, and it is quite easy to tell during those four weeks who will be the

Ch. Snaefells Limited Edition 3 years.

bullyboy. Dr Scott found it was always the largest male who was the dominant one. If it was an all-female litter, it was not the largest one, but the one who 'talked' the most. During these four weeks, the breeder must get the puppies used to people, giving them plenty of love. It is then considered that seven to eight weeks is the best age for puppies to go to their new homes, as the next critical period has arrived. With Shih Tzus, I consider eight weeks the earliest that they should leave their home, as many are not fully weaned before that.

A puppy can be affected both by not being with its mother up to seven weeks, and by staying with its mother too long. In the first case, they can become over-aggressive, and in the latter case, may lack boldness. Seeing how the Shih Tzu so loves her puppies and hates to be parted from them, this staying too long with the mother is a point to note. You may also get this lack of boldness by running on two litter mates together. One may be bold, but seldom both. However, this does not apply if two puppies of different litters or breeds are run on together, but this was something which had not been fully researched into. In the few cases of Shih Tzu I have heard of being run on in this unrelated way, there has certainly been no emotional upset.

You can start to train a puppy as soon as it is up on its feet. The sooner you train a Shih Tzu to be obedient to your call, the easier it will be when an adult. I feel sure this breed needs some very early training to obedience.

The third period is 49 to 84 days — seven to eight weeks. The puppy should meet as many people as possible during this period. (This can be difficult when a puppy is not fully inoculated). It is unusually susceptible to environmental influences. Although seven weeks is when the order of dominance starts, 11 to 15 weeks weeks is the critical time for this, and in Fox Terrier puppies where fighting was particularly bad, it was found that if male puppies were kept apart from seven weeks and re-introduced at 16 weeks, there was no fighting. Some male Shih Tzus do fight together, and when it is known that male dogs, particularly stud dogs, are to be kept together, this separation period may well be worth trying, though I have my doubts that it would work. It is considered essential during this period to give each puppy a small amount of individual attention and affection away from his siblings, and this should include basic training. If he does not have it, it may make him a life-long bully or an underdog.

As much teaching as possible should be done by 16 weeks. If the puppy has been taught, it can learn a great deal more later on. If it has never had any attention or teaching, it will be much more difficult to try to teach it anything later. It is enough to teach it how to learn, for remember that its brain is fully developed. Never expect it to learn too much — only play lessons are needed. More serious lessons can start at the fourth period from 16 weeks.

If you run a puppy on after eight weeks, take it where you can, and show it all you can before 16 weeks. It should be taken out in the car — this will prevent car sickness. Have it inoculated as soon as advised by your vet. Get it trained on the lead — six weeks is a good time for this, so long as you have first taught it to follow you off the lead. As soon as it is safe after inoculations, get it out to see people and traffic, and take it to 'puppy parties'.

Hereditary characteristics and environment go hand in hand, and feeding is a most important part of environment. It is considered by Burns and Fraser (Genetics of the Dog, 1966) that the changes of growth in a puppy are only partially controlled by its genes. Its growth is comparable to early

Ch Kareth Karisma age seven months.

maturing sheep, with high feeding during the first three months of life tending to produce heavy bones, large feet, a long back and relatively short legs and neck. This is an interesting point of view which I have found difficult to prove, though there is no doubt that different lines develop at different paces and this could possibly be due to the feeding.

The period from weaning at around eight weeks until 20 weeks of age is when pups grow most quickly. Between eight and ten weeks, they consume the highest proportion of food relative to the body weight.

Heavy bone is softer and less dense than light bone, for it bends more easily. The achondroplastic gene (a condition in which the limbs are abnormally short) affects heavy bone rather than fine, and this makes it more difficult to get short straight legs if the bone is thick. The standard does not call for massive bone, but 'muscular with ample bone . . . looking massive on account of the wealth of hair'. Great care is needed in the rearing of these dogs to obtain good fronts. Heavy bone is frequently the result of heavy feeding and restricted exercise. There has been evidence that heavy feeding favours the development of hip dysplasia, of which I am told there is more than there used to be in certain areas of the country. Equal damage can be done in other ways by under-feeding. Burns and Fraser go on to state that if moderate feeding up to five or six months of age is followed by heavy feeding, thickening of the long bones of the legs and coarsening of the skull are likely to result.

Rickets can also cause short, bent legs. Many knowledgeable people consider this a dietary as well as a hereditary condition. You can also get bone problems by overdosing with calcium and vitaminD.

It is inadvisable to follow a large meal by exercise in heavy-boned animals, since the weight of food in the stomach can cause bending of the legs. If there is a tendency for the legs to bow, it is helpful to raise the feeding bowl etc., up off the ground to a height whereby the legs do not have to bend to reach it. Another precaution is to avoid any walking down steps or stairs, and jumping from heights.

Results of genetical research on the conformation of the dog indicate it is rare for a purely Mendelian factor to be involved. There can be several different causes of one specific

Bad mouth with crooked teeth

result, i.e. 'the short leg may be due to a simple recessive gene, to partially dominant factors, to multiple factors not showing dominance, or even to rickets or to general poor nutrition' and it is thought that tooth and jaw size are inherited independently.

Under-feeding will produce faulty, weedy bodies prone to disease, and this practice should never be employed in the misguided idea that it will restrict an animal's size.

I hope this information will help people to realise that the growth of the puppy depends as much on satisfactory environment as on good breeding.

Your puppy is now four months old and fully immunised. At four months, a puppy has reached about half his adult weight, and by six months, two thirds of the adult weight. Factors of size and weight should always be considered in conjunction.

Now is the time to watch growth carefully and treat symptoms as they appear. Further full socialising is important. Between four and five months he is developing fast and will be more adventuresome, going out to do his business in the garden on his own (presuming you have been taking him out up to date, and telling him what he should be doing, and how good he is when he has done it!). If this is so, you will have him nearly house-trained. He will also wander farther afield, so it is important to keep him obedient to his call name — he will then come running when you call him. See that he keeps this up — Shih Tzus are not noted for their obedience.

Four to five months is the gawky age when his body may look out of proportion. You may despair, and wonder what has happened to your beautiful budding Champion. With care on your part, all may come well again, so don't pass him on to someone else now. Some things improve, but some cannot. I will try to list a few problems and how to deal with them.

Some growth problems

Teeth, jaw and bite

A puppy should have 28 teeth. The canines or eye teeth are the first to appear; there are two of these in each jaw placed at the side of the incisors. Next are the incisors in the front; there should be six of these in each jaw. There are pre-molars at the back — six in each jaw. There are no molars in the first teeth. It is quite normal for the teeth to be cut later than in the large breeds. The second teeth should be coming in from four to six months, and one anxiously watches hoping the new set will be good. There could well have been, and still can be, changes in the jaw. This can go on setting up to ten months. The underjaw normally continues to grow after the upper one has finished, but not always. We hope to have 1/8 inch under, but some end up much more. If they do not show the teeth when the mouth is closed, the dog should be alright. One should aim for improvement in the next litter. This would not be acceptable on the Continent. Sometimes baby teeth are late shedding. This can mean the second teeth do not come through in a straight line, but four in front and two behind, as they are blocked by the baby teeth. You can get your vet to remove the remaining baby teeth, which may help, but it means having an anaesthetic. There is always an element of risk, and a slight chance that the wrong teeth will get pulled out, or even that there are no second teeth. It is wisest to wait until the second teeth are showing. It is possible the dog may get only four incisors in each jaw. This happens more in some lines than others — it is an anomaly of the brachycephalic dog.

While we are on the subject of teeth numbers, there have been instances where there have been only three, or even two, very large incisors come through in each jaw; this is unacceptable and the dog must never be used for breeding. You can also get wry jaws. This can be due to one side of the jaw growing at a different pace from the other, or caused by an accident e.g. dislocation of the jaw through the puppy biting on too large an object. They can also be hereditary. Wry jaws are very undesirable. The full dentition of the adult dog is 42 teeth in all. Short-faced dogs frequently do not have this number owing to the shortening of the jaw, and it is usually the pre-molars which are missing.

There are several homoeopathic remedies which can be given to puppies having teething problems. Chamomilla is given when there is painful teething, and Calendula Lotion is used to soothe sore and inflamed gums. Calc. Carb or Calc. Phos can be given when there is delay in the teeth coming in. Calc Phos is said to help when the second teeth are appearing while the first are still in. It is given 6x four times daily for one month. When the gums and the mouth are sore, the puppies should be fed soft foods, though it is also useful to give hard objects (such as a baby's teething ring, or suitable bone) on which to chew.

Do keep a careful watch on the mouth, I have known it to become very infected. There can also be bleeding from the gums, and the throat will also become infected. These are rare conditions but they have occurred.

Tongue
This should not show. If he has only just started to show it, and just the tip, it should get better when the teeth are in. If he has always shown it badly, you had better teach him to keep it in as it is a fault.

Nose
Some noses grow out after the puppy is six months old. If it isn't too bad, you can try dressing the head to give the best effect. For example, experiment with the position you tie the top knot and puff out the hair below it. In some cases, a nose which is straight and slightly longer than it should be will improve with age. The head fills out particularly around the forehead and the cheeks. I have seen this happen to several youngsters after eight months old.

Many young puppies get tight nostrils during teething. This affects the breathing, especially with changes of temperature. Vitamin E may help to clear it up quickly. However, it does as a rule improve as the puppy grows, and is seldom a big worry. Badly pinched or deformed nostrils are quite different and bad for the animal, as the lungs are not getting a chance to expand fully. In this case, it is unwise to use the dog for breeding.

An elongated soft palate can cause snorting and poor breathing which is more pronounced during exercise as the air is not able to get through to the lungs sufficiently. This is something which happens in many 'pushed-in faced' breeds — one reason for not breeding for ultra-short noses.

Coat not good
Maybe he will never have a good coat, but there is a lot you can do to help. Feed the best of foods, and make sure he has enough, with sufficient fat in the diet. Polyunsaturated fats are best. Is he getting his dietary supplements? You can add extra Vitamin C with advantage, up to a total of 1gm, even more in some cases. Seaweed powder helps as it contains many needed minerals in a healthy

form. Mirror Coat is expensive but very good, though you need to be a little careful as it can make the coat soft, but it is better to have a soft coat than none at all. You can discontinue it after the coat has come through.

Are you over-grooming and removing too much coat, or breaking the ends? This often happens with over-zealous owners. Is your brush too harsh? Stop the daily grooming. Groom three times a week but keep him trained to it, and don't use that comb unless you really have to. Some puppies take much longer to coat up than others, and some colours take longer than others. For more information, see chapter 15 on grooming.

Loose-limbed and becoming bandy

Usually, this puppy is a very big-boned puppy. These bones are soft, and this trouble can be due to many things. Heredity is one, and environment another. Feeding can also play an important part. There is little you can do about the first, but plenty about the second and third. This fault frequently does not show up until 12 weeks. It is important not to do the wrong thing, so have a word with your vet. It could be rickets if your feeding is wrong, though this is unusual, particularly if he has been having his vitamin supplements or a complete dog food which should all necessary supplements in it. Too much Vitamin D and calcium can cause as much trouble as too little. Have you been giving too much? It is a known weakness among breeders to over do the calcium. Or maybe yours could do with some. Your vet will advise you. He may feel it is due to bone growth; the soft cartilage of the long bone ends may have had too much weight put on it. He may advise a two-week course of Cal-D. (Vitamin D and calcium, with the correct amount of phosphorous).

An over-fat, heavy puppy can be the cause. Running around too much after a heavy meal and climbing down stairs can tend to bend the elbows outwards, just as standing for long periods on the hind legs looking over a fence can bend the hind limbs.

Is your puppy very greedy? Try cutting down on calories. Give bran and brown rice instead of mixer meal.

Do you keep your puppy shut away in a cage with the mistaken idea that he will have a better coat or just to keep him safe? No matter what the reason, being shut away in a cage does nothing to help a good front. Even the way they will be sitting can cause the elbows to go outwards. How do you or other people pick up your puppy? Do you put your hand under the scapular (shoulder blade) instead of over it? If this is done repeatedly, the shoulder can be forced out. It's a funny thing, but I frequently used to see lovely dogs in the ring who were just a bit out on the left shoulder. I do not see it so much now. I wonder if it got bred out, or whether people handle their puppies better. I will never have the answer to that!

Sometimes, bandy legs are caused because the dog has too much of a barrel chest, instead of a broad, deep one. This can make the point of elbow come to the widest part, and great care is needed early on to exercise the puppy on the lead over a hard surface rather than allowing him to gallop around too much on grass. Of course, this exercise has to be in yards, not miles! Little and often should be the rule.

A loose-limbed puppy is rather different. It needs extra care while being tightened up. A puppy whose shoulders are slung, and not close to the rib cage, is likely to remain slung even when everything else has tightened up. Many puppies when under a year are still loose-limbed and are forgiven for it, but after that age, there is no excuse. The bones are no longer cartilage. You must put work into tightening your puppy before it is ten months old, or you may never have it right and it could end up not only loose but also bandy. Don't overdo it, or you could just end up by having 'bossy shoulders' and a 'tied front', which are equally bad. Many people don't worry sufficiently about the dog's front assembly, for in our coated breed, they think that it will be covered up, especially if they also 'string' the dog up. Others who have it strongly in their line tell people it is correct — it is not. It is far better to aim to have a correct body. It comes back to which is the most important to the breed — the dog who only looks good or the dog who is good? Why not have both?

There is another kind of loose limb which affect the joints, causing the dog to weave badly, nearly crossing its legs. This can occur in both the front and the back legs. Incorrect environmental conditions such as incorrect feeding and lack of exercise to help tighten up the ligaments can cause it. Loose joints can also be a hereditary condition.

Up behind

With luck, this is just growth. Some lines grow like horses, up one end and then the other. Don't get too worried unless it's due to a straight stifle; then it is unlikely to improve. Or it may really be due to him being 'down' in front because he has not come up on his pasterns.

Tail

Tails can be one of the most difficult parts of the dog to predict regarding maturity. Different lines do different things. Never discount a tail for going wrong during teething. Some tighten, some loosen, most go back to what they were before. Perfect early tails can end up all wrong — low and flat. In England, we like a high tail. A high 'set on' naturally helps. A low set tail can never end up right, though when the furnishing comes, you may well be able to disguise it, as with a too tight a tail, for the furnishing can be made to fall well over the back.

In America, they do not like a high tail — it is called a 'gay tail' . Maybe this is because so many of their tails are flat and they are not able to breed them out and have accepted them. With our dogs, I find the good high tail is dominant to the American flat tail, which is a great help. Some dogs who have a naturally good tail will tighten it when they are in the ring, owing to excitement or nerves. I find that this is one part of the anatomy where the genes seem happy to meet half-way! To correct a tight tail, I would try mating to a long tail which falls to the side, rather than a perfect pot handle.

The true pot handle comes over the back in a large ring, the tip just touching the back. Many longer tails fall to the side of the animal, the heavy furnishings often adding to this with their weight. The longer tail helps when you have a long-cast dog, for it will help give a better balance as it can be laid further along the back. These tails sometimes take a long time to come up and over with the puppy, and need working on. Stroke it lightly up and over the back several times a day. Some puppies hold their tails straight up in the air. These usually come right with age, though some don't and the handler has to hold it down by its feathering, but then it is up to the handler to make the most of their dog disguising its faults.

Different lines do different things at different ages with tails. At teething time, tight tails may loosen, but then tighten again. Other tails which start tight can loosen. Some perfect tails on baby dogs will flatten on the back as adults, particularly those which curl over the back very young. Others only tighten due to teething; these should become alright.

Eyes

Eyes can alter in shape and size from early days, but the colour remains once they have changed from 'puppy blue'. Light eyes remain light, as far as I know. They should grow in size with the puppy. If there is some white showing round, or in the corner of the eye early on, it might improve with age, but it could get worse. This depends on the bloodlines. It could be a squint, and the eye will lack co-ordination. The exercise of covering over one eye and making him follow your finger movement with the other can help. An adult with a big ring of white round the eyeball does not have the correct expression of the Shih Tzu but if the white does not show when the dog looks dead-ahead, do not worry. Many dogs show white of eye more when they become excited or nervous, such as standing on the judging table.

Weepy eyes are a nuisance as they leave the whiskers wet, and the tears cause staining. See your vet about this, as he may have some helpful advice to give you. It could be due to blocked tear ducts. Many dogs get very wet whiskers at shows. I think this is largely due to the various preparations being used on your or other peoples dogs which get into the atmosphere. If you do use any powder on the whiskers (strictly no powder is permitted by the KC) to dry them off, use cornflower or potato flour — never a scented powder.

Limping

Limping can, of course, be due to many things. It is not a part of natural growth but it does sometimes happen that puppies get up on tables, or are put on them for their grooming, and before you know what has happened, they have jumped down. This can cause injury to the forearm or shoulder. It may just be momentary, and better the next day, but if it is not, you should take him to your vet. It is most important that the right treatment is given now. He may need to be given some steroids. Obviously, it all depends on the injury, which is most likely to be due to a strained muscle or ligament. This will take time to get better, but don't despair. Give it until the bones are fully formed — around ten months. Always see your vet if there is limping due to an unknown cause during the growth period — things have been known to go wrong with the bones, particularly at the elbow joint. There is also a condition where the forearm bones do not grow at the same pace. In fact, one can stop growing. This will cause the foot to turn right inwards and the dog actually walks with its ankle on the ground. I have known of just three cases of this.

Too low on the leg

Has he had plenty of exercise? You should not take him for long walks until at least six months old, but puppies will exercise themselves in plenty, given the opportunity. I have one now who plays with his toy, a plastic can lid, throwing it all over the place and running after it in free exercise. Rushing around in the garden, chasing a ball if there are no other dogs to chase, is normal exercise for a Shih Tzu. This gives every opportunity for the limbs to expand and grow. Restrictive movement does not allow for this. Allow him to reach his maximum growth, but don't overdo it.

Too high on the leg

The opposite from the last. Are you over-exercising him for his age? His bones do not calcify until ten months. Maybe you are overdoing it a bit. Young puppies should not be taken for long walks.

What is his bone like? Are the long bones too fine? Is he terrier-fronted? If he is, there is nothing you can do about it. We do not want the legs too short, but often if they are over-long, it is because of incorrect long bones. Shih Tzus are achondroplastic. There always have been some English Shih Tzus with a slightly longer leg. People misguidedly blame height of leg on American imports. This can be so, and it is a point you need to watch when breeding, but there are also many top-winning English Shih Tzus with a higher leg. My own first English Champion, Li Chin Ku of Snaefell, was higher on the leg. Our earlier dogs had a reasonable length so they could move correctly. The ultra-short leg came with the 'Peke cross', which did not make it any more correct than the American higher leg. Both are wrong. However, every dog has some fault.

Length of back
Puppies usually grow out in length around four to five months, some earlier. Over-exercising too young can be the cause, but I think it is mostly genes that cause this rather than environment. Some lines grow out after six months, then everything grows out — even the nose!

Overall size and weight
The safest size to aim for is medium, neither the smallest 10lb or the largest 18lb. The dogs are not weighed in the ring — just as well, for many would be well over the top weight! They get away with it where a bottom weight of 10lb will be called too small!. Weight is not a good guide, anyway. Many show dogs are too fat for their health; this is frequently called 'good body'. It isn't at all. A Shih Tzu should be muscular and in hard condition, not flabby so your fingers sink into the flesh. Some oversized dogs can be too thin. Weight and size must be considered together. Never cut down on food to try to keep a dog smaller.

Throwing up the front feet. Padding
This is typical action of a very young puppy, but they should grow out of it. Is he down on his pasterns? Too much soft surface, like grass, can cause this, or even too much hard cement that has no 'give'. Get him onto a rough surface — tarmac or pebbles are good, and try a little road walking. You must get him up off those pasterns now, before it is too late. This can also be due to incorrect anatomy, like straight shoulders. If it is the anatomy, there is no real cure, though the walking and rough surface should help.

Testicles
There should be two of them, fully developed in the sac. This should have been checked early on. Some come down later than others. Many are down by eight weeks. They should be fully down, staying in the sac, by the time the puppy is a year old. If they are both still in the abdomen, they can become cancerous. See your vet. I think he will suggest that they should be removed. However, if one is down and the other is down but not fully in the sac, it is not likely to turn to cancer. When they are in the abdomen, they cannot mature as the temperature is too hot, which is why they are placed outside in the scrotal sac. The testicles should have descended before the puppy is born, and they can be felt early if you squat the puppy like a frog. The trouble is they can slip in and out, often retracting when the puppy is cold or excited. Around the age of four months, it can happen that one slips out — try massaging it back in daily. Sometimes, one testicle will be on a shorter cord, which prevents it from entering the sac although it can fully developed. Sometimes, the scrotal sac is too tight. A dog like this should not be shown, though now the Kennel Club does permit a dog to be

shown when BOTH testicles have been removed. Whether such a dog should win is a matter for each judge to decide.

Another condition is the 'floating' testicle, which is fully mobile and floats in and out of the sac. Usually, by the time it has matured (around one year), it has grown sufficiently to stay within the sac. The term for a dog with one testicle is unilateral cryptorchid (not monorchid as we so loosely call them!). Some vets will give a hormone injection, which helps in certain cases.

Head

Does the nice large head he had as a youngster seem to have stopped growing? How often I have seen this happen. Some really do stop growing altogether, while others stop and start again later. The head will be the last thing to mature on the dog, and could go on developing until he is at least 18 months old. It must always be remembered that not all lines develop in the same way, and I have seen many puppies with longer noses than one would like end up with a perfectly correct length nose. This being due to the head and foreface filling out around the nose area.

Puppy with bad pigment.

Poor pigment

Not much is known on the subject of 'lack of pigment'. Sometimes pigment does come very late, well after four months. If the flesh marks are bright pink at eight weeks, I very much doubt whether they will ever change to black, but if they are still white or pale pink, you have a chance. Whether this is due to genes, or purely a lack of melanin (the colour agent in pigment) or other minerals I can't say, but if you see the pigment is not good early on, apply treatment. The usual remedies are seaweed powder, elderberry, parsley and watercress, and the homeopathic remedies can be very successful too. For the next litter, you could try giving treacle as suggested in Chapter 8. Or try to improve the pigment in the next generation by breeding to a line with a good black, but be sure it is a black/gold, not a black/liver line. The latter won't do anything for the dog, particularly if the liver gene is in the antecedents of your bitch. Liver does not carry a black pigment.

The 'off black' nose is quite different from the liver nose, affecting golds in many breeds. They call this a 'winter nose', for it is only affected in the damp and winter weather and usually gets better again by May. It can also be caused by different things, such as hormones. In whelp, bitches get extra black noses, and liver ones go very dark brown. Stress can cause a nose to become light; this may be cured by giving ABIDEX vitamin drops. 'Colavet' and 'Lintox' have also been known to help. The subject of poor pigmentation around the nose area is even more perplexing. I have known of dogs whose pigment goes on filling in slowly for several years, until by the time they are five, it has become perfect!

Throwbacks to Tibetan Spaniels over the years.
1930s. Lord of Tibet (imported to Ireland from Kauffmann)
d. Ah Tishoo of Wey with throwback offspring.

Smooth-coated

It can occur that between eight weeks and three months. You may observe that your Shih Tzu does not have the correct coat, but it is smooth like a Cavalier King Charles, or a Tibetan Spaniel. In some cases, I know it to be a genuine throwback to the Tibetan Spaniel, for the breeds were mixed up and interbred in Tibet. In these dogs, the spaniel does seem to be the dominant one. Specimens have occured over the years.

There have been cases where the breeder has kept both Shih Tzus and K.C. spaniels. In such cases, one cannot but wonder whether there has been a misalliance and duel conception. However, even giving the benefit of the doubt, any such puppies should have their Shih Tzu registration withdrawn, or at the least endorsed 'progeny not eligible for registration', and sold purely as pets. If the puppy has already been registered, only the new owner can have that registration withdrawn. For the sake of the future of the breed, this should be done.

That is enough for your development problems. I'll now give you a few management problems which might occur.

Early 1970s :Two in a litter.

1984 at 10 months.

1985 at 12 weeks.

169

Problems of management

He won't walk on the lead

This needs to be done with kindness and bribery. It is no good saying you should have started early, but even now, follow out the method I gave for lead training, but it will be slower. Do not teach him to walk on the lead with a show collar; it should be a soft leather one, and have your light nylon lead or string attached. If you can get a helper, so much the better — let them hold the end loosely. Never pull him, but tempt him along. It does not matter with what — a favourite toy, or a titbit. Always call his name, and when he walks a few paces to you let the helper follow, holding the lead lightly. Give him terrific praise, and your toy or titbit if you want. You can do this in the house. Just persevere, making the distance he will walk a little longer each day, with the handler holding the lead. Eventually you will be able to dispense with your helper and take the lead yourself, maybe going a little bit ahead with the titbit and keeping the lead loose, and never forgetting the praise. It will come eventually!

He is biting

Many young puppies will bite in play or in their excitement at welcoming you, or when being groomed. They must be taught that this is wrong before they are 16 weeks old, for this is the age at which they learn who is the master, and a Shih Tzu will not be slow to decide that he is the master. If you have a real 'he-man' dog who does not like to be cuddled, respect this in him but on no account allow him to have his own way through growling; if you do, it is most likely to progress into biting. Puppies know when they hurt each other as one will cry out — this teaches the other one not to bite so hard. If the puppy bites his mother too hard, she will immediately reprimand him, usually by sitting across him with her mouth open over his head, but not biting him. If a puppy bites you, cry out 'no' as if in pain. He then learns not to play so roughly next time.

As I said, never let him get away with it when he is young. Don't just stop doing what you were doing (so long as you are not hurting him) — say 'no' and his name very severely. He should permit you to take anything away from him, and even out of his mouth. Much bad temper is often started by rough grooming, like using a wire or even a teasel brush against his skin. Never use these on puppies, and only carefully on adults. Tease out any mats — you would not like your hair pulled if it tangled up.

Growling must be nipped in the bud. Reprimand by stern voice, not by smacking — that is the worst thing you can do. Continue with what you were doing, but gently — don't let him think that by growling he can get away with it, for with his quick and intelligent brain he will soon know that this is how he can get his own way. Growling soon turns into biting.

Bad temper can also be caused through mismanagement and is sometimes due to excessive and unrestrained teasing and harassment from small children. There are people who buy a puppy as a live toy for their children; they train neither the puppy nor their children, and both turn nasty. It is, of course, the puppy who is blamed for this state of affairs. There is no better pet for a child than a Shih Tzu, but as a companion and not a toy. Given the right guidance, children are wonderful at training dogs, and love to feel that they have something of their very own who loves them and behaves better for them than for anybody else.

I hear too many reports of bad temper — this should never be. The Shih Tzu should be a good-tempered, friendly dog, so long as it has always been treated correctly and with loving care.

170

He won't stand up in the show ring

The best training is to go to puppy obedience classes, where he will learn to sit and stand at the command. I think these classes teach him to learn and use his brain better than 'show training'. You can still take him to the show training classes if you want to.

Get down on your knees to him in the ring so you can control him better. Hold the lead just a few inches above his neck so you have control. With the left hand, raise him to standing and gently tickle him on his tummy or thigh. Don't try to make him stand for the full class, just when the judge is coming round looking at the line-up. As he gets better, he can stand longer, and you will be able to stand up eventually.

He won't eat

Refer to Chaper 8 - Feeding

He is shy

If you are hoping to show your puppy, shyness is a great drawback and time and patience will be needed, but persevere. You will need to be extra gentle and patient. It is time to get him out meeting other dogs, for a dog may rule the roost in his own home, but be totally different away from it. It can be difficult with all the dog-restricted places, but take him everywhere you can, including buses and the railway station. Always encourage him, using a happy high-pitched tone of voice whenever he gets worried. Don't pick him up and cuddle him — this is the wrong treatment.

Many people now run 'puppy parties', where young puppies, (up to 20 months) can come and meet up with other puppies of different breeds, human adults and children. This is fine so long as you can manage it after the inoculation, and is far better for a young puppy than ordinary ring training classes; though they can be very good for show training. Sometimes the noise is overpowering for a shy puppy and does harm. Your vet is the best person to ask about the classes, for most of the good ones have contacted him.

You will have to be very patient and persevering. He needs to learn and be handled by strangers, who will go through the show procedure. He will have his mouth opened, but if he is teething and his mouth is sore, warn the handler who will be extra gentle. No matter how often you go to ring classes, it cannot give you the full atmosphere of the show. Do not over-train your puppy. You do not want him to get tired of showing before he starts.

The following things have been used successfully by some people to help overcome their dog's shyness — dog nerve tablets from herb farms such as Dorwest and Denes, homoeopathic remedies, aconite or tablets for shock and distress. I found these helped, given a tablet of 6x the night before and morning of a show. A little fresh baker's yeast daily, about the size of a hazelnut, is good — you can obtain this from some local bakers. Brewers Yeast tablets or Vetzyme; both these yeasts contain Vitamin B, which are tonic for the nerves. Cytocon from the chemist is another vitamin B product said to help. Vitamin C, which is an anti-stress vitamin, 250-500 mg. a day, can aid, but give a small dose first or it may upset the bowels. These on their own will not be sufficient. You must continue to get him used to things gently and kindly, and make his lessons fun.

Coprophagy

This is an unpleasant habit of dogs eating excreta, which is common in many breeds. It can be difficult to break. It is something which revolts people and is very important to try to prevent, especially if there are children around. No one is quite sure of the reason for this, except that it is quite normal for dogs to eat the excreta of animals feeding on grass, such as horses, cows and sheep. One suggestion for the cause is thought to be a deficiency of minerals or vitamins which are being sought by the dog in the proteins thrown out in the faeces. It has been suggested that the addition of a little more fat to the diet would help, by slowing down the progress of the food through the digestive tract and thus giving the proteins a better chance to become digested; fewer proteins then being discarded, the temptation would thus be removed.

Some think it is due to an insufficiency of the stomach enzymes to digest the excess of carbohydrates in present-day diets, these getting passed out in the faeces in unchanged form. The dog eats the faeces to replenish the enzymes. Another factor known to impede the action of the enzymes is lack of salt in the diet. Sometimes a very small pinch of salt in the food will help. It can be a hormone imbalance which can lead to digestive insufficiency.

The habit may have started early on by the puppy run not being cleaned up, and the puppies getting bored and playing with, then eating the excreta. All excreta should be picked up at once to break the habit. Roger Mugford, BSc., Phd. has written that he has applied the conditioned aversion paradigm developed by Garcia and others (1972) to some 20 cases of coprophagic dogs. The technique involves administration of a nausea-provoking drug (under veterinary supervision) to dogs shortly after they have ingested faeces. The dog feels ill within about ten minutes of eating the faeces, and makes a learned association with the item most recently consumed i.e. faeces. The dog is fully recovered within 2-3 hours of treatment and no adverse side-effects have been encountered. A second treatment may be required in a few cases but, he writes, only one dog has proved to be an unresponsive recidivist. It is not an unnatural habit, but revolting to us humans.

Try a higher protein diet, but make sure the dog is free from worms, or they will be eating it all up.

Some cases respond well to Vitamin B, particularly Biotin. One I know was treated and cured with pancreatic extracts. Putting meat tenderiser (containing papain not monosodium glutamate) on the food is also said to be a cure.

He is travel sick

Few dogs acclimatised to car travel when very young suffer from travel sickness. Some of this sickness is due to fear, and the association of fear. There are car-sickness travel pills you can get for dogs from the herbalists which can be very effective, though you need to try them out before any important occasion. It is sometimes best to give them the night before.

If the sickness is due to fear, the following is worth trying — first, try sitting in a stationary vehicle parked outside the house, to show your dog that no harm will come to him. A day or two later, take him for a short trip around the block, gradually increasing the time spent in the car.

Once the initial hurdle has been overcome, extend the time period, but give a small drink of milk and glucose half an hour before the journey and keep him on the floor of the car for a while so he doesn't notice the objects going by. The length of these trips should be gradually increased, and conversely, the time spent on the floor of the car decreased. Use anti-emetic tranquillising pills, which can be obtained from your vet and should be given about 30 minutes before the journey. Continue doing this for four to eight weeks — by this time, some satisfactory progress should have been made.

Grooming problems

There is quite a lot of mismanagement which can occur over grooming. The dog can be groomed so roughly that it becomes resentful and aggressive. Then the owner blames the dog because it has become bad-tempered and cannot be groomed. Very few Shih Tzus who are handled correctly with coats kept in good condition resent their grooming. Puppies may be difficult but they soon learn; you just have to persevere with them. If the breeder has not shown or told the new owner how to go about the grooming, many mistakes can be made. By the time the dog is starting to shed his undercoat — around ten months — it is liable to go into very solid mats if not watched carefully. This can happen very suddenly. Things then go from bad to worse, the dog gets bathed and the mats get thicker. This can be very uncomfortable for the dog. It becomes so bad that the only thing to do is to have the coat cut off. Refer to Chapter 12 for help.

Check you are using the right grooming tools. Seek advice from another owner. One of the club secretaries may be able to tell you of someone in your area who can help you. If you really cannot manage, do take him to a beauty parlour for professional attention.

He scratches

This can be a great problem. If you have a scratching Shih Tzu, it is unlikely to have a good coat, for the front will remain short and the back will grow long. The best thing to do is to eliminate the various causes one by one, and you might hit on the right one!

Check the anal glands, and for internal and external parasites. Combings from the coat will show the presence of fleas if none are to be seen otherwise. Some dogs are allergic to just one flea bite.

Incorrect diet is a frequent cause of scratching. In summer, a long-coated dog can easily become overheated, when it may be wise to cut down on his meat intake and give one teaspoon of milk of magnesia. If he is a salad-eater, try a salad recipe. Take him off all biscuit meals and give brown rice instead. There may be insufficient fat in the diet — this can give rise to scurf, which in itself can cause irritation and scratching. One teaspoon of corn oil added to the food, plus a bath with Seleen, (obtainable from your vet) will remove it.

Food allergy can also be the cause of scratching. This is covered in Chapter 8. For any scratching, if the cause is unknown, I would suggest a complete change of diet.

According to E P Stalling — a Houston veterinarian — as recorded in Dog World, there is a condition in dogs whereby the passage of food through the digestive system is prolonged owing to the ingestion of dust, swallowing of hair, various bacteria and indigestible materials. This prolonged process sets up a toxic condition and an alkaline pH of the skin is produced; the skin is normally slightly acid. This leads to a drop in the resistance of the skin to the invasion of bacteria and fungi and a susceptibility to allergens. To control this situation, it is suggested that one teaspoon of mineral oil to each 7-8lb of body weight should be given bi-weekly. This should be administered on an empty stomach, in the morning, no food or water being given until the afternoon of the same day. However, this treatment will not cure 'flea allergy dermatitis' if this is already established, and a thorough cleansing of the digestive system is necessary. I have known Shih Tzu owners to be in despair over scratching, when no amount of medicated baths and veterinary treatment seem able to cure the animal. Cider vinegar in the water or one teaspoon on the food can also help, particularly if the scratching is due to alkaline skin.

Irritation of the skin can also be caused by insufficient grooming. Matting of the coat means no air can get to the skin, so it is essential to use your comb. Scurf also collects under the hair and causes further irritation.

If the dog is scratching because of any skin lesion, your vet should be consulted for expert advice. It may be necessary to take skin scrapings. Through scratching, a simple irritation and breaking of the skin can very easily lead to a bacterial infection, therefore persistent scratching should never be neglected.

Staining of the coat
Are his whiskers getting stained? Some stain far more than others. Staining is due to various things. Firstly, do you wash his face daily? Particularly round the eyes, use a little 'No Tears' Johnson's baby shampoo in your water. Always wash his face after meals.

On what are you feeding him? Is the food staining his whiskers?

Does he have runny eyes? Both eye discharge and saliva cause staining. Speak to your vet about this — he should be able to help. Sometimes dribbling is due to a deep-seated infection in the throat. and when treated with a broad spectrum antibiotic, the staining clears up. After you have washed the whiskers, rub in some cornflour and Fullers Earth powder mixed with it, half and half. Or you can use $1/3$ each of cornflour, grooming powder and French chalk. Leave them in until they are dry, then brush them out. Potato flour is also good.

You can spend a fortune on buying stain-removing lotions, such as 'Diamond Eye' or 'Banish' by Doreen Page. Many people think the latter is really good but I have not had much success with it, so no doubt it all depends what has caused the staining! New products keep coming onto the market.

Leg staining
Long-coated dogs with white trousers stain easily, partly from urine or mopping up from cement or grass. Bathe the dog frequently, daily round his hindquarters is best if you can manage it. Between baths, spray on a powder whitener/cleaner like Bob Martin or Ring 5. Leave on for ten minutes, then brush out. Does he have sufficient water to drink? The urine may be too concentrated. Will the dog drink barley water?

Staining appears to be worse in some lines than others.

He rubs his face
Many like to do this. They will do it on the carpets, furniture or, if outside, along the cement or the wire netting, none of which is good for the growing of face furnishings.

If there is a lot of rubbing, not just after meals or when the face has been washed, then it is most likely to be an irritation, and you should get your vet to have a look.

Usually the rubbing is done after a meal — it's their way of wiping the face clean or dry. The face should be washed after a meal, for Shih Tzu do not like sticky food on their whiskers, which is why many prefer their food spread out on a flat surface. The trouble is after you have washed it, they consider you do not dry it properly, so they have a go themselves! Even if you pop them in their cage, they rub their face on the bedding. Try putting them up on a table for a few minutes until all has been forgotten, but first train to 'stay'. Most learn that very quickly — you do not want him to jump off.

Be careful how you put up the topknot. Be sure it is not dragging on hairs.

He is disobedient

At four months, he is getting bolder and has a will of his own. It is very important to teach him to 'stay' and to 'wait and come'. Take him to obedience training classes. He will thoroughly enjoy them and will learn quickly. If you are training him for show, mention this — he will be permitted to 'stand' while others 'sit'.

I think the dog enjoys these classes far more than ring training because he can show off how clever he is and does not get bored.

CHAPTER FOURTEEN

SELECTION

Selecting a Shih Tzu may be for the purpose of breeding and showing, or purely as a companion and pet. Whichever the reason, it is important that it should be treated as a pet and not as a breeding machine. It needs to be chosen to suit not only the environment in which it will live, but also your own personal preference and circumstances. The buyer who wants a companion Shih Tzu, but also hopes to have a litter, should follow the advice given for those who are selecting for breeding. It is not easy to keep the Shih Tzu in large numbers unless you have plenty of help, and are prepared to devote a great deal of your time to their care.

Large-scale commercialisation of the breed could well be its downfall. Its continuing popularity as a pet will be based on its fascinating character, thorough soundness, good temperament, and the fact that it is a very natural and unspoiled breed, rather than on its length of coat. Regrettably, it is now offered by some puppy farms and over-breeding is taking place, with the bitches confined to small kennels, where they spend their short life as a breeding machine. This is no life for any animal and certainly not for the Shih Tzu, who has always been a member of the family. It is impossible under these condition to be sure that the correct temperament and character is being maintained. Love and companionship is as important as food and drink to its full development; for this it repays amply with its increased intelligence and by giving devoted companionship for many years, not to mention hours of amusement, as well.

No one who is out at work all day should own a dog, least of all a puppy, unless they are able to take the animal with them. The Shih Tzu loves the car, which should be parked in a suitable shady place if you are leaving him in it; he will regard this as his own property. I know of several Shih Tzu who accompany their owners to work; they sit either in the office or the shop, and since their owners are nearby, they are perfectly happy. A house-bred animal is very content with his human companions, but it is kinder to have an older animal rather than a young puppy for such a life.

Selection of a puppy as a pet
If you have no intention of breeding or showing, your choice of pup is much wider. Money may be your governing factor, and most of the reputable breeders will vary their prices according to estimated show quality. An experienced breeder can recognise the potentially good specimen far better than the pet owner who just breeds an occasional litter for fun. It is true that many of these people seek advice on the quality of their puppies from the owner of the stud dog or the breeder of their bitch, and take great pride in rearing the litter to perfection. On the other hand, I have also known those who buy the cheapest they can find and then sell the whole litter for the top price!

You have an open choice over colour, purely to suit your fancy, but remember that colour breeding is not easy in this breed, and in many good bloodlines, the colours are very mixed. There are so many other points of more importance. Some black and whites and gold and whites breed true for colour. Solid black and solid golds can usually be relied on. Birth colours frequently fade.

Am Ch. Dragonfires Red Raider. Multi Group Winner USA.

If you have not decided about which sex to have, do not believe the uninitiated who tell you that a bitch is so much more affectionate than a dog; this may be true of some breeds, but as I have previously said, it is not so with the Shih Tzu, and Shih Tzu dogs are extremely affectionate and devoted. Another saying is that 'a bitch is not so likely to run off as a dog', but this is more a matter of family traits than sex; either may do so if the garden is not fenced in. I feel there are no grounds for basing your choice of sex on those reasons.

Size may be an important consideration to you. If you are a country lover who likes going for walks with your dog, you will be well advised not to pick too short a leg; even the small specimens will be very active walkers so long as they are not too low to the ground, for every half-inch makes a difference and there is more height of leg with some than others. However, if you live in a flat in a town and take your dog for walks in the park, this point will not worry you.

Character is most important, and by eight weeks of age, the puppies are showing their individual characteristics. There may be a 'bully' who has pushed the others out of the way to get the best place at the 'milk bar'; there may be a small one which has been pushed out, or another small one which is really sturdy, tough and intelligent, having had to work hard to keep up with the others. One puppy may have been hand-reared, or for some reason had more attention from the breeder; this one is likely to be more devoted to people than to dogs, and is often the ideal companion for a lonely owner, but not the one to choose for breeding as such animals can become too humanised and be difficult

177

to get into whelp. A puppy should not be shy at this age, but it is sometimes difficult to tell, as it will develop more when away from the dominant character. So much will depend on you, the way you rear it and introduce it to new things. The character frequently alters when it leaves its home kennel and siblings.

If you do not own a car, and are perhaps an elderly person who has to travel on a bus, then you will need to pick up your dog. Remember that a Shih Tzu is heavy for its size, and a specimen of 18lb is quite a weight to carry — a smaller one would be easier for you. Very often, the larger dogs have deeper barks and are more placid; although the Shih Tzu is not a yappy breed, they will nevertheless bark as well as guard dogs in the home.

Should you be buying a companion for an older male dog, I would advise a placid-tempered puppy — neither bully nor coward — over the age of 16 weeks. It is during the period between 12 and 16 weeks of age that the order of dominance is decided, and this can make a bully or a coward of any dog for life.

I have set out a few ideas specifically for the pet owner to consider, but those wishing to know more about the detailed points of the breed with regard to puppies should study subsequent sections in this chapter which deal with selection for show and breeding.

Starting a kennel with adult stock

You may have made up your mind what you intend to do, and be ready to go ahead without any further advice, but just in case you haven't yet done so, I will try to give you some.

I have already referred to the relative merits of house versus kennel at the beginning of this chapter, and have also condemned commercialisation. Everything depends on your individual circumstances and the amount of space at your disposal.

Commence with bitches, leaving the choice of a stud dog until you have gained more experience and knowledge of the lines and families in the breed. Using other people's dogs for stud purposes at this early stage will give you a much wider choice. Do not keep a pet dog and bitch in the same household unless you will be in a position to keep them separated when the bitch is in season. Otherwise, one should be spayed or castrated. It causes too many problems.

To own a kennel of Shih Tzu is very hard work, for the breed can be quite demanding if it is treated correctly. If you intend to breed as a hobby, and for the improvement of the Shih Tzu (which in my opinion is the only worthwhile way), you will certainly want to keep one of your own puppies, and this will happen not once but several times.

I think it is best to start with perhaps two adults only; more than this and you will require a breeders' licence. It is not always so easy to buy adult stock, but if you can afford it, some of the top kennels may have young show stock which they will sell, as they like to keep puppies for show and must restrict their numbers.

I must warn you that you will have to be very strong-minded not to end up with more than your original foundation stock!

Several Shih Tzu can live together quite happily and peacefully, unless the presence of one jealous animal causes fighting. Some stud dogs can be kept together, but there is likely to be trouble when the bitches come into season, and once fighting has started, it may well continue. In such circumstances, the only answer is separation or to find a new home for one of them, and this can be quite heart-breaking.

Having decided on the number and approximate ages of the animals with which you intend to start your kennel, you must set about choosing your stock. Obviously, those who are already breeders will know what method of breeding they intend to employ, so the following section is written for the newcomer into the world of dog breeding.

It is helpful to go round the shows, particularly to the breed-club championship shows, where you may have the opportunity to see the parents and grandparents, and also the progeny which they are siring in the puppy class.

If you are planning to build up your own strain, it is best that the animals you select should be of a similar type, for in this way you are less likely to breed stock resembling different lines. For this reason, it is helpful to have only the one common parent or grandparent, but antecedents further back are not so important as their influence is not so great.

There should be no outstanding faults, only those which can be bred out in one generation. The bitch you choose should, of course, be a very good representative of the breed, though you are unlikely to get perfection, for a breeder thinking that he or she has a perfect bitch would be unlikely to sell her to you unless you are prepared to pay very highly! Also, if you are new to showing, they may feel that you do not have the expertise and would waste the animal.

You may be able to obtain a bitch which a breeder has run on for show, but has decided not to keep. She might not be quite up to their show standard, but perfectly suitable for breeding. It is not always the best show bitches who throw the best puppies.

You may decide to go in for one or two different colour lines, which is always fascinating, but somewhat complicated in the breed at present. Gold would probably be the easiest, or black and white.

Selecting the stud dog

The same principles apply here as in the chapter on mating and whelping. Great care must be taken in selecting a stud dog for your own kennel use. He must suit your bitches, and although a study of pedigrees will be of considerable help, one cannot be sure until after the pups are born and grown up. It is far wiser not to buy your own stud dog at first.

Selecting a puppy for show or breeding

First, it should be made quite clear that 'any old throw-out' will not make a good brood bitch. She must be a good representative of her breed with a good pedigree, and although she may have some minor faults which you would prefer not to see in a show bitch, these must be ones she is unlikely to throw to her puppies, or can be improved on in one generation. In other words, buy the very best you can. A puppy from a good, even litter is likely to throw better stock than the only good puppy out of a poor litter.

No one can pick with absolute certainty at eight weeks of age, although with your own strain — or another with which you are familiar — it is obviously much easier. Different strains grow at different stages in various ways. Having kept different lines myself, I find this is very noticeable, therefore it follows that it is best to go to a breeder who knows his own stock and which he has reared carefully; not from a pet shop or puppy farm where the rearing and breeding are unknown to you. The dam of your future brood needs to have been well and carefully fed, or her litter will suffer — all of which costs more money than some people realise, and those people who are only in it thinking they will make money are sometimes reluctant to spend as much as they should.

You may be selecting for yourself from your own first litter, and hoping to retain the pick of the bunch. You will have had every opportunity to study your puppies, and in the course of observing their action, you may have found one which catches your eye — maybe because of its flashy colour, or because of that indefinable quality which is so often coupled with a correctly assembled body. A certain amount can be assessed at birth. For example, a good skull nearly always remains good, a very long thin body will fill out but is unlikely to shorten, but a short body may grow out.

Santosha Seren (F) age 11 months with young 11 year old owner Michael.

The longer you can defer making your final choice, the better, but in any case, do not come to a final decision before the pups are eight weeks old. At this age, you can feel the width of head, and depth of stop. I prefer a high forehead with a deep stop, this dome usually broadens out later on, although I have known the shallower, more sloping forehead fill out with the stop deepening later. I have also known a pointed skull to remain pointed rather than broaden out into width. The tipped-up nose will give the better expression, and though a Pekey type of puppy head often develops well, you do not want too short a nose, and it should be set level with the bottom rim of the eye.

If you want your puppy for breeding or stud purposes, do not choose one which had nostril trouble as a whelp, as this is likely to be inherited. However, if the nostrils have merely tightened up a little during teething, this is quite a common occurrence and will correct itself by the age of four or five months.

Preferably, there should be no flesh marks between the upper lip and nose. While not a compulsory proviso, and at this age there is still a chance for improvement, the absence of any such improvement can mean this will look worse as the puppy grows. One which is badly flesh-marked — and sometimes the upper lip is pink as well — is not so likely to be awarded top honours, with the present-day high standard in the ring. The pink tone can become quite vivid, and when the lip is affected, the animal looks as though it has been using lipstick! Pigment can be very strange and go on filling in slowly during the animal's life.

A round, well-spaced eye showing no white should be aimed for. In some lines, this white fills in as the puppy grows, but it is a difficult fault to breed out. Ideal head markings are a good white top-knot with white hair between the eyes, and an even white mask — or a plain black mask in some golds. These markings are not essential only preferable.

The teeth may not all be through, since some puppies cut these very late and the Shih Tzu is often later than other breeds, but they can be felt and counted. It is better to judge by the gums. The jaw should be broad and square, and either dead level or with the lower teeth only just outside the upper, since an undershot jaw tends to worsen as the puppy grows. In some lines, the bite will start by being slightly overshot; frequently, this is perfect by eight to 10 weeks, but if it is much over, I would not risk the chance of it correcting. Such puppies are usually sold more cheaply as pets, and are not suitable for foundation stock. If the first teeth are perfect, it does not mean that the second ones will be!

Watch for the ear set; low set, long, thick ear leathers are to be preferred and help to give width to the head. Long furnishings can disguise short ear leathers in the adult.

The rib cage will alter later, as the puppy bones are very soft, but the puppy should not be slab-sided. If excessively broad, it may have a roll in front, and while I think considerable care is needed in the correct rearing of such a youngster, all should be well with the right care. A very broad chest often drops down as the animal matures.

Kinks in the tail are likely to stay kinky, but tails are strange, and I suspect them to have late developing genes; I have known perfect tails to go kinky well after eight weeks. A large 'ring' without a kink may well end up a perfect pot handle. A long tail is good, provided it is set on high and well held. A tail set too low should be avoided in a show puppy as it will never look good, but remember that the tail is inclined to alter during teething; some tighten and others slacken, then become correct when teething is finished.

Some puppies are down in front, some never come up, and others develop this part late. A front which is constructionally bowed will not improve, but a loose front should tighten with care.
One cannot be sure of the length of back at eight weeks, since some lines grow long after six months. A very short back may remain that way, in which case you will not get the true breed action.
Some bones are heavier than others; you do not want a too fine-boned one. Some puppies are very loose-bodied and big-boned; these frequently grow large all over. The proportions of the leg bones do not appear to alter. The upper and lower bones of the limb are about equal in length, but the pastern bones should be shorter, otherwise the puppy will finish high on the leg. Much can be done to improve muscles and limbs with good rearing.

Most coats should be thick and dense by eight weeks, and a sparse coat is likely to remain so. The coarser coat may thicken later, and some gold coats are very late in maturing. With the introduction of American line, coat quality and texture have altered. Some of the very heavy coats 'blow' at six months and do not come back until maturity, and some thin coats thicken later.

Note how the puppy walks, although eight weeks is very young and action is not good in some lines at this age.

It is interesting to pick your puppy early on, but to leave the final choice as late as possible. Many times, your first choice is the right one.

Having paid due regard to the various points of the breed standard, check for hernias. Umbilical hernias are unfortunately very common in the breed. Some vets make a great thing about them and say such animals should not be bred from. This is difficult as no lines are completely free of them, though some are far worse than others, and if they are hereditary, one does not know how they are thrown. A large one will need to be operated upon. One with an inquinal hernias — felt as a lump in the groin — are fairly rare, and far more serious, and such animals having this should not be used for breeding. Sometimes early on, when this lump can be felt, it disappears as the animal gets older.

If you are choosing for show, I feel it is important to pick a bold temperament. The puppy who drops his tail at every new happening and does not come forward to strangers, is liable to be shy in the show ring. On the other hand, if this is the puppy which you feel you must keep — possibly because it is the only one in the litter of the sex you require, or is easily the best of the litter — you can do a great deal to help it, as explained in Chapter 7.

Mis-marked puppies with uneven black patches over their eyes do not necessarily throw this trait, but they are not suitable for show purposes and when it occurs in the pick of the litter, it is very disappointing.

All you can do is buy or keep the best possible, having regard both to the choice available and the amount you can afford. There is, however, one other way to obtain a bitch, and that is on breeding terms. These terms are set out by the bitch's owner, and I have known them to be quite disproportionate to the value of the animal, so you must be sure you are entirely in agreement right from the start. If you have the conditions set down in writing by the Kennel Club, this can save much unnecessary trouble later on. The most usual terms are to give two puppies to the bitch's owner, a first and third choice. You must appreciate you will be handing over the pick of the litter, but you may not have the experience and knowledge to recognise the best of the bunch yourself anyway, so it can be a great help to have a knowledgeable person taking an interest in your first litter while you gain valuable experience yourself.

Another point worth enquiring into when buying a bitch is the number of puppies in her own litter, for the size of the litter runs in families. The average is four, and this is a nice number with which a bitch can cope.

Be sure your puppy has been registered with the Kennel Club and that you are given the papers, and you then transfer the puppy into your name. If the puppy has not been registered with the rest of the litter, it will cost you a lot of money to do it separately at a later date. You will need to have the appropriate form (obtainable from the Kennel Club) signed both by the breeder and the stud dog owner. If it is your own litter you are registering, the following Kennel Club endorsements are often worth considering:

a) Not eligible for entry at shows, held under Kennel Club Rules.
b) Progeny not eligible for registration.
c) Not eligible for the issue of an export pedigree.
d) Name unchangeable.

Any endorsement shall only be lifted at the written request of the individual imposing it.

I hope I have given you the sufficient information to enable you to go ahead with confidence. The more you can learn about the various bloodlines, and the more you can observe at the shows, the better — but do be prepared for different judges to hold different opinions.

CHAPTER FIFTEEN

GROOMING AND COAT CARE

To the showman, the beauty of the Shih Tzu shines forth in his coat. To the pet owner, the coat can be a deterrent. Never glamourise the coat to the disadvantage of character, soundness and health. The beautiful coat does require care and attention. It is not difficult to keep two or three Shih Tzu in perfect condition, but it is very hard work to keep more than this number well groomed, especially if you have another breed to care for as well.

Moulting occurs in bitches twice a year, and in dogs usually only once. The guard hairs of the coat do not fall out except in special circumstances, such as illness, and sometimes after nursing a litter. It is the woolly undercoat which sheds, and this sheds into the coat, felting it up. Great attention to grooming is needed during this period, or you will have great lumps of wadded hair all over or the dead coat will mat into thick wads of wool. I will deal with how to get the coat out of this mess later in the chapter.

Coat colours

As stated, all colours are permissible, but fading or diluting ones make it difficult to breed for colour. In earlier days there were few true black and whites; these mostly changed to a dull iron grey. This is a colour of the past. Even the true pale greys are rare, more's the pity, for it is a lovely colour. There are far more solid blacks and golds now, which is not surprising as black is a dominant colour, and gold is the next colour to black. It is a mistake to breed your liver bitch haphazardly to black thinking you will get rid of your liver, for you can also have liver as the next colour to black, and this is recessive. If the black dog is black/liver, not black/gold, your liver bitch may well end up with a litter of liver puppies, for both parents have the gene. (A recessive gene will show up when it is carried by both parents.)

Solid Black. Dusky Rose of Bellakerne. Owners Tom and Sheila Richardson.
Photo: Russell Fine Art

The recessive black/liver gene covers the browns, dull golds and livers. These golds sometimes suffer from a 'Winter nose'. (This is a slightly 'off black' nose during the winter months.) The livers will have liver noses. The dominant black/gold lines carry the apricots and clear golds, all of which carry full black pigmentation. The solid golds have black masks, whilst most of the others have white. Both are permissible, but black masks do have the advantage of keeping cleaner, or at least appearing to do so! The solid colours win well in the show ring and are liked by many people; just as well, for once you have it, it is there to stay.

There do not seem to be as many diluting genes in the solid golds as in the parti colours, so many of the parti colours fade to a paler cream, very pretty but insipid; they do not stand out so well in the show ring. Golds come in numerous shades from pastel shades and pale honey to deep red-gold and chestnut.

Silver: If from this colour, it seems to remain. Others who change to silver, such as some born gold and the blacks with diluting genes, tend to change throughout their lives.

Rare colours and markings: Blue of the Persian cat, which carries a grey nose and light grey eye. The true black and tan marking, having black bodies with gold points and 'four eyes'. The only two litters containing these that I have heard of seem to have come through from the same source, and are very rare. All these colours have been sold as pets and never shown.

Good dark Liver. Kaolin Timu.
Owner Mrs Thelma Burnell (Australia).
Photo: Quicksilver Memories

One of the interesting things about Shih Tzus coat colour is how it changes over the dog's life. I have had a gold so dark at birth his pet owner breeders registered him 'bronze'. By 18 months of age, he slowly changed to silver, remaining that colour for a while before the coat gradually darkened. By the age of ten years, it has become almost black. That was Ch. Newroots Nankipoo of Snaefell.

The parti-colours can be in all colours and shades of colour — black and white, gold and white, gold/brindle (you can have solids in this, too), grey and white, and blues which are very rare. Liver in both solid and parti-colour needs to be a dark liver. I have not seen a chocolate-coloured dog for a very long time. They are lovely as puppies when a dark chocolate, but not so attractive in colour when older if they fade.

With the introduction into England of the 'red' American line of American Ch. Louwan Rebel Rouser, shades of this colour are creeping in, but there are many variations and diluting genes.

Many experienced breeders feel temperament and colour go together, and I agree to a certain extent. I have certainly found my gold/whites to be very loving and jealous. The brindles have been more placid. I do not think it is all to do with colour, but family characteristics in the genes play a big part as well.

Coat textures
It is now preferred for the coat to be straight. How times change. I remember when a straight coat was not liked at all and most dogs had wavy coats! The coat should not be dead straight, as in a Yorkshire terrier, but (as mentioned in the chapter on Standards) while a slight wave is permitted, a curl is not acceptable. A natural parting falls down the back.

A very brittle coat will break easily, and is more inclined to curl. A great deal of attention is required to get it back into condition. Some stripping out may be necessary, followed by careful treatment of the new growth. Additional vegetable oil and vitamins in the diet should help. Conditioning before and

Silver grey/white.
Ch. & Irish Ch. Mirazian Sweet Innocence.
Owner Mrs Margory Devine

after the bath will be necessary. Deep conditioning for such coats is a help, and possibly keeping the coat in oil for a while. For this, you can use such things as almond oil obtainable from the Body Shop. It is a thin oil — brush it on when you groom the dog. Or you can use the special oils obtainable from the stalls at dog shows. Petcetera will always send an order and give advice. Their telephone is 0192 684 3030. Wu Pi oil is a good and well-tried one. Saturate the dog's coat in these kinds of oils after the bath, and bathe weekly.

A healthy coat requires a healthy body, and, as in humans, the hair of a sick dog will be adversely affected. Good feeding and management are essential for a good coat.

Differently coloured coats carry different textures, some being stronger and easier to grow and manage than others.

The texture of the gold coat varies with the shade. Pastel shades grow thick and strong, with good undercoats, whereas the true deep gold is slow to mature and frequently carries less undercoat — it is soft, and more care is required in grooming.

As I mentioned earlier, there are some beautiful true black and whites. There does still seem to be different textures among them. Some grow enormously thick and strong coats, while others are grown very slowly, requiring great care in the grooming, similar to some of the gold coats. It would seem to be all in the genes. The white hair is stronger than the black. Sometimes just one hair will carry both black and white, and you can see the different textures in them.

Brindle shades and greys are usually very strong-textured coats, carrying good manageable under-coats. The brindle frequently changes to grey. Mine all finally end up black and white!

Tools

Good grooming is essential to stimulate hair growth and keep the dog's coat in a healthy condition. Most breeders have their own methods of grooming; there can be no hard and fast rules. Much depends on the way you use your tools.

Combs: A steel comb with wide teeth one end and narrow the other. Called 'greyhound', it is made in Germany. I consider some combing is essential, for the dead hair in the coat must be combed out, and the feet need combing. It should be used gently or you can drag out too much undercoat and break the ends of the guard hairs. Never try to drag out the mats with your comb, as this will only hurt the dog and cause him to dislike his grooming. You can also use the large wide-toothed sheepdog comb, which will take out less undercoat. Some people find the swivel tooth comb very good, especially for the last finish. Whatever comb you use, make quite sure the teeth are not overly sharp — test for this by clenching it in your hand.

Brushes: The type of brush used should vary with different coats. The woolly undercoated dogs need a firm brush such as the Maison Pearson nylon and bristle or Isinis. These are best for rather curly coats, as it will help straighten them. The finer softer coats may be better with the Hindes all-bristle brush. Hinds also make a very useful wire brush, which is more flexible than many and goes through the coat without hurting or damaging. These are obtainable from most pet shops in England. If you are wanting to show, you should buy the best wire brush suitable for Shih Tzus and other long coated breeds, which is the 'SweDog' Brush, or 'All Systems'. It is a very flexible wire, giving with the coat as you groom it, and removes static electricity. It is made abroad, but the agents in this country will supply you, along with the rest of the range of 'All Systems' grooming products such as shampoos and conditioners. The address is HUB International. The Butterflies, Peppard Farm. Peppard Common, near Henley-on-Thames, Oxon RG9 5JU. Tel 0491 628897. Wire brushes must always be used with great care; used too roughly, they will hurt the dog and cause him to resent his grooming. For the young puppy, a soft, old-fashioned type of bristle brush is the best; never use a wire on a young puppy.

Grooming

How much time you spend on the daily groom will depend on the thickness of the undercoat of your dog. Some have very thick woolly undercoats which must be gone through every day, while others can be left several days.

Method

A quick groom and a face wash should be carried out daily, with special attention being paid to the eyes, and a thorough grooming once a week.

You must train your dog to be groomed from puppyhood. It can be done by either lying him on his side on the table with a comfortable mat under him, or groom him on your lap. He will need to stand on the table for the final groom.

Be regular, and use brush and comb when you give the weekly groom, or mats will develop. For the daily groom, it may be sufficient to use the brush only. If you are gentle, and never pull the hair unnecessarily, the dog will enjoy the attention you are giving him and will allow you to tease out any mats and snarls. Accustom your puppy to grooming at an early age, training him to lie down so his underside can be done. Cut the elastic band which ties the top-knot — you will lose less hair this way. Do not groom the coat dry but use a wet spray, either one of the many coat conditioners available or water (rain water for preference).

If your Shih Tzu gets taken out for rough walking in the country, it is best to go over his coat thoroughly when you get home, for he is sure to get twigs, leaves and burrs (and, during the summer, grass seeds) stuck in his coat. If these are left in, they will make the coat more tangled than ever, and by working their way up to the skin surface, will cause irritation and scratching.

Full weekly grooming

Head: If there is any matting round the face, work in some de- matting solution such as Ring 5 Untangle, or if you have nothing else, try a hair-cream conditioner and leave it to soak in while you wash round the dog's eyes with warm water or an eye lotion. It is a good idea to flush out the eye, a practice which will remove any matter which might have collected. If the eyes are neglected, matter

Gold/white Int. Port. Span. Ch.
Snaefells Little Flower. Owner
Madame Monique Colombe (France.)
Photo: Jean Luc Lambert

collects in the corners by the nose; this discharge can not only rot the hair and stain it but also make a sore place on the flesh. It helps prevent this if you rub a little Vaseline round the eyes. If matting has occurred, do not comb, for you will pull all the hair as well and this will be very painful to the dog. The mats should have softened after working in the untangle lotion and be easier now for you to tease out with your fingers and thumb. Now wash the beard and whiskers. Use a 'no tears' shampoo round the whiskers. Take the comb through very gently. The best time for this is after feeding, as food deposits may collect under the chin. Some foods stain the whiskers. Brush and comb the ears downwards, not forgetting the area under the ear flaps which is a bad place for matting. See that the ears are clean, and that the hair which grows inside them is not caked up with wax. This hair should be pulled out. Do this gently by pulling just a few strands at the time.

At about five months, the hair on top of the head will have grown long enough to tie up, which prevents it from falling into the eyes, mouth and food. Comb it up from the stop of the nose and fix it with a small elastic band or slide. Be careful not to get other hair caught up in it, nor to draw the hair up too tightly, thus pulling up the eyes. Elastic bands are used for show. We never use bows, though they are used in some countries. Our dogs are not in the toy dog group, and we do not want them looking like 'toys'. The best bands to use are orthodontic, or latex, which can be bought from the clubs or at shows.

Wrapping the coat (See pages 194 - 195)

Body: Make the dog lie down on a table or in your lap. Use a conditioning spray. Brush from the skin first upwards, then down, in layers, using the comb only if necessary. Do not leave matted hair against the skin; this should be teased out, then brushed or combed if necessary. If you only top-brush and leave mats in, they will felt up and the dog will present a very bulky appearance, and become very uncomfortable, particularly when mats are under his thighs. The hair will pull every time he moves. While grooming, there is a good opportunity to make sure there are no signs of parasites. Fleas can be picked up from the grass very easily during the summer months.

If the dog has any persistent mats or snarls, use one of the useful 'anti-mat' preparations which I mentioned earlier. Work a little of the lotion into the mat with a small amount of light oil, then gently ease the hair apart; the guard hairs should then slip out of the mat and you can comb them through gently. Some hair will be inevitably lost in this process, but it should not show. If the tangle

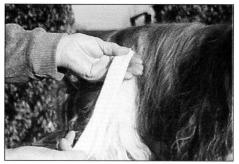

has become so bad that you cannot work it with your fingers, cut through it lengthways in several places — never cut across. You will lose more hair than by the teasing process, but at least it will hang correctly.

Brush the dog's stomach while he is lying down on his side. You can now go over the inside of his legs and under his armpits, two places where mats are always more likely to appear. Use your brush gently on his tummy, for it is tender. A dog should have his undercarriage sponged frequently, for this will keep him smelling sweet.

The trousers need careful attention. A change of diet or upset tummies can cause dirty trousers. If neglected, they may become stuck up, can block the anal passage and cause an abscess. If you are having problems this way, try adjusting his diet, or add a dessertspoon of bran or Allbran to help absorb the moisture.

Attend to the feet carefully, for they are sensitive. The lower leg and the feet mat easily, these being the parts which most frequently get wet. There is nothing like wet grass to build up mats on the legs. Do not catch your comb in the dew claws if they have been left on. Hair grows on the foot between the pads, and this needs watching because if the dog is always on grass, it can grow too long and become twisted up around the pads. It can also ball up with mud or little stones, and can be painful enough to cause lameness. Soak the hair and work on the mats, or cut them out. Keep a check on the nails, which should be kept short; if the dog is walking on hard surfaces, he will probably keep them down himself, but he cannot wear down his dew claws. For further details, see the next section.

Wrapping the coat (see pages 194-195.)

Anal Glands: These are two little glands are situated on either side of the anus. Some people consider they should be squeezed as routine with the general grooming. This can break down the surrounding tissues and can also be very painful, so they should only be squeezed if they feel full. Infected anal glands can poison the dog's whole system. If you are in any doubt about them, seek veterinary advice. Your vet will clear them out and show you how to do it.

Groom carefully, systematically and regularly all over, and your dog will look forward to this time with you and the attention he gets. If you have several dogs, they will practically queue up for their turn!

Ch. Harropine Chasing Rainbows. Bred and owned by Mr and Mrs Harper. (s. Champion Harropine China Town. d. Dragonfires Scarlet O'Hara – imp.)

For show dogs with some types of coats, a daily brushing may be too much. In such cases, three times a week may well be sufficient, but the head should still be attended to daily. Talk to your dog while he is being groomed, for he finds this soothing and enjoys it.

Nails: Dealing with the nails can be a painful operation and a dog which has once been hurt will always make a fuss. There is a section of 'quick' running down the nail and you must avoid this when clipping; if you should inadvertently cut it, bleeding will occur and it will be very painful. One is usually well-advised to keep a styptic handy, such as tinct benzoin co. (Friar's Balsam) or permanganate of potash crystals. It is best to cut off just a little at the time rather than risk cutting the quick and making it bleed. Some nails are black and others are pink. With a pink nail, you can easily see the pink quick, but it is not so easy to pick this out on the black nail — that is why it is advisable to cut off only the nail tip. I think the guillotine clippers or dew-claw clippers are the least painful, as they do not squash the nail together. If the 'quick' has grown too long to cut the nail, filing is best. File from base to the tip. With a puppy, I hold him firmly in my left arm, holding out the paw with my left hand, but if he struggles, assistance is necessary. You need to cut in a good light, for there is so much fur around the tiny claw and it must be done very carefully. Ordinary nail scissors may be used on very young puppies as their nails are soft.

When manicuring an adult dog, I prefer to cut the nails without assistance, unless the dog is particularly difficult, for I feel that an animal being firmly held by someone else becomes frightened and immediately begins to struggle. I make my dogs sit on the table in a good light, then pick up the paws one by one and just cut. They have been accustomed to this from puppyhood and have not been unduly hurt, so they seldom struggle.

The dew claws must be checked very carefully, for fur can easily mat around these and the comb can get caught in them during grooming. If allowed to grow long, they are liable to continue growing round in a circle, piercing and continuing to grow into the pad. This must be most painful and is likely to cause lameness. Dew claws are a nuisance and, although they may have been thought lucky by the Chinese, they usually prove unlucky to the dog. Therefore it is best to have them removed when whelps.

Solid gold with black mask. Weatsom Huggy Bear At Chadris. Owner David and Barbara Jessop

Bathing

Some people think this removes too much of the natural oil from the coat, and should be done only when absolutely necessary. It is more necessary with some dogs than others! Certainly a good regular grooming will keep many Shih Tzus clean and fresh. So much depends on where you live and the type of life the dog leads. Clay soil will brush out of the coat quite easily. My dogs get filthy and certainly need bathing as they roll in our black sandy soil, which works right into the coat and is inclined to stick.

During summer, it is a wise precaution to give a monthly bath to all dogs who run on grass, using an insecticidal shampoo — Vetzymes do one. If they have fleas, get a germicidal shampoo.

The first bath should be given with great care. Puppies can be bathed from eight weeks, if necessary, but it is essential to see they are thoroughly dry and remain in a warm room for several hours afterwards. A sink or hand-basin can be used when bathing a puppy, making it easier to control and less frightening for the animal. If it is frightened on the first occasion, there may always be trouble. It may be best not to use the shower for a puppy, as this may frighten it. Avoid bathing a dog in moult; at least groom it through first or you will have terrible felting.

Use a good dog shampoo, (the dog's HP is different from humans') or a baby-no-tears shampoo — the latter is wise for the head anyway — and a good cream rinse which will help to condition and separate the undercoat.

It is most important to prevent water from getting into the ears, so plug them with a little oiled cotton wool before bathing.

Always use a non-slip mat in the bath, or the dog will slip and slide around; this can not only be very frightening, particularly to a puppy, but will make your task more difficult. I prefer to use a spray when bathing an adult.

First of all, soak the coat all over, which in a full-coated dog like the Shih Tzu takes quite a bit of doing! Always wet the head last as most dislike this and it can frighten a puppy. Hold the head backwards with the ear flaps held down firmly against the side of the head while you spray the front.

Black/white. Ch. Santosha Tiger Lily.
Owners David and Susan Crossley

Give the coat two good lathers, with a rinse in between. Do not rub the coat, but 'milk' through the long hair; this way, it will tangle less. Be careful not to get soap into the eyes or water in the ears. In a hard-water area, rinsing is not so easy; you can either add a little borax to the final rinse or use rain or well water if you can get it. I like to do the final rinse in a baby bath full of water, and let the dog swim or float! You will be surprised how much more comes out of the coat. Now put on your cream rinse, leaving it for the required time before rinsing it off.

Wipe the surplus water off the coat with your hands, then pat the dog dry with towels. Do not rub in a circular action, for this will mat the undercoat. Let him have a good shake to remove more of the wetness. If I am bathing several dogs, I wrap one in a towel and put him in a towelling bag while I get on with the next. This absorbs much of the wetness and shortens the drying time.

Gold/white. Ch. Grandavon Ming Toi. Owner Mrs Yvonne Martin.

Dry cleaning

Cleaning with dry-cleaning powder is not used so much now with show dogs, as the Kennel Club rule forbids it to be used at shows. If used, the powder is rubbed well into the coat and left for an hour, then brushed out completely or, alternatively, brushed into the coat while the dog is being groomed. However, it does help to remove dirt and surplus grease, and is useful for separating any hairs when mats in the coat are being teased out while grooming.

A dog can be cleaned with spirit or with a foam shampoo. There are occasions when this is very useful, particularly for a small area of the coat, but it does not create the same effect as with wet bathing.

The show coat

A dog should not spend its life in a cage purely to grow the coat for show. Neither should it have a hamster water feeder as the main source of drinking water. If it has a drip feeder, and some like this, make sure you use a large puppy tube where the water drips freely.

Gold/brindle/white. Aust. Ch. Mudan Canada Dry. Owners Sheila and Tom Fitzgerald (Australia)

Naturally, more care needs to be taken than with the pet dog, for coat and presentation in the show ring are unfortunately of paramount importance. A poor specimen well presented in good coat will frequently win above a good specimen in poor coat and presentation. This is unfortunate for the breed, but there is no reason why you should not have a thoroughly sound and good dog in equally good coat and presentation. The action of the dog will be affected by being caging.

For the daily groom, use a wet spray — water, preferably rain water, or a special conditioner; there are many on the market and it is up to you to find out which suits your dog's coat best.

For the weekly groom, a light protein oil conditioner or rose water and glycerine (obtainable from Boots) can be used.

Your dog must be in good condition if it is to grow a good coat. This means good feeding with vitamin supplementation. Healthy exercise will give the natural bloom which so frequently just comes out of a bottle.

Gold/white. Int. Ch. Cherokee American Guy. Owner Anrick Laurent (France)

If necessary, condition the coat. Get rid of static electricity as
this causes breakage and split ends. If you use powder, it should be silicone. Talcum powder causes static.

Groom as previously mentioned, but bathing may need more care. There are almost as many methods of bathing as coat textures — find out which suits your dog.

Whether you groom prior to the bath is a matter for your own technique. If the dog has become very matted, I would advise doing it before. Otherwise, small mats can be teased out better when the dog is wet and the shampoo is in.

Bathing for show

Shampooing for the first time, use a product to remove oil (you can use lemon or even Fairy Liquid) if you have been using oil to help condition the coat. The second shampoo should be a special one to suit his coat. You find this out by trial and error. Whether you use a conditioner is again trial and error. Sometimes a conditioner can soften the coat too much; in other cases, it is needed and best not completely rinsed out. It will help prevent matting and also give the coat a sheen.

The following method is for coats which mat up badly after a bath; it is not so suitable for the oiled coat.

Half fill a baby bath with two gallons of warm water, adding your required amount of shampoo; a general one will do for the first wash. Stand the dog in the bath and bale the water over him for at least five to ten minutes. Rinse well with the spray.

For the second shampoo, fill the bath as before and use your 'special' shampoo. You should not need so much this time. Rinse well with the spray.

Make up your solution of cream rinse in a jug. Stand your dog in the emptied and cleaned bath and pour this solution down the centre line of the dog. Collect it in your jug and pour it over again to make sure it has gone right through the coat. Rinse well. Let the dog shake out the excess water. You should not have touched the coat at all.

Conditioning the coat: Bathe as normal. After the last rinse, mop out the surplus water and apply a conditioner such as Henna Wax or another deep conditioner. Place the body of the dog in a large plastic bag, secure it carefully and safely round the neck, put him in his cage in a warm place and leave him for 20 minutes before rinsing out. He may require further oiling before his next bath.

The very dry coat: This will require oiling, and give the dog a teaspoonful of corn oil with his food.

The curly coat: This is often due to a dry coat or it can be caused through the hair dryer being too hot or too close to the coat. After bathing, brush the hair down hard, holding the ends firmly as you dry. It is usually a strong coat, so you can use a strong brush without fear of removing too much coat.

Some show dogs are kept in oil — this helps to prevent ends from breaking and the coat matting. An oily solution or a little oil in the final rinse are poured over the dog. Dogs kept in an oiled coat need bathing every seven to ten days.

Drying

You can manage very well with an ordinary hair dryer. If you do not have a professional dog hair dryer, these are obtainable at shows, and you can get them fixed on stands, which is a great help as it leaves both your hands free for the dog. Brush the coat all the time to separate the hair. Be careful not to have the dryer too hot or too close to the coat, for this will damage it — a good blow is an asset. He may not like to feel his face and ears being blown, so help by drying these well with the towel. Wipe the inside of the ears with cotton wool. As the coat dries, blow the warm air up into it through the hair, which will help to dry it underneath and give it more body. Comb very carefully so as not to remove too much undercoat. Your method of drying must depend on the type of coat. If your dog has a very thick, woolly undercoat, you will need your nylon and bristle brush, parting the hair to the skin while you blow with the dryer.

If it is a wiry curly coat, pull the coat down straight and firm as you dry it.

If the texture is soft and there is little undercoat, you must be very careful and preserve all you have got. Do not use the brush or comb during the drying, but separate the hair with your fingers. Groom through gently the next day or after the dog is quite dry, using your special show-coat spray.

Wrapping the coat   (see pages 188-189)

Plait or wrap the top-knot to keep it from falling. If the long whiskers get into the food, then into the dog's mouth, you can tie them back with an elastic band. During feeding, the cut-off end of a stocking put behind the head will keep back the ears and whiskers.

The coat can be 'wrapped'. This is a big process and needs re-wrapping every three days. The dog does not mind it, but it is not satisfactory for a dog living a free life, which should be the way of a Shih Tzu, as wraps get pulled off by companions, and hair comes with them!

Eye and whisker stains: Some dogs stain more than others; it seems to be in the 'line'. Washing the whiskers daily helps, as does a special shampoo for white coats. After the daily whisker wash, powder with cornflower, potato flour or chalk, plastering it on. Leaving it overnight sometimes helps. There are many preparations on the market, few of which help. Some people find lemon juice good (this is good for stained teeth too, but the dog does not think so!). In some cases, staining is due to a

deep-seated infection in the throat, and a course of antibiotics solves the problem. Other people have found that milk of magnesia rubbed into the whiskers is good.

American top-not with bow - not used in Great Britain.
Photo: Isabelle France

If you have a dog which mats easily, there is a preparation called 'coat handler' which is excellent. There is both a shampoo and a conditioner. It certainly makes the grooming much easier. It is an American product obtainable from 'Sensational Products U.K.' Tel 0477 32241. They do attend some championship shows.

There are numerous coat preparations to choose from; these are sold at the championship shows. Be careful with some shampoos as they contain dyes, and this contravenes Kennel Club regulations.

Trimming the coat

The only acceptable trimming for the show ring is cutting the hair between the pads of the feet, and neatening the hair from underneath the foot to remove some of the longer hair. Never cut all round the foot to make it a neat around trimming the coat to floor length.

An easy pet trim.

Trimming the pet dog

Many dogs, owing to their lifestyle or their owners' lifestyle, need trimming, and it is far better to do this than to allow your dog to become full of mats. I do not like dogs to be clipped right back to the skin, though I know it is the quick and easy way. Many dogs do not like this; they feel bare (which they are) and disgraced. Besides that, it gives them no protection from heat or cold. I suggest you should always leave at least an inch on the coat, particularly in the winter. If you are having all his lovely coat taken off, at least let him have a pretty style. It is quite easy to do yourself and a lot cheaper, so long as you do it when the dog is groomed free of any mats. If you have it done at the beauty parlour, find out first how they intend to do it, or you can always tell them what you want. You would not go to the hairstylist without having some idea of what they intend to do!

I think one of the nicest and easiest of all is cutting the dog back to resemble a three-month-old puppy. Or you can leave it long on the tail and ear fringes and take the body hair short.

Some people keep the body hair and just cut the head back. This does save tying up the top knot daily, or even several times a day with some! I do not approve of vets who cut the Shih Tzu hair back around the eyes without asking or informing the owner. They do not seem to realise that once you cut the hair round the eyes you MUST keep it short all the time, for after it has been cut it will grow more spiky, and it will grow upwards into the eyes, doing just as much harm as before it was cut. Therefore, put Vaseline round the eyes daily — will help to soften the hair.

The old dog in particular often resents his grooming, especially on the head and round the eyes. It is much kinder to keep the head hair cut short.

If you wish to keep a long coat, or have it look as if you dog is in full coat, there are short cuts to help with the grooming. With your comb, take out all the undercoat you can, as this will leave in the guard hairs and will be unnoticeable. Cut the hair of the tummy well up to the sides of the ribs. This will help a great deal in wet weather. Cut the hair from under the thighs and axilla, where it can become very matted. None of this will show and your dog still looks in full coat. You can cut round the feet. Also cut the hair on top of the feet and let the hair of the leg fall down and it will cover up the cut hair of the foot.

CHAPTER SIXTEEN

SHOWING

Showing can be a fascinating hobby, so long as one retains a sense of humour and can take the bad with the good. It is also an opportunity to make many friends and have a good day out right away from other chores and worries of the world.

There is little monetary reward to be gained. Few shows pay any prize money and, if they do, it is barely enough to buy a drink or a new toy for your dog, whereas there is considerable expense involved on entry fees and travelling. Therefore, it is important that you should enjoy the day's outing even when your dog is not among the winners. Competition is keen, the standard is high, and it can be hard work to bring a dog into top show condition. Too many exhibitors can only see good in their own dogs and go about condemning other people's. Judging is by no means always good or fair. There can be a lot of dissatisfaction when people do not win, and obviously you can't win all the time as all judges see dogs differently; and the dog should be judged on the day, not by video many weeks before! As in all competitive sport, it has its seamy side, and if you intend showing then make up your mind not to have any part in it, as this behaviour just spoils the atmosphere and pleasure for everyone. It is a great sport, the majority of exhibitors are fantastic people and you will make many friends.

Your dog may not like showing — perhaps he has too good a life at home! But there are dogs who love to show off, and put everything into it, and others who immediately when they get into the vicinity of a show ground drop their tails and tell you in no uncertain terms that they do not enjoy showing and it is unkind to keep them in the ring. Pet dogs have been known to go 'lame' as soon

Bournemouth Championship Show 1993. Puppy bitch class.

as preparations commence — this is the Shih Tzu way of informing you that he is not going to play this game!

There are many different kinds of shows. It is best not to start with championship shows. The smaller shows are a better starting off ground. The competition is not so great and they are usually very friendly; there is more time to talk to other exhibitors who you will find most helpful if they know that you are new to showing. Also, they are a better training ground for both you and your dog.

Types of show

Primary shows
This is a new type of show recently introduced by the Kennel Club. The highest class at these shows is 'Maiden'. Dogs having won a first prize at any show, except as a puppy, are not permitted to compete. All entrants must be registered at the Kennel Club.

Sanction Show
This is the next smallest show. The highest class at these shows is Post Graduate and dogs having won a Challenge Certificate may not compete. Many big breeders show their young stock at these shows which ensures good competition. To enter, you must be a member of the society running the show, but your membership application will usually be accepted at the same time as your entry form.

Limited show
This is also limited to members of the society concerned and to dogs who have not won any Challenge Certificates towards becoming a Champion.

Open show

All dogs fully registered at the Kennel Club, including champions, are eligible for entry to open shows. The larger open shows are benched, i.e. the dog has a bench allotted to him which has the same number as his ring number, which is listed in the catalogue. The dog must either be on the bench in his cage, or tied on the bench with a collar and chain when not being shown.

If classes are not scheduled for your breed, there will be unclassified and variety classes for which you can enter.

Championship shows

These are the most important of all and are the only shows where Kennel Club Challenge Certificates are on offer. There are now 31 championship shows permitted to offer Challenge Certificates for the breed. Two Challenge Certificates and two reserve Challenge Certificates are given, one each for the best and best opposite sex. Five of these shows are held by the breed Clubs. Championship shows have the best classification and the largest number of entries. Entry fees are high and prize money is seldom given, then usually to top winners only.

Exemption shows

These are frequently held in aid of charities and are very popular, but show dogs should not be entered for them unless they are run under Kennel Club rules. There are, invariably, classes for mongrels and dogs who are not registered at the Kennel Club.

Four classes are permitted for registered dogs. These attract large entries and winning show dogs frequently enter, naturally, with charitable aims in mind the object is to get as many entries as possible to raise a little much-needed money. They can be great fun, entries need not be made until the day of the show, and there is a generally happy and carefree atmosphere.

Junior handling

Over the latter years, this has become a good sport for juniors (human, not dog). They have their own Kennel Club Junior Organisation, and most shows have 'junior handling classes' which are very popular and competitive, the winners going on to compete for yearly finals. They have competitions with other countries, and are encouraged in many ways.

One of the weekly dog papers (Dog World or Our Dogs) will give you all the information you need regarding forthcoming shows, together with the secretary's address so you can send for a schedule, but remember your puppy must be at least six months of age and fully registered in your name at the Kennel Club. The closing date for entry is usually one to two months before the show.

You now have your schedule and entry form, and are wondering which classes to enter. For a first show, it is unwise to enter more than two classes, for your puppy may be nervous and his first show should be a pleasure. If he is under nine months old, and there is a minor puppy class available, then this is the best for him. All the entrants will be young and a very young puppy is not expected to show like a veteran.

I would advise you to give the junior class a miss since very experienced dogs can enter this one. The maiden and novice classes are the next best to enter. If there are no breed classes scheduled, you can enter the non-classified variety class which will be smaller than the 'Any Variety'. Your schedule will give you the qualifications necessary for the various classes.

If your dog has not been fully registered or not transferred from the previous owner, this must be done before the last date of entry for the show. Write to or telephone the Kennel Club at 1 Clarges Street, Piccadilly, London W1Y 8AB, obtain the required form and fill it in immediately. Strictly speaking, you should have had this form given to you and signed by the previous owner or breeder when you purchased your puppy.

If you have not had your registration or transfer papers back from the Kennel Club when completing the entry form for the show, add the letters NAF (Name applied for) or TAF (transfer applied for), whichever is applicable. Send off the entry form before the closing date. If you want a reply to know that your entry has arrived include a stamped addressed postcard, or get a 'proof of posting' from the post office. If an entry goes astray, a proof of posting will be accepted by the Kennel Club, but not the stub receipt of your cheque. If you have not already done so, now is the time to proceed with training your dog and yourself. You need to know your job to show your dog at its best.

Training

If you have followed the suggestions in my chapter on training, your dog will be walking well on the lead and will have learned to obey you and be well socialised. Ring training is only a short step from this but it does give your dog a chance to feel the atmosphere of a show and mix with many other breeds.

Many canine societies hold ring-craft classes, and it is well worth attending these. It will help you to show your dog with more confidence, and this confidence of yours will be transmitted to your dog through the lead. Your dog will have had the advantage of socialising with other dogs and being handled on the table by many different people. This can be very nerve-wracking for an animal, and if it is put off at its first show, it may have a lasting affect.

Preparation for show

Besides the necessary training for the ring, you will want to ensure your dog's coat is at its best. Each exhibitor has his or her special technique, and here again you may get very confused if you ask too many people exactly what you should do, for the advice is bound to be conflicting. If I pass on some general hints, so you can decide what best suits you and your dog.

There is nothing like a wet bath to give a dog's coat that gloss and bloom which helps him to stand out above others. A dry-bath preparation is useful when shows are close together and you do not wish to bathe the dog again so soon. If you wet-bathe your dog, you need to find out which is the best time to do it. Some require bathing early so that the coat has time to regain its 'body'. Others are best bathed the day before and brushed hard to make the coat lie down. The softer coat which may carry less undercoat is sometimes best done a few days before or it will hang very limp. After the bath, the dog needs to be kept clean, which is not always easy! Chapter 15 on Grooming and Coat Care gives more details.

The Kennel Club has strict rules on show preparation. No colouring or lacquer must be used on the coat, and no powder can be used at the show (if this has been used at home, it must all be brushed

Crowvalley The Chancer with owner Betty Williams after winning his first CC at Birmingham 1993

out before the dog gets to the show). Remember to keep the nails clipped since long nails have an adverse effect on the dog's action. For cleaning the dog's teeth, you need special dog toothpaste as this does not require rinsing — never use human toothpaste for dogs. Clean the teeth with a swab wrapped round an orange stick. There are various preparations on the market for cleaning dogs' teeth, and specially made toothbrushes which are very helpful.

Equipment for show

These days most of our Shih Tzus are brought to the show in a cage, (you will find there are many stalls at the shows which sell suitable cages) The cage can go on the bench with your number, which is provided at championship shows.

Delmarvey Cleopatra of Janmayed with owner Anne Pickburn, and judge Susan Johnson winning graduate bitch class Builth Wells 1993

Take a bag containing the following:

Show lead and collar: There are many types and colours from which to choose, generally on sale at most shows. Do not choose the harsh nylon slip or very fine round ones — both of these cut into the dog's neck when you pull up the head and frequently are the cause of the dog not walking happily. There are soft woven nylon ones which do not hurt. Accustom your dog to t h e show collar and lead before taking him to the show. Never use a harness on your dog. I prefer to start a puppy off with a special soft leather collar, as this gives more control.

Cotton wool and water or optrex to wipe the eyes.

Tissues for many purposes.

Drinking bowl and water. Although there is water at the show, it is wiser to bring your own to prevent tummy upsets.

Towel. If it is wet at the show or there is dew on the grass, the dog will need wiping down after he has exercised to relieve himself.

Clip to hold on your ring number; these can be bought at the show.

Dry-cleaning product in case your dog gets dirty.

A plastic bag in which to put your rubbish.

Do not forget to take your tickets. Few shows besides championship shows send out tickets, so if you have several dogs, make sure you have marked your schedule with the name of the dog you have entered.

Wellingtons and Mackintosh for the outdoor shows. Even in the marquees, the ground gets wet after heavy rain.

If it is one of our rare hot summers, you will need to come prepared with ice packs and ice to keep your dog cool. If you stay outside in the grooming area by the ring, come prepared with a heat blanket (usually on sale at Championship Shows) and a sunshade.

There is a lot of show equipment you can buy such as grooming tables, and trolleys for wheeling your dogs and equipment into the show from the car park. I would advise you not to buy any of this until you know you will continue with showing. The items are very expensive and not essential with just one dog. If you have a small, lightweight card-table, bring it with you for it will do just as well; or if you have a travelling cage, you can groom your dog on that.

Most Championship Shows give prior notice as to which dogs are first in the ring, and the time of their judging. As a rule, this is announced in the dog papers a week beforehand. Always arrive in good time; an hour before judging is due to start is not too early. You may have a long walk from the car park, and then some trouble in finding your bench. Your dog will need to relieve himself — if he goes in the ring uncomfortable, he may not walk well. It will not help your dog if you become flustered and rush him into the ring ungroomed. Buy a catalogue, settle your dog on his bench, ascertain (if you do not already know) when you may expect to be in the ring, and prepare to have your dog groomed for that time.

There is always last-minute grooming to be attended to with a Shih Tzu. The extent of this final preparation will depend on how much you have done beforehand, and on your mode of travel. If you travelled by train, and your dog was not boxed, he is unlikely to arrive in the immaculate condition in which he left. This is where your cleaning materials are needed. Even if he has remained clean, he will still require another groom before actually entering the ring. The better the presentation, the greater are his chances of winning. A dog whose thick undercoat is matted will not look so good, even though the guard hairs are long and well groomed, for the body line will be spoiled and he may even look out of proportion.

Groom the head and re-tie the top-knot, being careful not to pull in the hair too tightly above the eyes, which would not only be uncomfortable but also alters the expression. Comb the whiskers neatly, wipe round the eyes with a damp swab, or a dry one if time is short; the whiskers need to be dry by judging time. Potato flour or cornflour will help to dry them, then brush it out. Pay attention to the inside of the legs which are often forgotten, and comb the hair of the feet. Check that the trousers are clean and well combed down; if they are bunchy and sticking out you will be adding an inch to your dog's length, and his legs will look too far under his body. All these small details are of the greatest importance and will be learned by experience. Put the show collar and lead on your dog, remember the clip for attaching your number, and you are ready for your class. You are allowed to take a brush or comb into the ring with you.

Tying the top-knot.

Ring procedure

When your class is called go into the ring. If your ring number was on the bench or had been sent to you, be sure to put it on, otherwise the steward will hand out the numbers. Then line up with the other dogs and handlers but position yourself down the line if you can, so as to have the opportunity to watch procedure. Not all judges use the same method for walking the dog.

Talking to the judge is not permitted in the ring, unless you are spoken to first. If you have any queries, address these to the steward.

The judge may ask for the dogs to be walked round. You will then follow each other in a large circle, so be sure to keep your dog on the inner side. You should never position yourself between the judge and your dog. After this, each dog is judged separately. The first in the line stands their dog on the judging table, where it will be examined by hand for various anatomical points. The head will be felt, the eyes inspected and the mouth opened. If the puppy has not been trained to expect this, he may resist, and if he is frightened and upset, it could well cause him to dislike showing. (Grooming on the table at home is a good start to training, and if you have a few friends who are willing to help by handling him lightly at this time, it will not come as an alarming experience at his first show.)

His age may be asked, and you will be asked to 'walk your dog' while the judge watches his action from all angles — hind, front and side action which is so important in the Shih Tzu. Training for this will have helped considerably, both for you and the dog; if you walk sloppily, so will he! He needs to walk smartly with his head and tail held up. It should not be necessary to rush the dog round the ring, but take him at his best steady pace. If the judge is watching side action, remember to keep the dog between you and the judge.

After all dogs have been examined and walked, they are lined up again and the judge makes his final choice. It is important that your dog remains in the standing position at this point in proceedings, after which the winning dogs will be called out to the centre of the ring. In a very large class, a shortlist is often picked out before the final choice made.

A few words of advice may be timely here. As I said before, it is not sufficient to have a basically good dog; it is up to you to learn how to make the most of it, in coat, presentation, training and ringcraft. Other breeders are usually most helpful to novices, unless the latter seem to think they know it all, in which case, they will get little help!

Do not make the mistake of asking too many people for their opinion of your dog. They will all tell you willingly, but you will be very confused by possibly contradictory comments, and the dog's faults will be pointed out to you to such an extent that you will wonder if there is anything right about him at all! You will soon find out the most knowledgeable breeders, but unfortunately, even they do not always agree about the quality of each other's animals. The judge at a show is usually willing to give an opinion if approached after the judging is completed.

If you are fortunate enough to win at your first show, do not imagine you will win every time. Not all judges come to the same conclusions, and what is important to one may be unimportant to another. If you do not win, the experience will still be valuable, and you will probably learn far more in your efforts to ascertain just why you were not successful; this may even be obvious to you straight away, and will help you to avoid becoming 'kennel blind'. Learn all you can about handling and presentation. The good handlers know their dogs' faults and virtues, and handle each dog to its best advantage.

People who wear gimmicky clothes usually do so to attract the judge's attention, but this can work two ways and also detract from the dog. Flat or low-heeled shoes are best. Wide skirts are not suitable at outdoor shows as the wind can blow them in the way of your walking dog.

If you do not win this time, there is always another time and a different judge. If you have faith in your dog, don't give up; his time will come when he is ready for it. Just keep improving both your handling and presentation.

Never show an in-season bitch at shows where there are mixed dog and bitch classes. A bitch having a false pregnancy may not be happy showing, particularly at the time after her season when the puppies would have been born.

Spayed Bitches and Castrated Dogs.
The Kennel Club rules have been relaxed here, and permit these to be shown but wish to be informed beforehand.

Junior warrant

A dog may only compete for this title between the ages of one year and 18 months. To qualify, 25 points have to be won. They are awarded as follows: One point for a first in a breed class at an Open Show. Three points for a first at a Championship Show.

Many a promising youngster has been ruined through being over-shown by the owner trying to get sufficient points to attain this title, yet it has no real significance, except to prove it was a very nice youngster. At one time, it was expected that a Junior Warrant holder would become a Champion. This is not always so, for some very good youngsters do not mature as you want. The great danger is in over-showing the dog in order to win this title, and this can create boredom for the dog and it stops giving of its best in the show ring. It is very tempting to 'over show' a promising junior. A puppy should not attend two shows each week-end, for week after week, as some do, but should have sufficient relaxation to grow. It is surprising how much a good show dog will put into showing; the dogs do know what they are doing, and the next day, they should be permitted to relax and rest, not be dragged off to another show. This is particularly the case with a puppy who is still growing.

Dog and bitch CC winners Builth Wells 1993. Vicky Grugan with Jardhu The Republican, judge Susan Johnson, Sheila Richardson with Ch. Bellakerne Misty Do.

Champions

It is harder for a dog to gain its title in Britain than in other countries, for the systems are quite different. In Britain, a dog gains the title of Champion by winning three Challenge Certificates under three different judges, one of which must be gained after the dog is over 12 months old. Challenge Certificates are only on offer at Championship Shows and, to win, the dog may have to compete against a formidable array of champions, for they are all entered in the open class. We do not have separate Champion classes, as they do in many other countries. Many a good dog is unable to become a Champion. It is as well to remember that it is by no means always the champions who throw the best stock.

CHAPTER SEVENTEEN

HEALTH

Many ailments have already been dealt with in their appropriate chapters. The Shih Tzu is by nature a very robust little dog, and illness and disease do not come his way as often as in some small breeds, although weaklings can be found in any variety. The weakling will pick up infection easily.

I wrote the above paragraph for the first edition of my previous book in 1974. Twenty years on, I am glad to say I think it still stands, but at the same time I do not think on the whole that they are as robust as in the earlier days. I cannot tell why. It could be modern feeding, or a less healthy lifestyle; for I do not think quite so many lead the healthy country life they used to. There is so much anti-dog feeling about that dogs are more restricted for exercise than in the past. Food has certainly changed a lot, both ours and dogs'. On the whole, it is not so pure as it used to be. It would be very difficult to feed several dogs on a good variety of healthy human fresh food; which is essential to obtain all the necessary vitamins and minerals and anything else which has not as yet been discovered. So owners fall back on feeding a convenience commercial 'complete' diet, many of which are excellent, and better than an insufficient home made diet. But who really knows what is complete?

The best way to guard against infection is to feed well, keep the dog and its living conditions clean, and let the dog lead a healthy life. Unfortunately, some dogs will still succumb whatever care you take. Cancer has taken toll of many dogs, and each year one hears of more cases. Why? Nobody knows, but it is tragic, more so when one does not know how to guard against it.

I will mention mostly diseases which I have known to have affected Shih Tzus. I am not a vet, and a good veterinary book should help you more. The one, of many, which I have found to be most helpful in the home is 'Dog owners Home Veterinary Handbook'. Never neglect a condition which requires veterinary attention by experimenting, for often, the sooner you seek advice, the quicker the cure. When a condition is left too long, secondary complications can set in. Vet fees are very high and best avoided by keeping your animal healthy.

Giving pills: It sounds simple until you try to do it! To open the dog's mouth, you should hold either side of the upper jaw with your left hand on top of the jaw, the thumb at the right and the middle finger at the left. Press gently behind the canine teeth. This will open the mouth. With your other hand, depress the tongue and slip the pill to the back of the throat. Some dogs are good at taking pills, some are not. Shih Tzus are stronger than you might think, and if they do not want to take the pill, they struggle, and they are strong. The pill becomes slippery with saliva. They may not go down and the dog will keep it in its mouth, and, when you are not looking, spit it out! I have not yet mastered the art and avoid giving pills if I can, so if you have difficulty, this is what I do. If you can get your dog to take the pill enclosed in a titbit, that is easier, or crush it and dissolve it in a little milk, then give it by spoon or a small syringe. No problem!

To take the temperature: The best way to take a dog's temperature is rectally. Keep the thermometer specifically for the dog — do not use your human one! You need a blunt-ended thermometer, for you do not want it to break inside the dog if he moves suddenly. The best thermometers are digital ones. Although more expensive, they are far safer and easier to read. Grease the thermometer, (use KY jelly for a digital one). Raise the dog's tail and insert the thermometer about an inch. Leave it a minute or according to the instructions with your thermometer, as they can vary. The dog's normal temperature is around 101.5 deg F (38.2 deg C).

Nursing a dog: Naturally, the nursing will depend on the nature of the disease. Any sick animal must be kept warm and comfortable, and away away from all disturbances, though it will like to be in close touch with its owner. The bed should be dry and comfortable. Vet beds or some similar material are best as they give warmth and remain dry as any urine or moisture from the dog will go right through the material. Drinking water must be accessible, and if the dog cannot drink on its own or reach the bowl, it should have it offered frequently. If the animal is unable to move, it should be regularly turned on its other side. The diet naturally has to be according to the disease, but a tempting light diet of fish or chicken is indicated particularly if the dog has a rise of temperature. If necessary, this may have to be liquidised and fed by spoon or syringe. There are now many very good invalid diets made by Hills and Pedigree Petfoods obtainable from the vet. If the dog likes them, they may well be the best as they will contain all the necessary ingredients and are concentrated so the dog does not require so much.

It is most important to note whether the dog has its bowels open and passes urine. If the dog is under the vet, you will be given any special instructions, follow them carefully. Broken bones, slipped discs or eye injuries among other things may need special treatment. With eye injuries, it is often necessary for a 'collar' like a flower pot to be put round the dog's head to prevent him rubbing his eyes. This is not very comfortable for the dog, but most necessary. It will need to be removed for the dog to drink or eat as it will have to extend beyond the muzzle. For some conditions to stop the dog from constant licking, it can help to put it into a baby-grow suit. I have found using a cotton pillow case very useful to stop it licking any body sores. It will not be able to move around much, but sometimes drastic measures need to be taken. I put the dog up to his neck into it, and thread a drawstring at that end which I tie securely. This is far more comfortable than a collar. Putting socks on the feet helps to stop scratching. I find the best way to keep these on is by binding micropore bandage round the top of the sock, or you can use prestoband, or even strapping with the sticky side out. Never get strapping on the dog's hair, as you will have to cut it off.

Any animal suffering an infectious disease should be moved away from the other animals.

Inoculations: These are given from eight weeks. They should not be given if the animal is at all under the weather. Shih Tzu puppies often suffer from snuffles at that age, possibly due to teething. The inoculations are given for protection against hard pad and distemper, canine virus hepatitis and leptospiral jaundice. Parvovirus is added to this and sometimes a protection against some of the bacteria which cause kennel cough. Whether it is wise to have everything given in a multiple inoculation must be your vet's decision. Some vets do not give all together. The inoculation is repeated at 12 weeks. Some like to repeat it again at 16 weeks. When it is felt that this is necessary, one wonders whether it would be better to delay the first a couple of weeks; but this does depend on home conditions and whether the puppies are likely to pick up infection due to proximity of other animals. The danger is that the puppy still has immunity from the mother and that the injections are not therefore giving the full protection. It is advised that booster injections are given every year. Occasionally an animal has an adverse reaction to the injections, but this is rare.

Abscesses

These can occur anywhere. They are extremely painful. The first signs may be that the dog has a rise of temperature. The abscess forms and eventually bursts, letting out all the pus, giving relief to the animal.

Treatment: Apply heat to try to draw the abscess to a head. The dog should be put on antibiotics. These may make the abscess subside without coming to a head. I frequently hear of anal abscesses. These are very painful and unpleasant and may require surgical treatment. The dog may have half an aspirin to help with the pain, but he should be under the vet and you must carry out his instructions.

Acupuncture

There has been considerable success with this treatment for various illnesses, including disc trouble.

Anal glands

There are two of these glands situated just inside the anus, one on either side. They contain a very smelly fluid. The dog should clear them during defecation. They may also get expressed if the dog is suddenly frightened. When the glands become over-full, they need to be attended to. It is a sign that they require expressing when a dog skids across the floor on his bottom. The beauty parlour will attend to it if your dog goes to one. Otherwise, get your vet to do it and ask him to show you how so that you can do it yourself another time. It is not pleasant. Raise the dog's tail, grasp behind the sacs or glands and squeeze outwards. You should have a wad of cotton wool in your hand in front of the anus as this unpleasant smelling fluid — which sometimes becomes thick — will shoot out when you squeeze. Some people do this whenever they give the dog its full groom. I do not consider it should be done unless the sacs are over-full as continual squeezing breaks down the surrounding tissues. If this is very painful or you suspect there is pus and an abscess, take the dog to your vet.

Biting feet

This is a problem that many people's dogs have had. It can be just that they are bored and it has become a habit. It is more likely that there is an irritation due to harvest mite, or some other mite.

Treatment: Try washing the feet in Pot Permanganate, or Benzyl Benzoate. It is likely to be due to mite of some sort. If it is due to a bad habit, you can try applying bitter apple. The trouble with this is that the bitter taste does not last very long and needs to be used frequently.

Bloat

This is rare but not unheard of in small breed. It is largely the big breeds which suffer with this dangerous condition. However, Shih Tzus have had it, though it is not so likely to be accompanied by a twist or torsion when the stomach twists on itself. It is an emergency condition. The signs are the dog will look very distressed, and be salivating. Its stomach will blow up like a balloon. The cause is due to a build-up of air and gases in the stomach, and must be relieved straight away. Get on to your vet at once. If your dog has had this once, it may recur. It will help to avoid it by not feeding dry foods. Give two meals instead of one large one. Remove water during meal time, and do not let the dog exercise vigorously after its meal.

Constipation

If your dog keep straining but does not pass a stool, it is likely that he is constipated. Straining can also occur with diarrhoea. If you have been giving him bones he can chew, this will cause constipation, but be sure there are no fragments of bone lodging at the anus which he cannot pass. You should not give cooked bones, but only long bones, such as rib bones and marrow bones, and do not leave your dog chewing them for too long if you find he is managing to break them up. Bits of bone can also cause impaction, which might cause blood to be passed. You can feel for this with a well-greased gloved finger.

Treatment: So long as you are sure it is constipation, you can give milk of magnesia. If your dog suffers from it frequently, you should look to his diet. Adding a little liver to the diet will have a laxative effect.

Coprophagy

This is something which affect all breeds, not just Shih Tzus. It is the disgusting habit of a dog eating excreta, and I do not think anybody has found a cure although there are many many suggestions! I have dealt with this fully under Problems of Management in Chapter 13.

Cysts

These can occur in many different areas:

Sebaceous cysts are cysts on the body in a lump which contains a fluid. Some can be drained, but most eventually need to be removed or they become infected.

Interdigital cysts occur between the toes. I do not think this is as common in Shih Tzus as some breeds but they are very painful and difficult to cure. Long-term antibiotics sometimes affect a cure or an autogenous vaccine may be necessary. These are vaccines specially prepared from the bacteria affecting that individual animal.

Dermoid cysts are cysts containing hair and body tissue. I have also mentioned dermoid cysts under 'eyes'.

Cystic ovaries will cause a bitch to be infertile. They usually have overlong seasons, due to the ovary producing an excess of oestrogen.

Ranula cysts are caused by a block on the salivary glands. There may be a small lump in the mouth at the side of the tongue.

Diarrhoea and vomiting gastro-enteritis

This can be very serious, especially for puppies and old dogs. Many diseases start this way, parvovirus being one. Dehydration can set in very quickly and if at all severe, the animal needs to be on a drip to counteract the dehydration. There are other bugs besides parvo, and some of them can be just as drastic, so do not delay in getting on to your vet.

If this is mild and just a tummy upset, it may be something due to what the dog has eaten rather than infection or poisoning. Take him off food for a day, even if he wants to eat. If he is better the next day, give boiled rice only. If he turns his nose up at it, just take it away and let him go without. A short starvation will do no harm. You can offer honey and water, but do not give milk. Give him a probiotic.

Ears

If you see the dog shaking his head, or holding it to one side, you may be sure he has pain in his ear. Rather than attempting to attend to it yourself, it is safer to get your vet to see to it, for there are many things which could be wrong — an abscess, grass seed or otodectic mange to mention a few. Never go poking down the ear canal — you could easily damage the ear drum. If he is repeatedly scratching behind it, ear mites are likely to be causing irritation. Mats form easily behind the ear. Much of the trouble is caused by the hair which grows in them, becoming matted up and clogging the narrow ear canal.

The best way to prevent ear trouble is by keeping the ears clean. When you groom your dog, take a swab of cotton wool and a little olive oil, carefully wipe the external part of the ear and just inside. Keep the hair which grows inside the ear free from mats, and if there is much of it, gently pull it out a few strands at the time. Never do this if the ear is inflamed in any way, but clear it of wax so there can be a free flow for any discharge. When grooming your dog, it is a good idea to smell the ears. You will soon recognise the smell of canker or ear mites. These are the cause of the nasty brown discharge in the ear. Otodex drops are quite good for clearing this. If you find it difficult to pull the hair yourself, get your vet or beauty parlour to show you.

Eyes

All breeds of dogs with large front facing eyes are vulnerable to trauma as they have little or no protection.

General treatment: The eyes are very vulnerable to damage as they face frontwards. They should be washed out daily. I find the best method for this is to first wipe round the eye with cotton wool to remove any 'sleep'. You can do this at the same time as you wash the whiskers. Then irrigate the eye with a soothing solution.

To irrigate the eye: You can either irrigate the eye by using a small jug with a reasonable length of fine spout. (a small teapot or a long spouted invalid cup are good), or you can do it with a largish swab of cotton wool. Use a different swab for each eye. If you have washed round the eye with the swab, do not dip it back into the lotion, but use a fresh swab. These precautions will save infecting the eyes. The lotion should have the chill taken off. Incline the dog's head to one side so that the fluid is passed from the outer side towards the nose. It is as well to have a towel or a dish in which to catch the lotion. A soothing lotion to use is camomile, which you can make up camomile tea from tea bags bought at the heath shop. Cold tea is also very good. Never touch the eye ball with a dry swab.

To insert eye drops: Holding the bottle of eye drops in your warm hand before inserting them will take the chill off. Gently pull up the upper lid exposing the cornea and squeeze the drop on to it without touching the eye.

To insert eye ointment: Pull down the lower lid and squeeze the ointment along the bottom of the eye. Do not touch the eye.

Cataract

The older dog frequently suffers from this. The lens becomes opaque and gives a bluish white appearance to the eye. The condition can be operated on. It now has a higher success rate as new methods are used. It is a very expensive operation and not suitable to all dogs. If this senile condition of cataract is seen in its early stages, it is said to be inhibited with the homoeopathic treatment of:

calcarea fluorica 6x

natrum muraticum 12x

magnesia carbonica 6x

Three doses of one remedy daily in rotation, continuing for four weeks.

Juvenile cataract

A puppy may be born with a 'juvenile' cataract. It seems uncertain why this occurs. Some say it is hereditary, while others that it occurs in the womb.

Conjunctivitis

The eye will look red, due to infection or inflammation. Hair rubbing the eye is a frequent cause. There may be discharge or pus. The condition needs treating to save further damage to the eye, so try to find the cause. It could be due to the powder you have used on the whiskers, or coat sprays. If you use boric acid for bathing the eye, make quite sure all the crystals are completely dissolved, for they may cause irritation. Drafts can also cause conjunctivitis. If the dog keeps rubbing the eye, it is likely to cause an ulcer.

Dermoid cyst

These small cysts, which contain hair, can grow on the eyeball. They are likely to cause irritation of the eye and should be removed. This is usually quite a simple operation and of the few cases of which I have heard, the eye has not been affected.

Dry eye

Dry eye is a condition where there is a lack of tears and the eye surface becomes dry. It needs bathing or irrigating daily to remove all matter which may have adhered to it. Always use a very wet swab. One is usually advised to put in artificial tears, which are obtainable from the chemist. This is not wholly satisfactory, for to be of any use, they need to be put in at least hourly. There is an operation which is sometimes performed to relieve the situation. Within recent years, it has been discovered that Cyclosporin drops and vitamin A, are more lubricating than tear drops, and there have been good results on many dry eyes. The disadvantage is their high cost. One drop twice daily is all that is required. They are meant to help promote the increase of tears. It is well worth asking your vet about them.

Entropion

This is a condition of the eyelids, when the rims turn inwards. It is not a condition I have heard affects Shih Tzus. It is considered a hereditary condition and any animal affected should not be bred from. It can be corrected surgically.

Harders gland, or cherry eye

This is a small gland situated in the third eyelid. A large red swelling like a cherry appears in the inner corner of the eye. It does not cause discomfort but is very unsightly and will need to be removed.

Ulcers

The first signs that your dog has an eye ulcer may be that he is obviously in some pain, he may rub his eye, which aggravates the condition. He may close his eye, and feel so miserable and in so much pain that he goes off his food. You may be able to see the ulcer or the eye will have a bluish white tinge covering it.

Ulcers can be due to many things — irritation from some object, injury, ill health and infection. Do not delay in getting him to your vet — if left it will become worse and the dog may end up losing its eye. The vet will put in a dye to test for an ulcer. A shallow ulcer will respond to the correct ointment. If it is a severe, deep ulcer, it may be necessary to have the eye stitched up and left for a week to heal. This will need an anaesthetic. The healed ulcer can leave a white mark on the eye. This is scar tissue. Some people have found the homoeopathic treatment of Silicea 30x has cleared up the scar tissue.

Warts (papillomas)

These are small pimple-like lumps on the eye lid, usually caused by a constitutional problem. Once this is solved, the warts will disappear. If they do not, it may be necessary to have them surgically removed. Homoeopathically, they suggest, after treating the disturbed metabolic equilibrium, to try thuja 6x three times a day — this is said to cure about 50% of warts.

Watery eye syndrome

This is a condition where there are a normal amount of tears secreted but there is inadequate drainage, and they continually overflow. For some reason, there is an obstruction in the lacrimal ducts. These ducts are very tiny and can easily become blocked with a foreign body or even grass seed. There may be congenital absence of ducts or even congenital narrowing. Your vet may be able to flush them out it is certainly worth getting advice.

Flea dermatitis or flea allergy

Many dogs suffer this without the owner realising the dog has been bitten by a flea. The trouble with fleas is that they can stay around a long time unless severely dealt with. That means treating the whole house, all the dog's bedding, etc, and not just the dog. It is wise to consult your vet about this as there are many forms of dermatitis. For a dog who suffers with a flea allergy, just one flea bite is sufficient to cause intense irritation for a long time. Refer to chapter 6 - General Management.

Fungus

Dogs who lie around on damp grass or earth often get little black spots, which are a minute fungus. These stick into the skin in places where there is no coat, especially round the nipples of bitches. To get rid of them, you can either wash with sulphur soap, rub them with a swab wrung out in saline solution (salt and water) or use a cloth wrung out in a mixture of two parts of alcohol to one of chloroform, which you can have made up by a chemist. Two or more applications may be sufficient, with an interval between. I have never heard of them doing any harm.

Grass seeds

Hardly an illness, but it can end up as one. You need to watch your dog carefully during the summer months when the grasses are seeding. Barley is the worst — it is long and spiky. Never cut it down in your garden without clearing it away, or it will dry out and get into your dog's coat. From there, it soon travels upwards lodging itself in soft tissues such as between the pads of the feet, under the arms, in the ears or round the eyes and even up the nose. Once it has got under the skin, it is most difficult to find. It always travels well ahead of the track it leaves. Eventually, an abscess will form. Grass seeds are very dangerous.

Heart disease

I do not hear of many Shih Tzus suffering from this these days. In the past, I did. It is very difficult to tell what the heart condition is. Symptoms do not always show, the dog may be listless and not good at walking. An elderly dog who suffers from heart condition usually has a dry cough. A young dog with a heart 'murmur' may continue to lead a perfectly normal life without any medication, while others may require treatment, which is likely to be for life. Some have died suddenly without the owner ever having known the dog had a heart condition.

Heat stroke

This mostly occurs when dogs have been left in cars in hot weather with insufficient ventilation. It can also occur with dogs shut in small kennels with poor ventilation and insufficient water. It is particularly our flat-faced dogs which are affected. It can also occur at dog shows in over-powering heat. The marquees become very hot and airless. If you are staying outside in the grooming area, you should come provided with a heat blanket. Many people have large sunshades attached to their grooming tables, which is fine so long as consideration is given to other people wishing to see the dogs in the ring.

The symptoms are great distress, rapid panting and drooling. The tongue and lips become very red. The dog rapidly becomes weaker, the temperature rises and the dog collapses and dies if nothing is done.

Treatment: As soon as there are any signs of heat stroke, remove the dog from the area. Cold water should be applied to the skin to get the temperature down. The dog can be immersed in a bath of cold water. The temperature must not be lowered too far as this can damage the brain mechanism. If you have a thermometer, stop when it reaches 102.5 F (39.2C). The cooling off usually continues for a while. Let the dog rest in the cool and watch that the temperature does not start to rise again Prevention is best. Never leave dogs in cars during hot weather. When attending shows during the summer heat, take ice blocks or ice with you and give the dog frequent drinks of ice-cold water. If you do not have ice with you, buy him an ice cream — most dogs love it. If you are able to do so, get the dog to your vet immediately where it can be treated properly. Many dogs have died of heat stroke.

Hair balls

Shih Tzus can suffer quite badly from hair balls, even puppies, who love to pick up bits of fluff and hair in their mouths and swallow them. An accumulation can become a hard mat in the stomach and can cause problems, one of which is a very indifferent appetite. An animal will frequently vomit this horrible wad of mixed hair and other accumulated objects. If it is not too large, it will pass out of the stomach through the intestines.

Treatment: The best thing to do is try to prevent it happening. Keep your animal well groomed so there is less loose hair for it to lick and pull at. Give the dog one teaspoonful of olive oil daily with its food to lubricate and pass objects through the stomach to the intestines. If you know your dog suffers with this, it is worth giving the cat remedy of VRX Petromalt.

Hernias
See Chapter 11 - The First Three Weeks

Hip dysplasia
This is a condition which affects the hip joint. The head of the femur does not fit into a too-shallow socket of the hip joint. This can causes great pain, and lameness in the hind legs. There are varying degrees, and X-ray diagnosis is required for which the dog needs an anaesthetic. I am told that there is a greater incidence of this disease than previously, though I have not personally heard of cases. Not many Shih Tzus have had their hips scored in this country as far as I know, though many do in America.

Hot spots
These are painful raised patches of skin which exude pus. Sometimes it is a secondary infection from a flea bite which has become infected through the dog nibbling or scratching at it. It is also referred to as wet eczema. The hair needs cutting away — it will be lost anyway as it will come away with the scab. This lets the air get to it and makes it easier to clean the sore and treat it. Many remedies have been suggested — the cure really does depend on the cause. Panolog cream (obtainable from the vet) usually clears it up. Sulfadene, obtainable from pet shops, is said to be good. People whose dogs suffer from this usually have their own pet remedy, but what cures one may not work on another.

Kennel cough
This is a very infectious disease as the bacteria are airborne. You can also carry it on your clothes. Although it is not looked upon as serious to adult dogs, it can be very serious when the old or very young catch it. You can inoculate your dog against some of the bacteria which cause it, but like influenza in humans, not all the virus and bacteria have been isolated. Now it appears that clinical signs are changing. It is more of a generalised illness than just the horrible cough. The animals have a high temperature and refuse food. The infection hangs around a lot longer than was previously thought. Bordetella bacteria is found in the respiratory tract of infectious dogs for up to three months after the initial infection. The dog must be kept away from mixing with others, and most definitely must not be taken to shows. Young puppies have died of collapsed bronchial tubes through the coughing.

Treatment: For mild cases, treatment is based on trying to keep the dog from coughing by not letting it get over-excited, preventing exercise and keeping it warm. If the throat is sore, give liquidised foods. The vet may prescribe antibiotics. Cough medicines are sometimes given but do not appear to help much.

Kidney dysplasia or renal cortical hypoplasia
Breeders should be aware of this condition for although there have been very few officially reported cases in England, there have been several unofficial ones of which I have been given notice. In both America and Scandinavia breeders are alerted to it, and it is more openly spoken of and looked out for. It is looked upon as a familial disease; mode of inheritance is still unknown though it has been decided that it is a recessive factor rather than dominant. It is also suggested that the cause could be

environmental, diet and a predisposition to the disease. Stress is another big factor. Little was heard of it before convenience feeding of dry foods became popular; it is most important that dogs fed this way have a supply of water always available from a bowl not a hamster feeder. Unfortunately the symptoms seldom show until after weaning, so it may not be suspected before the puppy is sold.

There may have been early deaths of affected whelps, but few people have these biopsied. The symptoms do not show until 75% of the kidney nephrons are affected. The first signs are excessive drinking, passing large quantities of dilute urine and intermittent loss of appetite. Most animals severely affected die before the age of two. When less severely affected they can live to an older age.

When first signs of excessive drinking are seen, and suspicions are aroused, the urine should be checked and the BUN test — Blood urea nitrogen — and the blood plasma creatinine tested. Before the tests, the animal should be starved of food and water for 12 to 18 hours to be sure of accurate results. If there is an abnormality, it is not necessarily an accurate indication of disease at that given time. Neither of these are proof positive. The only positive proof of this condition is examination of the kidneys, for there are many different kidney diseases and one should not jump to conclusions. X-ray will show up the size of the kidney, which is likely to be shrunken and small. If both are affected, it is presumed that dysplasia is present. When an animal dies young of kidney failure, an autopsy should be performed, though this is seldom done as the owners are too distressed. The kidneys should be placed in ten times the quantity of formalin and sent for identification of this disease.

It is said that a dog requires half an ounce of water per 1lb body weight. For dry feeding when 8-10 weeks old, the normal consumption is 1oz water per 1lb of body weight based on dogs fed commercial dry food in proportion of 1 cup of food to $1/3$ of a cup of water. If the disease is severe the puppy may drink five times that amount.

Lameness
There are many bone diseases which can cause lameness, such as hip dysplasia, slipping hock, luxation of the elbow joint etc. I am told on good authority that more Shih Tzus suffer from luxation of joints than in the past. Few Shih Tzus have their hips scored in England. If there is any doubt, this should be done. It does require an anaesthetic for the X-ray.

Limping is also caused by the hair which grows between the pads of the feet becoming matted up with mud and stones. It can also tangle up around the nails, especially the dew claw, which can cause pain and makes walking most unpleasant. It is best to cut this hair out or at least wash the feet regularly and make sure they are free from mats. It has been found with some dogs who have been taken to their vet because they are limping, that the nails, especially the dew claws, have become so long that they are growing round and into the flesh of the dog. I have even heard of them piercing right through to the other side. Not only must this be terribly painful but is likely to become infected.

Metritis
See chapter 11 — First Three Weeks.

Parvovirus
This is too big and general a subject for me to go into. The conditions are very serious. The dog will have excessive diarrhoea, which will be very offensive. The dog is also likely to be vomiting. You must

contact your vet immediately. The dog will become dehydrated very quickly and must be treated for this with a drip. Separate the infected dog and disinfect all the area where it has been. Get Trigene or some other disinfectant from your vet. Be particularly careful if you have puppies. It is the old and the young which will be worst affected.

Pasteurella infection

This is something which is often overlooked. It goes in cycles of five years and during 1992, a large number of dogs suffered from the infection. It can be picked up from sheep-grazing ground. Show dogs can pick it up from agricultural venues. They can also pass it on to each other by sniffing and licking. Although it is to be found in the nose and throat, it can be transmitted to the vagina and uterus by licking. It can cause eye ulcers and tonsillitis, with secondary infection in the lungs. Bitches can lose their litters and should be treated with a broad spectrum antibiotic such as oxytetracycline, or in case of chest infection, paediatric Panomycin. An immunity is built up but this wears off and they can catch it again during the next cycle.

Pseudomonia

This is another bacteria affecting our dogs in 1992. Like pasteurella, it is spread by contact, and can get into the womb, causing abortion and puppy loss. At the time I am writing this, there is only one antibiotic for this infection — Gentamycin.

Poisons

If you suspect your dog has been poisoned, get on to your vet immediately. Slug bait and Warfarin are both very poisonous and should never be left around where the dog can get hold of them.

The contents of the rubbish bin can be a great attraction to a young mischievous puppy — watch out for them taking old tea bags. They contain caffeine, which will make them very hyperactive. There is no antidote for caffeine. Valium may be needed to quieten them. To make dogs vomit in an emergency, give a small knob of household washing soda.

Pyometra

This is a very serious condition. The first signs are often a very prolonged season. This should always make one suspicious. It is commonest in older bitches. Once it was thought that if a bitch had a litter, it would prevent pyometra. Now it is known that this is not so.

An early birth control injection (promone) caused pyometra, and as soon as this was discovered, it was removed from the market. It is thought to be caused by a hormonal imbalance.

It usually appears one to 12 weeks after a bitch goes out of season.

You can have an open pyometra where the cervix relaxes and large amounts of blood-stained pus come away; or a closed pyometra, in which case the pus stays within the uterus causing painful swelling in the lower abdomen — this is the most serious. Sometimes open pyometra is treated with antibiotics, and it appears to clear up. Sadly, rather than clearing up, it can turn into a closed pyometra. If your bitch has had any sort of infection after her season and has been treated and appears to have cleared up, do not breed from her on the next season, but make quite sure all is clear, for if the condition has turned into a closed pyometra, the bitch is in for trouble. The other signs of pyometra are the bitch refusing to eat. She appears depressed and lethargic and will drink and urinate more than normal.

The treatment for most cases is surgical, and it is far better to have the uterus removed before she has reached this septic state. There is now treatment for young bitches, but not all are suitable for this and it has many painful side-effects which will necessitate her staying at the vet surgery under observation.

Sinus, dermoid

This is something that affects Ridgebacks and, according to an American paper, also Shih Tzus. I have never heard of it affecting any Shih Tzus in this country, but I quote from the Kennel Gazette of October 1993:

'The Dermoid Sinus is an inherited condition in Ridgebacks. It is caused by a defect in the formation of a nerve canal during embryonic development of a puppy. The defect is thought to be inherited as a simple recessive gene'. They go on to say animals affected should be neutered. It is often not detected until the dog is adult. It is a cavity running from the skin down into underlying tissue as a cul-de-sac which fills up with the secretion from the sebaceous glands. If it remains continually open, it can become infected and if it goes down to the spinal cord, it will be very serious, if not fatal. Such dogs should not be bred from.

Maxillary sinus

The most usual of these nasal cavity sinuses, but you can also have frontal and paranasal. They come through from the root of a tooth and out into the cheek where they continually discharge, and do not heal up until the offending tooth has been attended to.

Skin diseases

This is too big and difficult a subject. So many things can cause skin problems. What you can try yourself is to check for allergy. Change the diet completely. Start with rice, then slowly add other food to it, but try each for several days. Also change all your grooming preparations, as they may have something in them which is causing the problem. Try the mildest shampoos, though I have heard of a Shih Tzu who was allergic to Johnsons Baby Shampoo. Don't leave it too long before getting professional advise. Even the vets find this a very hard one to diagnose, so a skin specialist may be your best bet.

Slipped discs

This is a very misleading name for this back problem. The intervertebral discs are in the spine separating and helping to cushion the spinal vertebra. The disc does not actually slip out of place, but its fibrous outer membrane becomes thin and the soft centre escapes, causing great pain, which can lead to paralysis. This mainly occurs either at the neck, the cervical vertebra, or further down the back between the cervical and lumber. When it is in the neck, it is very painful for the dog to lower its head.

This has been the cause of some dogs refusing their food, for it was too painful for them to lower their heads to their dishes. When the dish was raised, the dog could manage to eat. Pain killers are usually given, and the dog needs to be confined for at least two weeks. Steroids and Butazolidin may be given to relieve the inflammation. If you know your dog has this weakness and you see him looking in pain and roaching his back, a good emergency treatment is to apply an ice bag. The sooner the inflammation is down, the quicker the cure.

Acupuncture has been given with success. Surgery is also performed with remarkable success in many cases. But dogs can recover without surgery if they are not seriously affected. However, do get your dog to the vet straight away for early diagnosis and treatment is important.

Slipping patella or patella luxation
The patella is the knee cap, and it is very small and just held in place by ligaments. In some dogs, these are loose and the knee cap slips out. If the joint is loose, you can hear it click. A dog who suffers from this will often walk about three steps then hop or extend its leg to allow the patella to slip back in.

Snorting
I call this very distressing condition by this simple name as I cannot think of another one for it. The dog appears to both snort and choke, making a terrible noise and being unable to get its breath. It is something like an asthma attack. It is often brought on by excitement. If your dog does it frequently and the condition appears to be getting worse, do see your vet for it can be due to many things, such as enlarged tonsils, elongated soft palate, infected teeth which have caused gingivitis and have infected the tonsils. Once the cause has been treated, the dog will get much better. It is not a good thing to have the soft palate shortened, as this can leave the dog worse as food is liable to come down the nose.

When the dog has an attack, the best thing to do is put your finger down his throat, which will relieve any mucus and open up the airways.

Soft palate
An elongated soft palate is to be found in brachycephalic dogs, due to the face having been pushed back. If the dog suffers from this, it is very likely to affect its breathing as it can obstruct the airways. This is particularly noticeable when the dog takes exercise. As I said above, do not have the soft palate cut back unless absolutely necessary, as you can get further problems of food coming down the nose.

Stings
Shih Tzus love to catch anything which flies around. Unfortunately, sometimes it is a wasp or a bee, and they get stung on the lip or more seriously in the mouth or throat, though I am assured by my vet that this seldom happens. However if it does occur, antihistamine drugs should be given, such as adrenaline or even cortisone injections to relieve the swelling. These should be given as soon as possible. Bees leave their sting in and the poison sac is at the bottom of the sting. If you can remove it carefully with the sac intact, that is a great help. The area can be bathed with a concentration of one tablespoon of household bicarbonate of soda in one to two pints of water. This is quite harmless if accidentally swallowed. Ordinary washing soda may be used instead. For wasp stings, you should treat with an acid such as vinegar, or onion is said to be good. Do these treatments for about ten minutes and they can be repeated every further ten minutes until the irritation has subsided. The other likely place to get stung in on the foot. I would give immediate homoeopathic treatment of a tablet of Apis Mel 6x and repeat it within the hour if necessary. This will not affect anything else your vet may prescribe.

Stones

These are most commonly found in the bladder and are unfortunately quite common in Shih Tzus. Some lines are more prone to them than others, but it is thought this breed is predisposed to them. The first signs you may notice are of the bitch or dog passing urine more frequently than normal. Also, it may appear to be taking rather a long time only to pass a tiny puddle, or you may see small blood spots. Other things besides stones can cause these symptoms, such as infection. Your vet will investigate first to eliminate the other possibilities. If it is 'gravel', you may well be able to make a positive diagnosis yourself. Sometimes the tiny stones which are passed adhere to the hair round the vulva or penis. If you see these, collect them and take them to your vet. This is proof positive and will save the necessity for further expensive investigations. An operation to remove them may be advised. Stones will be sent away to the laboratory to find out which kind they are. Struvite are the most common, but there are other kinds. Once an animal has had stones, it is likely to get them again. Hill's Science Diets makes a special diet for dogs suffering with bladder stones, but they need to know which type they are. Certain stones or gravel can be dissolved by the diet, which they remain on for about a month, then continue with the next diet on which they need to stay all their life. This is better than having frequent dangerous operations. These diets are only obtainable from your vet. The homoeopathic theory is that the cause is either constitutional or genetic. If constitutional, they can be treated by first treating the constitutional condition of the animal. Many are caused through a too-alkaline urine, so giving one teaspoonful of apple cider vinegar daily in food or water helps to keep the pH balance slightly acidic and is worth giving as it is said to help in many conditions, such as scratching and keeping away fleas.

Stress

Many people do not give enough thought to stress. Our dogs are subjected to a great deal of stress, which lowers their resistance and leaves their bodies wide open to infection and disease. Puppies and older dogs are under stress at shows, and they should be allowed to rest the following day, not rushed off to another show, particularly bitches. During any stressful times, it helps to give your animal extra vitamin C.

A gram of vitamin C can be given but it may cause a loose bowel so you should start off with a small dose. Puppies are under stress when they go to their new homes, and very likely to have a reaction.

Teeth anormalities

(See Chapter 13 - The Puppy, under *Teeth, jaw and bite.*)

In recent years, there has been a growing awareness of the importance of oral hygiene for dogs as a means of preventing certain dental problems. This subject is large enough to warrant a book in its own right, and there is an increasing amount of literature on the subject. One such publication, *Dog owner's guide to proper dental care*, is available free of charge from:
Nylabone Ltd, PO Box 15, Waterlooville, PO7 6BQ.

Tight nostrils and snufflies

I have written at some length about this in Chapter 12 - Rearing The Litter, under *Snuffly puppies* and Chapter 11 - The First Three Weeks, under *Nostril trouble.*

APPENDIX A

Breed Registrations at the Kennel Club

Year		Year		Year		Year		Year	
1934	39	1951	60	1968	771	1985	1576		
1935	20	1952	53	1969	1037	1986	1532		
1936	31	1953	41	1970	1526	1987	1743		
1937	18	1954	71	1971	1453	1988	1755		
1938	28	1955	80	1972	1441	1989	3896		
1939	47	1956	97	1973	1583	1990	4603		
1940	11	1957	110	1974	1940	1991	4426		
1941	11	1958	132	1975	1613	1992	4320		
1942	7	1959	133	1976	937*	1993	3992		
1943	2	1960	153	1977	716*	1994	4466		
1944	12	1961	226	1978	1380				
1945	3	1962	276	1979	2013				
1946	5	1963	355	1980	1823				
1947	10	1964	447	1981	1528				
1948	28	1965	499	1982	1397				
1949	42	1966	498	1983	1425				
1950	40	1967	540	1984	1531				

*On Active Register

APPENDIX B

Breed Clubs

THE SHIH TZU CLUB
Secretary: Mrs Josephine Johnson, Holmcroft, Brook Road, Bassingbourn, Royston, Herts.
        Tel: Steeple Morden (01763) 852338

THE MANCHU SHIH TZU SOCIETY
Secretary: Mrs V. Goodwin, Collards,Bexon Lane, Bredgar, Sittingbourne, Kent, ME9 8HD.
        Tel: Milstead (0179583) 247

THE SHIH TZU CLUB OF SCOTLAND
Secretary: Mrs J Grugan, Friarside, Clessnock Road, Galston, Ayrshire.
        Tel: Galston 820247

THE NORTHERN COUNTIES SHIH TZU CLUB
Secretary: Mr R Metcalf, Metadale, High Moor Top, Cononley, Nr Keighley, West Yorkshire BD20 8PD.
        Tel: Crosshills (01535) 33934

THE SHIH TZU CLUB OF SOUTH WALES AND WESTERN COUNTIES
Secretary: Mrs D B Harding, Ithaca, Newbury Road, Baydon, nr Marlborough, Wilts.
        Tel: Marlborough (01672) 40929

THE ULSTER SHIH TZU CLUB
Secretary: Mrs Iris Cumming, 10 Crawford Place, Belfast, Northern Ireland. BT6 973.
        Tel: (0232) 799219

APPENDIX C

General Appearance - The Shih Tzu is a sturdy, lively, alert Toy dog with long flowing double coat. Befitting his noble Chinese ancestry as a highly valued, prized companion and palace pet, the Shih Tzu is proud of bearing, has a distinctively arrogant carriage with head well up and tail curved over the back. Although there has always been considerable size variation, the Shih Tzu must be compact, solid, carrying good weight and substance. Even though a Toy dog, the Shih Tzu must be subject to the same requirements of soundness and structure prescribed for all breeds, and any deviation from the ideal described in the standard should be penalized to the extent of the deviation. Structural faults common to all breeds are as undesirable in the Shih Tzu as in any other breed, regardless of whether or not such faults are specifically mentioned in the standard.

Size, proportion, substance - *Size* - Ideally, height at withers is 9 to 10 inches; but, not less than 8 inches nor more than 11 inches. Ideally, weight of mature dogs, 9 to 16 pounds. *Proportion* - Length between withers and root of tail is slightly longer than height at withers. The Shih Tzu must never be so high stationed as to appear leggy, nor so low stationed as to appear dumpy or squatty. *Substance* - Regardless of size, the Shih Tzu is always compact, solid and carries good weight and substance.

Head - *Head* - Round, broad, wide between eyes, its size in balance with the overall size of dog being neither too large nor too small. *Fault:* Narrow head, close-set eyes. *Expression* - Warm, sweet, wide-eyed, friendly and trusting. An overall well-balanced and pleasant expression supersedes the importance of individual parts. Care should be taken to look and examine will beyond the hair to determine if what is seen is the actual head and expression rather than an image created by grooming technique. *Eyes* - Large, round, not prominent, placed well apart, looking straight ahead. Very dark. Lighter on liver pigmented dogs and blue pigmented dogs. *Fault:* Small, close-set or light eyes; excessive eye white. Ears - Large, set slightly below crown of skull; heavily coated. *Skull* - Domed. *Stop* - There is a definite stop. *Muzzle* - Square, short, unwrinkled, with good cushioning, set no lower than bottom eye rim; never downturned. Ideally, no longer than 1 inch from tip of nose to stop although length may vary slightly in relation to overall size of dog. Front of muzzle should be flat; lower lip and chin not protruding and definitely never receding. *Fault:* Snipiness, lack of definite stop. *Nose* - Nostrils are broad, wide, and open. *Pigmentation* - Nose, lips, eye rims are black on all colors, except liver on liver pigmented dogs. *Fault:* Pink on nose, lips or eye rims. *Bite* - Undershot. Jaw is broad and wide. A missing tooth or slightly misaligned teeth should not be too severely penalized. Teeth and tongue should not show when mouth is closed. *Fault:* Overshot bite.

Neck, Topline, Body - Of utmost importance is an overall well-balanced dog with not exaggerated features. *Neck* - Well set-on flowing smoothly into shoulders; of sufficient length to permit natural high head carriage and in balance with height and length of dog. *Topline* - Level. *Body* - Short-coupled and sturdy with no waist or tuck-up. The Shih Tzu is slightly longer than tall. *Fault:* Legginess. *Chest* - Broad and deep with good spring-of-rib, however, not barrel-chested. Depth of ribcage should extend to just below elbow. Distance from elbow to withers is a little greater then from elbow to ground. *Croup* - Flat. *Tail* - Set on high, heavily plumed, carried in curve well over back. Too loose, too tight, too flat, or too low set a tail is undesirable and should be penalized to extent of deviation.

Forequarters - *Shoulders* - Well-angulated, well laid-back, fitting smoothly into body. *Legs* - Straight, well-boned, muscular, set well-apart and under chest, with elbows set close to body. *Pasterns* - Strong, perpendicular. *Dewclaws* - May be removed. *Feet* - Firm, well-padded, point straight ahead.

APPENDIX C

Hindquarters - Angulation of hindquarters should be in balance with forequarters. *Legs* - Well-boned, muscular, and straight when viewed from rear with well-bent stifles, not close set but in line with forequarters. *Hocks* - Well let down, perpendicular. *Fault:* Hyperextension of hocks. *Dewclaws* - May be removed. *Feet* - Firm, well-padded, point straight ahead.

Coat - Luxurious, double-coated, dense, long, and flowing. Slight wave permissible. Hair on top of head is tied up. *Fault:* Sparse coat, single coat, curly coat. *Trimming* - Feet, bottom of coat, and anus may be done for neatness and to facilitate movement. *Fault:* Excessive trimming.

Color and Markings - All are permissible and to be considered equally.

Gait - The Shih Tzu moves straight and must be shown at its own natural speed, neither raced nor strung-up, to evaluate its smooth, effortless movement with good front reach and equally strong rear drive, level topline, naturally high head carriage, and tail carried in gentle curve over back.

Temperament - As the sole purpose of the Shih Tzu is that of a companion and house pet, it is essential that its temperament be outgoing, happy, affectionate, friendly and trusting towards all.

Approved May 9, 1989

APPENDIX D - **WHELPING TABLE**

| Served Jan | 01 | 02 | 03 | 04 | 05 | 06 | 07 | 08 | 09 | 10 | 11 | 12 | 13 | 14 |
| Due to whelp Mar/Apr | 05 | 06 | 07 | 08 | 09 | 10 | 11 | 12 | 13 | 14 | 15 | 16 | 17 | 18 |

| Served Feb | 01 | 02 | 03 | 04 | 05 | 06 | 07 | 08 | 09 | 10 | 11 | 12 | 13 | 14 |
| Due to whelp Apr/May | 05 | 06 | 07 | 08 | 09 | 10 | 11 | 12 | 13 | 14 | 15 | 16 | 17 | 18 |

| Served Mar | 01 | 02 | 03 | 04 | 05 | 06 | 07 | 08 | 09 | 10 | 11 | 12 | 13 | 14 |
| Due to whelp May/Jun | 03 | 04 | 05 | 06 | 07 | 08 | 09 | 10 | 11 | 12 | 13 | 14 | 15 | 16 |

| Served April | 01 | 02 | 03 | 04 | 05 | 06 | 07 | 08 | 09 | 10 | 11 | 12 | 13 | 14 |
| Due to whelp Jun/Jul | 03 | 04 | 05 | 06 | 07 | 08 | 09 | 10 | 11 | 12 | 13 | 14 | 15 | 16 |

| Served May | 01 | 02 | 03 | 04 | 05 | 06 | 07 | 08 | 09 | 10 | 11 | 12 | 13 | 14 |
| Due to whelp Jul/Aug | 03 | 04 | 05 | 06 | 07 | 08 | 09 | 10 | 11 | 12 | 13 | 14 | 15 | 16 |

| Served Jun | 01 | 02 | 03 | 04 | 05 | 06 | 07 | 08 | 09 | 10 | 11 | 12 | 13 | 14 |
| Due to whelp Aug/Sep | 03 | 04 | 05 | 06 | 07 | 08 | 09 | 10 | 11 | 12 | 13 | 14 | 15 | 16 |

| Served Jul | 01 | 02 | 03 | 04 | 05 | 06 | 07 | 08 | 09 | 10 | 11 | 12 | 13 | 14 |
| Due to whelp Sept/Oct | 02 | 03 | 04 | 05 | 06 | 07 | 08 | 09 | 10 | 11 | 12 | 13 | 14 | 15 |

| Served Aug | 01 | 02 | 03 | 04 | 05 | 06 | 07 | 08 | 09 | 10 | 11 | 12 | 13 | 14 |
| Due to whelp Oct/Nov | 03 | 04 | 05 | 06 | 07 | 08 | 09 | 10 | 11 | 12 | 13 | 14 | 15 | 16 |

| Served Sep | 01 | 02 | 03 | 04 | 05 | 06 | 07 | 08 | 09 | 10 | 11 | 12 | 13 | 14 |
| Due to whelp Nov/Dec | 03 | 04 | 05 | 06 | 07 | 08 | 09 | 10 | 11 | 12 | 13 | 14 | 15 | 16 |

| Served Oct | 01 | 02 | 03 | 04 | 05 | 06 | 07 | 08 | 09 | 10 | 11 | 12 | 13 | 14 |
| Due to whelp Dec/Jan | 03 | 04 | 05 | 06 | 07 | 08 | 09 | 10 | 11 | 12 | 13 | 14 | 15 | 16 |

| Served Nov | 01 | 02 | 03 | 04 | 05 | 06 | 07 | 08 | 09 | 10 | 11 | 12 | 13 | 14 |
| Due to whelp Jan/Feb | 03 | 04 | 05 | 06 | 07 | 08 | 09 | 10 | 11 | 12 | 13 | 14 | 15 | 16 |

| Served Dec | 01 | 02 | 03 | 04 | 05 | 06 | 07 | 08 | 09 | 10 | 11 | 12 | 13 | 14 |
| Due to whelp Feb/Mar | 02 | 03 | 04 | 05 | 06 | 07 | 08 | 09 | 10 | 11 | 12 | 13 | 14 | 15 |

APPENDIX D - **WHELPING TABLE**

15	16	17	18	19	20	21	22	23	24	25	26	27	28	29	30	31
19	20	21	22	23	24	25	26	27	28	29	30	31	01	02	03	04

15	16	17	18	19	20	21	22	23	24	25	26	27	28	(29)
19	20	21	22	23	24	25	26	27	28	29	30	01	02	(03)

15	16	17	18	19	20	21	22	23	24	25	26	27	28	29	30	31
17	18	19	20	21	22	23	24	25	26	27	28	29	30	31	01	02

15	16	17	18	19	20	21	22	23	24	25	26	27	28	29	30
17	18	19	20	21	22	23	24	25	26	27	28	29	30	01	02

15	16	17	18	19	20	21	22	23	24	25	26	27	28	29	30	31
17	18	19	20	21	22	23	24	25	26	27	28	29	30	31	01	02

15	16	17	18	19	20	21	22	23	24	25	26	27	28	29	30
17	18	19	20	21	22	23	24	25	26	27	28	29	30	31	01

15	16	17	18	19	20	21	22	23	24	25	26	27	28	29	30	31
16	17	18	19	20	21	22	23	24	25	26	27	28	29	30	01	02

15	16	17	18	19	20	21	22	23	24	25	26	27	28	29	30	31
17	18	19	20	21	22	23	24	25	26	27	28	29	30	31	01	02

15	16	17	18	19	20	21	22	23	24	25	26	27	28	29	30
17	18	19	20	21	22	23	24	25	26	27	28	29	30	01	02

15	16	17	18	19	20	21	22	23	24	25	26	27	28	29	30	31
17	18	19	20	21	22	23	24	25	26	27	28	29	30	31	01	02

15	16	17	18	19	20	21	22	23	24	25	26	27	28	29	30
17	18	19	20	21	22	23	24	25	26	27	28	29	30	31	01

15	16	17	18	19	20	21	22	23	24	25	26	27	28	29	30	31
16	17	18	19	20	21	22	23	24	25	26	27	28	01	02	03	

APPENDIX E

Name	Sex	D.O.B.	Sire	Dam	Breeder	Owner
TA CHI OF TAISHAN	B	05 06 45	SUI YAN	MADAM KO OF TAISHAN	Lady Brownrigg	Breeder
YU MO CHUANG OF BOYDON	D	01 08 39	YANGTSE OF TAISHAN	HSUEH LI CHAN OF TAISHAN	Mrs. H. Moulton	Lady Brownrigg
1950						
CHOO LING	D	30 05 44	SANUS CHING-A-BOO	SING-PU	Gen. Telfer-Smollet	Lady Brownrigg
1951						
MAO-MAO OF LHAKANG	B	13 06 48	LYEMUN OF TAISHAN	MEE-NA OF TAISHAN	Mrs. G. Widdington	Breeder
SHEBO TSEMO OF LHAKANG	D	29 04 48	PU OF OULTON	LINDI LU OF LHAKANG	Mrs Widdington	Mrs. S. Bode
SING TZU OF SHEBO	B	11 10 47	CH. CHOO LING	SING HI	Mrs. G. Garforth-Bles	Mrs. S. Bode
1952						
HONG OF HUNGJAO	D	10 12 46	PU OF OULTON	SING-PU	Gen. Telfer-Smollet	Mrs. M. B. Eaden
PA-KO OF TAISHAN	B	06 04 50	CH. YU MO CHUANG OF BOYDON	CH. SING TSU OF SHEBO	Mrs. S. Bode	Lady Brownrigg
1953						
LING-FU OF SHUANGHSI	B	16 02 51	LYEMUN OF TAISHAN	WU-LING OF SHUANGHSI	Mrs. J. Hopkinson	Mr. & Mrs. K. B. Rawlings
TENSING OF LHAKANG	D	23 07 52	CH. YO MO CHUANG OF BOYDON	CH. MAO-MAO OF LHAKANG	Mrs. G. Widdington	Mr. & Mrs. K. B. Rawlings
1955						
MAYA WONG OF LHAKANG	B	23 07 52	CH. YU MO CHUANG OF BOYDON	CH. MAO MAO OF LHAKANG	Mrs. G. Widdington	Breeder
WANG-POO OF TAISHAN	D	29 02 52	CH. CHOO LING	CH. PA-KO OF TAISHAN	Lady Brownrigg	Breeder
1956						
LILY-WU OF LHAKANG	B	23 07 52	CH. YU MO CHUANG OF BOYDON	CH. MAO-MAO OF LHAKANG	Mrs. G. Widdington	Mr. & Mrs. K. B. Rawlings
YI TING MO OF ANTARCTICA	D	11 03 53	CH. SHEBO TSEMO OF LHAKANG	TANG OF OULTON	Mr. & Mrs. K. B. Rawlings	Breeders
1957						
SHU-SSA OF MICHELCOMBE	B	11 05 54	CH. SHEBO TSEMO OF LHAKANG	CHUANNE TU OF ELFANN	Miss O. Nichols	Mrs. R. A. Clarke
YANO OKIMA OF ANTARCTICA	D	28 03 55	PERKY CHING OF THE MYND	CH. SING TZU OF SHEBO	Mr. & Mrs. K. B. Rawlings	Breeders
1958						
ELFANN TA-TO OF LHAKANG	B	13 02 52	YENMO OF LHAKANG	CHENMO OF LHAKANG	Mrs. Mather	Mrs. Murray-Kerr
SHU-SHE YU OF LHAKANG	B	23 07 52	CH. YU MO CHUANG OF BOYDON	CH. MAO-MAO OF LHAKANG	Mrs. G. Widdington	Mrs. Haycock
SINDI-LU OF ANTARCTICA	B	02 10 56	CH. YI TING MO OF ANTARCTICA	CHAO MENG-FU OF ANTARCTICA	Mrs. A. L. Dadds	Mr. & Mrs. K. B. Rawlings
1959						
CHOO CHOO AT CATHAY	D	30 05 57	WEN SHU OF LHAKANG	TA LE SHIH OF TAWNYRIDGE	Mrs. J. Ross	Mrs. A. O. Grindey
1960						
SHEBO WEN YIN OF LHAKANG	D	07 06 57	WEN SHU OF LHAKANG	CH. MAYA WONG OF LHAKANG	Mrs. G. Widdington	Mrs. S. Bode
SUKI OF MAVESYN	B	28 05 57	CH. YI TING MO OF ANTARCTICA	YET MING OF MAVESYN	Mrs. M. Cope	Mr. & Mrs. K. B. Rawlings
TIEN MEMSAHIB	B	16 06 56	BIMBO	MU HO	Mrs. T. Morgan	Mrs. G. Widdington
TZU-AN OF LHAKANG	B	12 06 58	JO-JO OF LHAKANG	MEI-HUA OF LHAKANG	Mrs. F. M. Bunk	Mrs. A. O. Grindey
1961						

Name	Sex	Date	Sire	Dam		
CLYSTVALE KARI OF SNOWLAND	D	27 08 59	KHAN JANMAYEN	TZU HSI OF CLYSTVALE	Mrs. A. L. Westcott	Miss E. Clark
JOU-LI OF LHAKANG	B	11 05 55	BIMBO	CH. MAYA WONG OF LHAKANG	Mrs. G. Widdington	Mr. P. Beeley
KUAN TI OF ANTARCTICA	D	27 02 57	CH. YI TING MO OF ANTARCTICA	CH. LING-FU OF SHUANGHSI	Mr. & Mrs. K. B. Rawlings	Breeders
1962						
ELLINGHAM KALA NAG	D	20 07 59	TACKLA SAHIB OF LHAKANG	DARZEE OF CLYSTVALE	Lady Haggerston	Mrs. J. Lovely
PAN WAO CHEN OF ANTARCTICA	D	18 05 60	CH. YI TING MO OF ANTARCTICA	DAN GAU OF SHANGHOO	Mrs. St. John Gore	Mr. & Mrs. K. B. Rawlings
1963						
LI CHING KU OF SNAEFELL	D	04 02 60	YIBBIN OF ANTARCTICA	MISSEE LEE OF SNAEFELL	Mrs. A. L. Dadds	Breeder
SU SI OF SNAEFELL	B	28 10 59	TZU-HANG OF SNAEFELL	CHUNG OF SNAEFELL	Mrs. A. Dadds	Breeder
SUMI SAN OF DARLI	B	26 02 59	LUND HOUSE PONG	CORAL OF AIRLEA	Miss S. Gill	Mr. & Mrs. W. Jobson
TERESA OF TINKERTOWN	B	13 01 62	CH. KUAN TI OF ANTARCTICA	AN MEI OF LHAKANG	Mr. P. Beeley	Mrs. Balmforth
1964						
MEI SAKI OF GREENMOSS	B	05 01 63	GREENMOSS YU LI CHING OF WYNDTOI	SASHA MING OF WYNDTOI	Mrs. E. Roberts	Mr. & Mrs. A. Leadbitter
SHANG WU OF ANTARCTICA	B	12 05 63	CH. PAN WAO CHEN OF ANTARCTICA	CHIA OF ANTARCTICA	Mr. & Mrs. K. B. Rawlings	Mr. J. Moody
SHIRAZ OF ELLINGHAM	B	17 05 60	TACKLA SAHIB OF LHAKANG	MICHELCOMBE CRYSTAL OF CLYSTVALE	Lady Haggerston	Miss E. M. Evans
SOONG OF LHAKANG	B	01 11 61	CHUANGSTE OF LHAKANG	CHING YO OF ELFANN	Mrs. G. Widdington	Breeder
SUSIE WONG OF ANTARCTICA	B	10 11 59	SHEBO WEN YIN OF LHAKANG	CH. SUKI OF MAVESYN	Mr. & Mrs. K. B. Rawlings	Breeders
TALIFU FU HI	D	11 01 62	LHAKANG LI-SHAN OF ELFANN	LOTUS BUD OF RICKSOO	Mr. & Mrs. C. Boot	Breeders
1965						
CATHAY NICHOLAS OF KASHMOOR	D	15 08 62	PAN PIPES FENG-YA	KANDY OF KASHMOOR	Mrs. Ross	Mrs. A. O. Grindey
CHI-MA-CHE OF ANTARCTICA	D	23 05 61	JUNGFALTETS JUNG MING	ELFANN TARA OF CLYSTVALE	Mrs. M. Longden	Mr. & Mrs. K. B. Rawlings
DOMESE OF TELOTA	B	26 10 63	CH. TENSING OF SHANRETA	SIEW SING OF PAGODALAND	Mrs. Preedy	Mrs. O. Newson
TALIFU BOSSY BOOTS	D	23 01 63	CH. TALIFU FU HI	LOTUS BUD OF RICKSOO	Mr. & Mrs. C. Boot	Breeders
TENSING OF SHANRETA	D	17 11 62	TENSING TU OF TELOTA	NECTARINE OF LOCHNAGER	Mr. & Mrs. J. R. Smith	Breeders
1966						
DOTT OF GORSEYCOP	B	01 09 63	SNAEFELL HUCKLEBERRY FINN	SUKIE TONG OF DAPPERLEE	Mrs. Bennett	Mrs. M. Hoare
GREENMOSS CHIN KI OF MEO	D	18 01 62	CHOO T'SUN OF TELOTA	ELFANN MAYA WEN OF RICKSOO	Mrs. V. Reynolds	Mr. & Mrs. A. Leadbitter
KATRINA OF GREENMOSS	B	09 09 65	CH. GREENMOSS CHIN KI OF MEO	MEI LU LU OF WYNDTOI	Mr. & Mrs. A. Leadbitter	Breeders
KUANG KUANG OF ANTARCTICA	D	03 09 62	CH. CHI-MA-CHE OF ANTARCTICA	SING-TZU OF ANTARCTICA	Mr. & Mrs. K. B. Rawlings	Breeders
LING FU OF ANTARCTICA	B	17 05 64	LONGLANE TELSTAR	DOMUS YANDA	Miss E. L. Bennett	Mr. & Mrs. K. B. Rawlings
1967						
ANTARCTICA CHAN SHIH OF DARITE	D	07 08 65	CH. CHI-MA-CHE OF ANTARCTICA	FU CHI OF DARITE	Mrs. Copplestone	Mr. & Mrs. K. B. Rawlings
QUAN-SHU OF EDSVILLE	D	27 12 63	GREENMOSS YU-LI-CHING OF WYNDTOI	SHANG TSI OF MANJUARI	Mr. E. Openshaw	Breeder
SUSELLA OF BANWEE	B	22 07 65	SYCHIM OF BANWEE	MING LU OF SHANRETA	Mesdames Tomlinson & Godson	Mrs. T. E. Morgan
1968						

Name	Sex	D.O.B.	Sire	Dam	Breeder	Owner
AH HSEUH LI-CHAN OF CATHAY	D	14 04 64	CATHAY NICHOLAS OF KASHMOOR	KIN PO OF CLYSTVALE	Mrs. A. O. Grindey	Breeder
FLEETING YU SING OF ANTARCTICA	D	19 08 65	CH. PAN WAO CHEN OF ANTARCTICA	FLEETING BANWEE MING	Mrs. M. Garrish	Mr. & Mrs. K. B. Rawlings
GOLDEN PEREGRINE OF ELFANN	D	20 02 66	SING HI OF LHAKANG	GOLDEN BOBBIN OF ELFANN	Miss E. M. Evans	Mr. & Mrs. A. Leadbitter
LOCHRANZA CHOO-LING OF CATHAY	B	16 05 66	CH. CATHAY NICHOLAS OF KASHMOOR	LOCHRANZA LOLITA OF BARUSANN	Misses MacMillan & Coull	Mrs. O. Grindey
1969						
CHERHOLMES SINGING LADY OF WYSARGE	B	04 05 66	GREENMOSS YU-LI-CHING OF WYNDTOI	CHERHOLMES BUCKDENE KIN YIN HWA	Mrs. Reithermann	Mrs. M. Coppage
YUH CHIN WONG	B	01 04 65	TENSING TU OF TELOTA	TIGER LILY OF MYARLUNE	Mr. C. Howe	Breeder
1970						
CHA-SAKI OF ANTARCTICA	B	16 04 68	CH. ANTARCTICA CHAN SHIH OF DARITE	GINA OF ANTARCTICA	Mr. & Mrs. K. B. Rawlings	Breeder
CHE KO OF ANTARCTICA	B	10 04 67	CH. ANTARCTICA CHAN SHIH OF DARITE	CH. SHANG WU OF ANTARCTICA	Mr. & Mrs. K. B. Rawlings	Breeders
DOMINIC OF TELOTA	D	02 07 68	CH. ANTARCTICA CHAN SHIH OF DARITE	CH. DOMESE OF TELOTA	Mrs. O. Newson	Breeder
GREENMOSS GOLDEN SUNBEAM OF ELFANN	B	26 04 68	INT. CH. GOLDEN PEREGRINE OF ELFANN	ELFANN SUNSHINE OF GREENMOSS	Miss E. M. Evans	Mr. & Mrs. A. Leadbitter
JEN KAI KO OF LHAKANG	D	03 03 67	SING HI OF LHAKANG	JESSAME OF LHAKANG	Mrs. G. Widdington	Mrs. E. Fox
SUE LING OF BRIDGEND	B	08 12 68	GREENMOSS CHIN KI OF MEO	TRICINA KYLIN	Mr. & Mrs. E. Carter	Breeders
YA TUNG OF ANTARCTICA	D	01 05 69	CH. FLEETING YU SING OF ANTARCTICA	SUSANAH OF ANTARCTICA	Mr. & Mrs. K. B. Rawlings	Breeders
1971						
ANTARCTICA DON JUAN OF TELOTA	D	16 02 69	CH. FLEETING YU SING OF ANTARCTICA	CH. DOMESE OF TELOTA	Mrs. O. Newson	Mr. & Mrs. K. B. Rawlings
CHIN LING OF GREENMOSS	D	01 09 68	CH. GREENMOSS CHIN KI OF MEO	HSIANG CHIEH OF LIDDESDALE	Mrs. J. Mangles	Mr. & Mrs. A. Leadbitter
FEI YING OF GREENMOSS	B	25 01 69	INT. CH. GOLDEN PEREGRINE OF ELFANN	BROWNHILLS YU HONEY	Mrs. & Mrs. A. Leadbitter	Breeders
KO KO SAKI OF GREENMOSS	B	06 07 69	CH. JEN KAI KO OF LHAKANG	CH. MEI SAKI OF GREENMOSS	Mr. & Mrs. A. Leadbitter	Breeders
TRICINA WEN MO OF BRIDGEND	B	08 12 68	CH. GREENMOSS CHIN KI OF MEO	TRICINA KY LIN	Mr. & Mrs. E. Carter	Breeders
1972						
BOWSTONES SHAPUR OF CATHAY	D	21 06 69	CH. CATHAY NICHOLAS OF KASHMOOR	BOWSTONES KO KO	Mrs. I. Booth	Mrs. A. O. Grindey
CHERHOLMES GOLDEN SAMANTHA	B	20 03 68	INT. CH. GOLDEN PEREGRINE OF ELFANN	INT. CH. CHERHOLMES DEBUTANTE	Mrs. Reithermann	Breeder
KUIRE HERMES OF ANTARCTICA	D	24 02 71	CH. YA TUNG OF ANTARCTICA	DUCHESS OF TELOTA	Mrs. R. D. Johnson	Mr. & Mrs. K. B. Rawlings
MU T'ANG OF ANTARCTICA	B	02 05 70	CHOO YAU FONG OF ANTARCTICA	ANTARCTICA CHAN SOPHIE OF AKABEN	Mr. & Mrs. K. B. Rawlings	Breeders
1973						
NEWROOTS NANKIPOO OF SNAEFELL	D	04 12 70	CH. GREENMOSS CHIN KI OF MEO	HO YAN OF NEWROOTS	Misses D. Fenner & E. Thomas	Mrs. A. Dadds
WHITETHROATS CHINESE GEM	B	11 06 70	CH. JEN KAI KO OF LHAKANG	WHITETHROAT MEI LING	Mrs. E. Fox	Breeder
ZEUS OF BRIDGEND	D	08 12 68	CH. GREENMOSS CHIN KI OF MEO	TRICINA KYLIN	Mr. & Mrs. E. Carter	Mrs. Thornton
ANTARCTICA TA T'UNG FU	B	15 10 70	CH. YA TUNG OF ANTARCTICA	CHIH SHIH OF ANTARCTICA	Miss K. Willeby	Mr. & Mrs. K. B. Rawlings
GREENMOSS SOKET TUMI	D	05 03 71	CH. GREENMOSS CHIN KI OF MEO	CH. GREENMOSS GOLDEN SUNBEAM OF ELFANN	Mr. & Mrs. A. Leadbitter	Breeders

Name	Sex	Date	Sire	Dam	Owner	Breeder
KEYTOR SWEET CHARITY	B	17 11 71	CH. GREENMOSS CHIN KI OF MEO	KEYTOR SUKEE SUE OF HYNING	Mrs. E. M. Johnson	Breeder
KUSHI PALHI OF SHASHEEN	B	24 11 70	CH. CHIN LING OF GREENMOSS	SHAWALA KULA	Miss D. Bridge	Mrs. M. Turnbull
SANTOSHA RAMBLING ROSE	B	06 07 70	CH. CHIN LING OF GREENMOSS	MARNIE OF MYARLUNE	Mr. & Mrs. D. Crossley	Mr. & Mrs. V. Wilkinson
SARAWANA CHIU MEI OF TAONAN	B	23 08 68	CH. GREENMOSS CHIN KI OF MEO	SARAWANA BUCKDENE MITSUKO	Mrs. I. E. & Miss S. M. Wigglesworth	Mrs. D. B. Harding
SIMONE OF SANDOWN	B	19 04 70	BUDA BUDA OF RAWSTOCK	SAN YEN OF SANDOWN	Mrs. W. E. Donaldson	Mr. B. Halton
WYSARGE CHIN KI TUO OF GREENMOSS	D	20 06 69	GREENMOSS CHIN KI OF MEO	FRANWIL KIKI DEE	Mr. & Mrs. A. Leadbitter	Mrs. E. M. Johnson

1974

Name	Sex	Date	Sire	Dam	Owner	Breeder
GOLDEN SUMMERTIME OF ELFANN	B	23 06 69	CH. GREENMOSS CHIN KI OF MEO	GOLDEN BOBBIN OF ELFANN	Miss E. M. Evans	Mr. T. Hoyle
GREENMOSS GLORY BEE	D	07 07 71	INT. CH. GREENMOSS GOLDEN GAYLORD OF ELFANN	GREENMOSS CHANTILLY LACE	Mr. & Mrs A. Leadbitter	Breeders
KEYTOR MIDAS	D	28 11 71	CH. CHIN LING OF GREENMOSS	MARIETTA OF SHASHEEN	Mrs. E. M. Johnson	Breeder
PATSY DO OF HYNING	B	17 08 71	CH. CHIN LING OF GREENMOSS	LINDY LOU OF HYNING	Mrs. M. Rowling	Mr. & Mrs. T. Richardson
SAMPA KE-KE-RU ZIMBA OF SHASHEEN	D	03 03 72	GREENMOSS SAKIS LEGACY	SHAWLA KULA	Miss D. Bridge	Mrs. M. Turnbull

1975

Name	Sex	Date	Sire	Dam	Owner	Breeder
SCHERZO OF SHIMISU	D	12 09 71	CH. FLEETING YU SING OF ANTARCTICA	PILTDOWN POPINJAY	Miss K. Willeby	Miss M. Cole
SU TUNG PO OF ANTARCTICA	B	12 09 71	CH. YA TUNG OF ANTARCTICA	LU CHE OF GORSEYCOP	Miss K. Willeby	Mr. & Mrs. K. B. Rawlings
TRICINA TAI HAKU	D	24 05 72	ELFANN GOLDEN SUNRISE OF TRICINA	TRICINA KYLIN	Mr. & Mrs. E. Carter	Miss J. Papps
ELFANN GOLDEN POSY OF LANSU	B	09 01 72	CH. ZEUS OF BRIDGEND	CHIN-EE-LEE OF ELFANN	Mrs. E. M. Evans	Mr. T. Hoyle
GOLDEN HEIDI OF ELFANN	B	26 04 68	INT. CH. GOLDEN PEREGRINE OF ELFANN	ELFANN SUNSHINE OF GREENMOSS	Miss E. M. Evans	Mr. T. Hoyle
KARETH KRISHNA	B	07 11 72	CH. WYSARGE CHINKI TUO OF GREENMOSS	KHUMAR TOFFEE ROYAL	Mr. J. Peat	Breeder
MERRYGARTH MAI-SUZI	B	01 02 73	CH. KUIRE HERMES OF ANTARCTICA	TELOTA DOMINI	Mr. & Mrs. R. Atwill	Breeders
SANDOWN YOLANDE	B	20 10 70	CH. CHIN LING OF GREENMOSS	YEN-TING OF GRANDAVON	Mrs. W. Donaldson	Mr. B. Halton
WHITETHROAT SUNA OF BERINSHILL	D	05 04 74	LHAKANG PAN FROM WHITETHROAT	WHITETHROAT PRECIOUS JADE	Mrs. E. Fox	Mesdames Waugh & Boyle

1976

Name	Sex	Date	Sire	Dam	Owner	Breeder
CROWVALLEY TWEEDLEDUM	D	13 10 73	ELFANN GOLDEN SUNRISE OF TRICINA	CROWVALLEY YAMEETO	Mr. & Mrs. L Williams	Breeders
GORSEYCOP TURNIP TOP	D	11 10 74	CH. DOMINIC OF TELOTA	GORSEYCOP ARAMINTA	Mrs. M. Hoare	Breeder
GREENMOSS CHINKI'S FLING	D	17 05 74	CH. GREENMOSS CHIN KI OF MEO	CH. KO KO SAKI OF GREENMOSS	Mr. & Mrs. A. Leadbitter	Breeders
GREENMOSS GIDEON	D	08 12 70	TAN TAN OF LHAKANG	HONEY BEE OF LHAKANG	Mrs. I. Duncan	Mr. K. Thompson
HARTEND DILL	D	12 03 72	LANSU EASTERTIME OF ELANZO	HARTEND AMANDA	Misses Overend & Hartham	Mrs. G. Moston
KHUMAR CHINA SILK OF DARRALLS	B	24 04 73	TOMTRU OF LHAKANG	KHUMAR KOBWEB	Mrs. J. Edwards	Mrs. D. C. Gurney
MERRYGARTH KAN DO OF CATHAY	D	17 09 74	CH. SCHERZO OF SCHIMISU	TELOTA DOMINI	Mr. & Mrs. R. Atwill	Mrs. O. Grindey
SANDI QUAI LU OF ANTARCTICA	D	08 07 73	CH. KUIRE HERMES OF ANTARCTICA	YAR-MIN T'SING	Mrs. J. Broadbent	Mr. & Mrs. K. B. Rawlings
SHASHEEN LORELEI	B	11 10 71	GREENMOSS SAKI'S LEGACY	SHASHEEN BROWNRIDGE LADY ROSEMARY	Mrs. M. Turnbull	Breeder

Name	Sex	D.O.B.	Sire	Dam	Breeder	Owner
WHITETHROAT LITTLE MISSEE	B	10 06 73	CH. TRICINA TAI HAKU	WHITETHROAT LOTUS BUD	Mrs. E. Fox	Breeder
1977						
JAMART KI MING	D	15 04 72	CH. ANTARCTICA DON JUAN OF TELOTA	ANTARCTICA TENG T'UNG	Mrs. M. L. K. Fourt	Breeder
JULING MINGS GOLDEN SLIPPER	B	02 06 72	CHERHOLMES DIPPERTY-DO	MING YEN OF LIDDESDALE	Mrs. W. Elder	Mrs. R. Barlow
KHUMAR KISS ME KATE	B	16 04 74	NEWROOTS NANKIPOO OF SNAEFELL	KHUMAR KISMET	Mrs. J. Edwards	Breeder
MONTZELLA'S TSI CHOU	D	11 06 72	CH. DOMINIC OF TELOTA	SHU-SHU-MING OF MONTZELLA	Mr. & Mrs. J. Carter	Breeders
PENSMOOR JADE PRINCE	D	07 11 73	CH. DOMINIC OF TELOTA	MANDU ANNETTE	Mrs. P. Younger	Breeder
UNISTEV MEI WAY	B	23 04 74	CH. GREENMOSS GLORY BEE	CH. SIMONE OF SANDOWN	Mr. B. Halton	Breeder
1978						
BELLAKERNE INCA DO	B	30 10 75	HYNING YES SIR	CH. PATSY DO OF HYNING	Mr. & Mrs. T. Richardson	Breeders
BELLAKERNE SUKI SUE	B	12 07 75	CROWVALLEY YENISIE	BELLAKERNE BUTTON	Mr. & Mrs. T. Richardson	Breeders
BELLAKERNE ZIPPITY DO	D	30 10 75	HYNING YES SIR	CH. PATSY DO OF HYNING	Mr. & Mrs. T. Richardson	Breeders
BOWSTONES CROWVALLEY SHAN TUNG	B	12 01 76	CH. YA TUNG OF ANTARCTICA	CROWVALLEY YAMEETO	Mr. & Mrs. L. Williams	Mrs. I. Booth
BOWSTONES MEENA OF ATTOCYL	B	06 08 74	HYNING GOTCHA OF GREENMOSS	BOWSTONES CHETSUNG OF ANTARCTICA	Mrs. I. Booth	Mrs. M. Kaye
CROWVALLEY POSEIDON	D	31 08 76	CH. CROWVALLEY TWEEDLEDUM	AUST. CH. CROWVALLEY MINERVA	Mr. & Mrs. L. Williams	Breeders
LANSU FRAGRANT CLOUD	B	31 07 75	ELANZO GOLD DIGGER	CH. ELFANN GOLDEN POSY OF LANSU	Mr. T. Hoyle	Mrs. S. Hoyle (Rawlings)
LINGCHEE JAY TUNG	D	20 12 76	TELOTA LEE TUNG SOO	SHESTABYE SAKOTA	Mrs. G. Ling	Breeder
MERIADOC KAHEDIN	D	08 04 74	CH. DOMINIC OF TELOTA	MEADOWBLUE MARY POPPINS	Miss J. Wray	Breeder
SANTOSHA BEWITCHED	B	21 07 75	TOMTRU OF LHAKANG	SANTOSHA DOUBLE DIMPLE	Mr. & Mrs. D. Crossley	Breeders
SHOU SHANG OF ANTARCTICA	B	12 10 75	CH. KUIRE HERMES OF ANTARCTICA	CH. ANTARCTICA TA T'UNG FU	Mr. & Mrs. K. B. Rawlings	Breeders
TRISULA CHIOH KOH OF ANTARCTICA	B	07 07 75	SUI YANG TI OF ANTARCTICA	SPRING MAGIC OF TRISULA	Mrs. B. Todd	Breeder
1979						
FISHPONDS SOO SZE	B	15 09 75	FISHPONDS SAN YEN	FISHPONDS SHENG YIN	Mrs. E. Coulson & Mrs. B. Carey	Breeders
GREENMOSS BEE IN A BONNET	B	12 02 77	CH. GREENMOSS GLORY BEE	WYSARGE JADE LOTUS BUD	Mr. & Mrs. A Leadbitter	Breeders
KADWEN YAN TSI	D	25 02 73	TRICINA CHI FU	KADWEN FU PAN CH'AO	Mrs. E. Sellers	Mrs. M. Devine
PHILWEN MI BOI OF ANTARCTICA	D	14 03 75	CH. SANDI QUAI LU OF ANTARCTICA	SI-TSUNG OF ANTARCTICA	Mr. & Mrs. Behan	Mr. & Mrs. K. B. Rawlings
SANTOSHA SUNDOWN	B	28 08 77	ELFANN GOLDEN SUNRISE OF TRICINA	SANTOSHA GENEVIEVE	Mr. & Mrs. D. Crossley	Breeders
SHIRWEN HAN-SUM-BEE	D	03 07 76	JULINGS MING HAN-SUM-SUN	SUSIE BEE OF GREENMOSS	Mr. & Mrs. R. Lewis	Breeders
TELOTA ANOUSKA	B	17 03 76	TELOTA DOMINGA	TELOTA DOMDARSCHE	Mrs. O. Newson	Mrs. D. & Mr. M. Harper
1980						
BUTTONS OF SNAEFELL	D	21 11 75	CH. ZEUS OF BRIDGEND	SNAEFELL FLAME	Mrs. I. May	Mrs. A. Dadds
CROWVALLEY PEGASUS	D	21 11 77	INT. CH. CROWVALLEY POSEIDEN	TRICINA KAY	Mr. & Mrs. L. Williams	Breeders
DARRALLS FELICITY	B	24 06 80	CH. YA TUNG OF ANTARCTICA	CH. KHUMAR CHINA SILK OF DARRALL	Mrs. D. C. Gurney	Breeder
DELRIDGE GOLDEN GEMINI AT CROWVALLEY	D	05 03 79	CH. CROWVALLEY PEGASUS	DELRIDGE KWAN YIN	Mesdames Budd & Wilson	Mr. & Mrs. L Williams & Mrs. E. Wilson

Name	Sex	Date	Sire	Dam		Breeders
GREENMOSS BEES KNEES	D	27 11 78	CH. GREENMOSS GLORY BEE	WYSARGE JADE LOTUS BUD	Mr. & Mrs. A. Leadbitter	Breeders
JAIVONNE GLIMMER OF HOPE	B	10 03 76	CHERHOLMES REGAL SPLENDOUR	WEN-DEE OF RUBYDALE	Mrs. S. Yates	Mrs. E. Stephenson
KARETH KESTREL OF RITOUNG	D	16 06 77	WHITETHROAT CHINESE PANDA	YANTOREEN SZE MOO	Mr. J. Peat	Mrs. M. Young
TELOTA SIMON CHEN	D	26 10 75	CH. DOMINIC OF TELOTA	TELOTA TA-MAH	Mrs. O. Newson	Mrs. & Miss Greves
TERCERO'S ENCHANTRESS	B	05 01 78	CROWVALLEY FALSTAFF	LADY BEE GOOD OF GREENMOSS	Mrs. E. Egan	Mr. D. S. Iley

1981

Name	Sex	Date	Sire	Dam		Breeders
BELLAKERNE ZOE DO	B	04 11 78	CH. GREENMOSS CHINKI'S FLING	CH. PATSY DO OF HYNING	Mr. & Mrs. T. Richardson	Mrs. T. Morgan & Mrs. G. Dolphin

Name	Sex	Date	Sire	Dam		Breeders
CROWVALLEY JESSICA	B	28 05 77	TRICINA CHI FU	CROWVALLEY SIWEL SING LU	Mr. & Mrs. L. Williams	Breeders
EASTERN PROMISE OF HONEYLEE	D	01 05 79	CH. TRICINA TAI HAKU	TAONAN TAMARA	Mr. & Mrs. J. Foster	Miss J. Papps
ELANZO CHAO FU OF SAROSIM	B	31 07 78	ELFANN SUMMER SUNSHINE	ELANZO TRACE OF GOLD	Miss A. Martin	Mrs. P. A. Brook
GORSEYCOP SPLENDID SUMMER	B	08 10 77	CH. DOMINIC OF TELOTA	GORSEYCOP GEORGETTE	Mrs. M. Hoare	Mrs. A. Pickburn
HIONA HOOSA BABEE OF CIJENA	B	17 01 78	CH. BELLAKERNE ZIPPITY DO	HIONA HIGH FALLUTIN	Mrs. G. Moston	Mrs. J. Moir-Heath
KELTINA SSU SHIH WEN SHU	B	26 01 78	CROWVALLEY MANDARIN	KELTINA BAMBINO	Mrs. & Miss Johnson	Breeders
KEYTOR SWEET DREAMER	B	08 12 78	CH. GREENMOSS CHINKI'S FLING	KEYTOR SWEET MIRABELLE	Mrs. E. Johnson	Mrs. E. & Miss S. Johnson
KEYTOR TRISHE TRASHE	B	12 09 79	CH. GREENMOSS GLORY BEE	TRICINA ROSS OF KEYTOR	Mrs. E. Johnson	Mrs. E. & Miss S. Johnson
MONTZELLAS CHINK TO CHEN	D	04 08 78	CH. MONTZELLA'S TSI CHOU	MONTZELLA'S LU CHIA	Mr. & Mrs. J. Carter	Breeders
QUEENSFIELD TUTSI WONG OF CHELHAMA	B	18 12 75	ALAK KUM KOI OF MIDDLETUNE	POOKSHILL WONG	Mrs. F. Wood	Mrs. V. Goodwin

Name	Sex	Date	Sire	Dam		Breeders
RAGOOSA GOLDEN RAFFLES	D	12 10 77	CH. GREENMOSS GLORY BEE	FURAHA FLORSHO OF RAGOOSA	Mrs. C. M. Lewis	Mr. P. Seier-Sorensen
SANTOSHA SUNKING	D	09 02 79	LHAKANG BABU OF BODINIC	SANTOSHA SUNSET	Mr. & Mrs. D. Crossley	Breeders
WENTRES JAYCEE VALENCEE	D	29 05 79	CH. CROWVALLEY TWEEDLEDUM	MIRAZIAN ZISKA	Miss W. Greves	Breeder
YAKEE CHANG YEH	B	01 11 78	CH. GREENMOSS GLORY BEE	KEYTOR SINGING WIND OF YAKEE	Messrs Easdon & Martin	Breeders

1982

Name	Sex	Date	Sire	Dam		Breeders
BELLAKERNE MELISA DO	B	04 11 78	CH. GREENMOSS CHINKI'S FLING	CH. PATSY DO OF HYNING	Mr. & Mrs. T. Richardson	Breeders
CLAROPIE PETER PAN AT CROWVALLEY	D	18 08 80	CH. CROWVALLEY PEGASUS	CLAROPIE PANDIE	Mrs. A. Aitkin	Mr. & Mrs. L. Williams

Name	Sex	Date	Sire	Dam		Breeders
EASTELMS TEO CHI	B	20 07 80	SITZENDORF BLACK BRYONY OF EASTELMS	TRISULA CHI LING OF EASTELMS	Mrs. N. Gardner	Breeder

Name	Sex	Date	Sire	Dam		Breeders
EMROSE SPINNING WHEEL	D	13 07 78	SARIK SEHOFE	EMROSE SHADY LADY	Mrs. R. & Miss J. Howard	Breeders
FERNELL MISTA MAGIC	D	16 04 79	CH. FERNELL SPRING BANDIT	LADY FAYRE OF NOVASKAYA	Mrs. J. Ellis	Mrs. J. & Mr. D. Ellis
KARETH KHOIR ANGEL	B	14 06 79	LHARING BABU OF BODINIC	SANTOSHA SERAPHIM	Mr. J. Peat	Breeder
PAORA SUKI SHOO OF CHAULIN	B	14 06 79	PAORA CHEROKEE	DENROMA HARVEST GOLD	Mr. & Mrs. K. Draper	Mr. & Mrs. P. Jackson

1983

Name	Sex	Date	Sire	Dam		Breeders
CHARKA OF KUIRE	B	26 06 80	SANTOSHA CHARLEMAGNE OF KUIRE	BOTREE GEMINI TU	Mrs. L. Smetherham	Mrs. J. Johnson

Name	Sex	D.O.B.	Sire	Dam	Breeder	Owner
GRANDAAVON MAELI	B	14 04 79	CH. GREENMOSS GLORY BEE	JANKERI JEZEBEL OF GRANDAVON	Mrs. Y. Martin	Breeder
GREENMOSS SURELY BEE	B	12 10 79	CH. GREENMOSS GLORY BEE	WYSARGE JADE LOTUS BUD	Mr. & Mrs. A. Leadbitter	Breeders
HARROPINE CHINA TOWN	D	20 09 80	TARRALENKA CHUNG TIEN OF TRISULA	CH. TELOTA ANOUSKA	Mrs. D. & Mr. M. Harper	Breeders
HYNING BARNABY BEE OF RABART	D	26 07 78	CH. SHIRWEN HAN-SUM-BEE	HYNING BIM-BAM-BOO	Mrs. M. Rowling	Mr. R. Slater
JARDHU WAFFLES WU	D	04 04 79	CH. GREENMOSS GLORY BEE	WEN CHENGSIAN OF GLENGALL	Mrs. V. Grugan	Mr. & Mrs. J. Grugan
LYNTOR EASTERN MAGIC	D	26 02 79	LYNTOR BLACK BEAUTY	DENROMA MINTI-LING OF LYNTOR	Mrs. R. Barlow	Breeder
MORT OF BELLAKERNE AT LHARING	D	09 06 80	CH. GREENMOSS CHINKI'S FLING	BELLAKERNE ABBA DO	Mrs. T. Morgan	Mr. & Mrs. T. Harvie
SANTOSHA BEWITCHING OF JANMAYEN	B	09 02 79	CH. GREENMOSS CHINKI'S FLING	CH. SANTOSHA BEWITCHED	Mr. & Mrs. D. Crossley	Breeders
SNAEFELL CHARM	B	16 01 78	CH. BUTTONS OF SNAEFELL	NEWROOTS PITTI SING OF SNAEFELL	Mrs. A. Dadds	Breeder
SNAEFELL IMPERIAL IMP	B	26 01 81	CH. NEWROOTS NANKIPOO OF SNAEFELL	SNAEFELL QUEEN OF THE SNOW	Mrs. A. Dadds	Breeder
1984						
CHELHAMA AJAX OLYMPIUS	D	06 07 77	CH. DOMINIC OF TELOTA	CH. QUEENSFIELD TUTSI WONG OF CHELHAMA	Mrs. V. Goodwin	Breeder
CROWVALLEY PERDITA	B	13 01 82	CH. CROWVALLEY TWEEDLEDUM	CH. CRWOVALLEY JESSICA	Mr. & Mrs. L. Williams	Breeders
GREENMOSS YU TU	D	06 06 82	GREENMOSS KNEE BREECHES	CH. GREENMOSS BEE IN A BONNET	Mr. & Mrs. A. Leadbitter	Breeders
HARROPINE CHRISTMAS CAROL	D	09 10 82	SNAEFELL CARRY ON REGARDLESS	TANZU MIE ECC-LAIRE OF HARROPINE	Mrs. D. & Mr. M. Harper	Breeders
KUIRE SECRET SIMON	D	01 10 82	CAMGLIA FUZZACKER	CH. CHARKA OF KUIRE	Mrs. J. Johnson	Breeder
LHAKANG CASSIUS	D	29 01 81	TOR RA LON	CHERUBIM OF LHAKANG	Mrs. G. Widdington	Mrs. Y. Brooker
LINGCAPE GEMINI	B	06 09 80	CH. GREENMOSS CHINKI'S FLING	LINGCAPE GENESIS	Mr. P. Capeling	Breeder
MONTZELLAS ROSA LIN	B	27 10 81	CH. MONTZELLA'S TSI CHOU	MONTZELLA'S CHITA-TOU	Mr. & Mrs. J. Carter	Breeders
SENOUSI ROSALITA OF ROSSVALE	B	18 12 80	CH. DELRIDGE GOLDEN GEMINI AT CROWVALLEY	CH. TERCERO'S ENTRANTRESS	Mr. D. Iley	Mrs. S. Brown
SNAEFELL KATRINA OF JANMAYEN	B	03 07 80	CH. NEWROOTS NANKIPOO OF SNAEFELL	CH. SNAEFELL CHARM	Mrs. A. Dadds	Mesdames Pickburn & Duke
1985						
GOLD 'N' DELICIOUS OF ROSSVALE	B	20 11 79	CH. GREENMOSS BEES KNEES	SHIRWEN MISS CHIEF	Mr. Orchard	Mrs. S. Brown
JANMAYEN BIANCA	B	22 10 83	SNAEFELL CARRY ON REGARDLESS	BOWSTONES TZULAH OF JANMAYEN	Mesmames Pickburn & Duke	Breeders
JORHECAS KEVIN'S FEELINGS	D	15 09 81	CH. GREENMOSS GLORY BEE	JORHECAS BABY JANE	Messrs. Saevich & Caram	Mrs. M. A. Newell
KARETH KUMUPPANCE	D	04 06 82	KELTINA SHENG TAN CHIEH	SANTOSHA SEPHARIM	Mr. J. Peat	Breeder
SANTOSHA ROYAL FLUSH	D	06 12 82	CH. SANTOSHA SUNKING	CH. SANTOSHA SUNDOWN	Mr. & Mrs. D. Crossley	Breeders
SUNNY BOY OF TANIBET	D	04 10 81	CH. SANTOSHA SUNKING	HANSHI LOVIN LASS	Mrs. P. Whitehead	Miss D. Howland
SWEET CINDY LOU OF FERNELL	B	26 04 82	FERNELL MISTA CHAN-LIN-LI	GAR GUZELL KIPRIS	Mr. & Mrs. Nafi	Mrs. J. Ellis
VALARDY CHAN TING	B	05 06 81	JULING MINGS HAN-SUM-SUN	VALARDY CHANTANA	Mrs. K. Alteroff	Breeder

Name	Sex	Date	Sire	Dam	Owner	Breeder
YAKEE JOIE DE VIVE OF MERACON		29 09 82	CH GREENMOSS BEES KNEES	CH. YAKEE CHANG YEH	A. Easdon	Mrs. S. McNab

1986

Name	Sex	Date	Sire	Dam	Owner	Breeder
AMYLOTS WAI WAI WONDER	B	18 09 83	SHANIMEL BLONDE BOMBER	POPSU-WOPSU OF AMYLOTS	Mr. & Mrs. D. Williams	Breeders
ANIBES PUTTIN' ON THE RITZ	B	25 02 85	S. UCH. WHITETHROAT JARVIS	INT. CH. YRINGHA NO STUFFED TOI FOR ANIBES	Mrs. A. Berggren	Mesdames Dolphin & Berggren
BOUFALLS THE BRIGADIER AT CROWVALLEY	D	10 10 83	DARRALLS FIDELIO	CEDARHYTHE LITTLE JEWEL	Mrs. B. Taylor	Mr. & Mrs. L. Williams
FIREFOX OF SANTOSHA	D	08 04 84	CH. SANTOSHA ROYAL FLUSH	CH. YAKEE CHANG YEH	Messrs. Easdon & Martin	Breeders
HARROPINE CHARKA KHAN AT ANTARCTICA	D	21 12 84	SISTASU SILVER BULLET	HARROPINE ODYSSEY	Mrs. D. & Mr. M. Harper	Mr. & Mrs. K. B. Rawlings
HARROPINE LORD OF THE RINGS	D	01 09 83	CH. HARROPINE CHINA TOWN	TRISULA CHIA CHING OF HARROPINE	Mrs. D. & Mr. M. Harper	Breeders
HARROPINE ODYSSEY	B	15 06 83	CH. HARROPINE CHINA TOWN	TANZU MIE ECC-LAIRE OF HARROPINE	Mrs. D. & Mr. M. Harper	Breeders
HARROPINE SUPER TROOPER	D	20 09 80	TARRALENKA CHUNG TIEN OF TRISULA	CH. TELOTA ANOUSKA	Mrs. D. & Mr. M. Harper	Mrs. P. Lord
KEYTOR ANY QUESTIONS	D	13 08 84	WYVERN ON A PROMISE OF KEYTOR	FIDDLE DE DEE OF KEYTOR	Mrs. E. & Miss S. Johnson	Breeders
ORLANDO OF KUIRE	D	22 08 81	KUIRE LU BOZ	BENQUIN SWEET HONESTY OF CHRIKENDAR	Mrs. M. Droogan	Mr. & Mrs. N. Stevens
ROSARIL MODESTY BLAIZE	B	21 11 80	ROSARIL BLACK IS BEAUTIFUL	JAIVONNE IRRESISTABLE MISS	Miss A. Stephenson	Breeder

1987

Name	Sex	Date	Sire	Dam	Owner	Breeder
BOWSTONES SHU SHAN	B	03 04 82	CH. CROWVALLEY TWEEDLEDUM	CH. BOWSTONES CROWVALLEY SHAN TUNG	Mrs. I. Booth	Mrs. P. Maule

1988

Name	Sex	Date	Sire	Dam	Owner	Breeder
KARETH KISMET OF LYRE	B	24 03 85	CH. FIREFOX OF SANTOSHA	KARETH KHAMELEON	Mr. & Mrs. F. Hickey	Mr. J. Peat
KOUN BILLY BUNTER OF YASHNEE	D	11 01 84	YASHNEE PAO SHENG	BELLAKERNE TINKABELLE OF KOUN	M. Ross	Mr. & Mrs. K. Dyson
LHARING MOON MISCHIEF	B	11 02 84	CH. MORT OF BELLAKERNE AT LHARING	LHARING GOLDEN MOONCHILD	Mr. & Mrs. T. Harvie	Breeders
SENOUSI BE-BOP DELUX	B	12 11 85	CH. KEYTOR ANY QUESTIONS	SENOUSI BOW WOW	Mr. D. S. Iley	Breeder
WENDOLYN WILD GINGER	D	14 10 83	CH. SANTOSHA SUNKING	KADWEN KRISTOBELLE	Mrs. J. W. Wood-Jones	Breeder
ZUTHIS MOONLIGHT SHADOW	B	03 06 83	BELLAKERNE BRADY OF ERDDIG	ZUTHIS ONLY DREAMING	Mr. & Mrs. Roberts	Breeders
BELLAKERNE PAGAN DO	B	10 10 85	BELLAKERNE BRADY OF ERDDIG	SAMANTHA OF BELLAKERNE	Mrs. S. Richardson	Breeder
CAMLIEN TOUCH OF CLASS	D	09 02 84	TOR RA LON	CAMLIEN CABRINA	Mr. & Mrs. J. McNeill	Breeders
HARROPINE TIMPANI OF HASHANAH	D	14 09 85	CH. HARROPINE LORD OF THE RINGS	TANZU MIE-ECCLAIRE OF HARROPINE	Mr. M. Harper	Mrs. J. Franks
KARETH KHARISMA	B	18 10 87	CH. KARETH KUMPPANCE	CLARRISSA OF LHARING	Mr. J. Peat	Breeder
REUBICIA BECKA OF HUXLOR	B	04 12 84	HARROPINE CASSIDY OF HUXLOR	TYPROS YING TONG	Mrs. P. Jackman	Mrs. P. Lord
ROSARIL THE CHIMNEY SWEEP	D	05 01 86	CH. SANTOSHA SUNKING	CH. ROSARIL MODESTY BLAIZE	Miss A. Stephenson	Mrs. E. Stephenson
CSANTOSHA TIGER LILY	B	15 03 86	KEYTOR CHATTERBOX	SANTOSHA SUNBEAM	Mr. & Mrs. D. Crossley	Breeders
SEBASTIAN OF KEYTOR	D	07 07 85	TOM FOOL OF KEYTOR	KEYTOR JIBBA JABBA	Mrs. Beecham	Mrs. E. & Miss S. Johnson
TATSANNA ROCK N ROLL	D	12 09 84	YAKEE THINK AGAIN	TATSANNA SHIMMERING LIGHT	Mr. & Mrs. D. Anderson	Breeders
WEATSOM MY FAIR LADY OF HASHANAH	B	08 06 85	TANZU PERFECT PARTNER AT WEATSOM	WEATSOM MAGIC MOMENTS	Mrs. M. Stangeland	Mrs. J. Franks

Name	Sex	D.O.B.	Sire	Dam	Breeder	Owner
WEATSOM ONLY YOU	B	13 04 85	TOUCH OF CLASS AT WEATSOM	HARROPINE FLASHDANCE	Mrs. M. Stangeland	Breeder
1989						
CEDARHYTHE YEU HEU OF SAROSIM	B	04 06 87	CH. FIREFOX OF SANTOSHA	SAROSIM TSENG FWO AT CEDARHYTHE	Mrs. J. Clifford	Mrs. P. Brook
HARROPINE ICARUS	D	16 06 86	CH. SANTOSHA SUNKING	HARROPINE THORNBIRD	Mrs. D. & Mr. M. Harper	Mrs. D. & Mr. M. Harper
MARSHONG SPECIAL GUY	D	19 07 84	KEYTOR WELL TO DO	SALEDEN SIMPLY SPECIAL	Mrs. S. Fox	Breeder
MIRAZIAN SWEET INNOCENCE	B	25 03 82	CH. KADWEN YAN TSI	MEISHKA OF MIRAZIAN	Mrs. M. Devine	Breeder
WEATSOM LITTLE BIG MAN OF HASHANAH	D	19 11 86	CH. HARROPINE CHINA TOWN	WEATSOM A DREAM COME TRUE	Mrs. M. Stangeland	Mrs. J. Franks
1990						
CEDARHYTHE LOVE 'N' PRIDE AT SOCORRO	D	23 05 85	HARROPINE CASSIDY OF HUXLOR	KELTINA SUN PRINCESS OF CEDARHYTHE	Mrs. J. Clifford	Messrs. Hutchins & Evans
CHANIKOS YU KIZZY OF TOMOLLY	B	16 03 88	LEJUSANO FOO WIN	CHANIKOS OH DIANNA	Mrs. A. Spooner	Mesdames Turner & Hennessey Smith
CROWVALLEY ANNIVERSARY	B	22 06 86	CH. CROWVALLEY PEGASUS	ROSAYLEEN MINSTREL	S. Fortun	Mr. & Mrs. L Williams
DELBILLIE COCOA THE CLOWN	D	13 04 87	CH. SANTOSHA ROYAL FLUSH	LHAKANG CAPRICE	Mr. & Mrs. Butterworth	Breeders
DENROMA TIARA AT TAMANU	B	15 07 86	PAORA HEZA KU-TEE	BELLAKERNE STACY DO	Mr. D. Munford	Mr. & Mrs. S. Ford
HUXLOR ESCUDOS	B	02 09 85	CH. HARROPINE LORD OF THE RINGS	WEATSOM POCKET MONEY OF HUXLOR	Mrs. P. Lord	Breeder
ROSARIL DELILAH	B	30 09 87	CH. FIREFOX OF SANTOSHA	CH. ROSARIL MODESTY BLAISE	Miss A. Stephenson	Mrs. E. Stephenson
ROSSVALE PRETTY IN PINK	B	09 02 87	CH. KEYTOR ANY QUESTIONS	CH. SENOUSI ROSALITA OF ROSSVALE	Mrs. S. Brown	Breeder
SUEMAN SHIHATZU CHAZ AT EMROSE	D	17 04 87	MANDABET GOLDEN DREAM	KIZZY WONG	Davies	Mrs. J. Howells
TATSANNA THE CHARMER	D	13 12 87	KARETH KINGS CONSORT	TATSANNA SHIMMERING LIGHT	Mr. & Mrs. D. Anderson	Mrs. J. Lovely
WENDOLYN WUNDA WIZARD OF JARDHU	D	02 04 87	CH. SANTOSHA SUNKING	WENDOLYN WILMA	Mrs. W. Wood-Jones	Mr. & Mrs. J. Grugan
1991						
BOWCHILD PROMISES PROMISES	B	09 07 87	CH. FIREFOX OF SANTOSHA	CH. AMYLOTS WAI WAI WONDER	Mrs. P. Woodbridge	Breeder
CEDARHYTHE LITE MY FIRE	B	04 06 87	CH. FIREFOX OF SANTOSHA	SAROSIM TSENG FWO AT CEDARHYTHE	Mrs. J. Clifford	Messrs. Carter & Donnaby
CHELHAMA PERICLES	D	13 11 84	CH. CHELHAMA AJAX OLYMPIUS	CHELHAMA PERSEPHONE	Mrs. V. Goodwin	Breeder
EDSVILLE CRACKERJACK	D	30 06 87	PAORA WEE DAVIE BAKER	TA MEI OF EDSVILLE	Openshaw & Booth	Breeders
GRANDAVON MING TOI	B	17 02 88	ZUTHIS BUGSY MALONE	PRIMA DONNA OF GRANDAVON	Mrs. Y. Martin	Breeder
HASHANAH HOT PURSUIT	D	22 12 88	CH. WEATSOM LITTLE BIG MAN OF	CH. WEATSOM MY FAIR LADY OF	Mrs. J. Franks	Breeder

Name		Date	Sire	Dam	Owner	Breeder
HASHANAH						
HASHANAH TAKE ME TO THE TOP	B	22 12 89	CH. WEATSOM LITTLE BIG MAN OF HASHANAH	CH. WEATSOM MY FAIR LADY OF HASHANAH	Mrs. J. Franks	Mrs. J. Franks
JARDHU MYZ-SUNN	D	06 02 88	SANTOSHA ROYAL FLUSH	JARDHU MISCHEVOUS MI-ZEE	Mr. & Mrs. J. Grugan	Breeders
MAGIQUE MAGPIE OF CHELHAMA	B	24 11 87	HUXLOR KING OF GLORY AT CHELHAMA	LEITHILL LUCINDA	Mrs. Goodwin & Miss Cormack	Mrs. V. Goodwin
MINGROVIA ELITE PETITE OF TAMERON	B	31 01 84	CH. LHARING CASSIUS	MINGROVIA MADELINE	Mrs. C. Soulsby	Mrs. L. Howard
SNAEFELL LIMITED EDITION	D	11 10 88	AM CH. DIN HO RUPERT T BEAR	SNAEFELL IRMA LA DOUCE	Mrs. A. Dadds	Breeder
WEATSOM MADAM BUTTERFLY	B	25 10 88	CH. WEATSOM TOM THUMB AT COWLEY	WEATSOM CALL ME MADAM	Mrs. M. Stangeland	Breeder
WEATSOM TOM THUMB AT COWLEY	D	02 08 86	TOM FOOL OF KEYTOR	MARMALADE ATKINS AT TANZU	Mrs. M. Stangeland	Breeder
1992						
BELLAKERNE MISTY DO	B	17 05 90	ZUTHIS MOONWALKER	CH. BELLAKERNE PAGAN DO	Mrs. S. Richardson	Breeder
CABBALA BEAUTIFUL DREAMER	B	30 01 90	CH. SNAEFELL LIMITED EDITION	SHE WHO DARES OF WEATSOM AT CABBALA	Mrs. G. Goodwin	Mrs. G. Goodwin
CHELHAMA DE COURCEY	D	22 09 88	CH. FIREFOX OF SANTOSHA	CHELHAMA PERSEPHONE	Mrs. V. Goodwin	Mrs. V. Goodwin
GREENMOSS PRAISE BEE	D	18 08 88	CH. CAMLLIEN TOUCH OF CLASS	GREENMOSS DAISY TU	Mr. & Mrs. A. Leadbitter	Breeders
LOUWAN WINNING COLOURS AT HUXLOR	D	30 09 88	AM. CH. LOUWANS REBEL ROUSER	AM. CH. LOUWAN TOOTSIE	Louis & Wanda Gec	Mrs. P. Lord
MEGGY'S PROMISE FOR LHARING	B	10 12 88	YAKEE GRAND FINALE AT LHARING	LHARING LITTLE LADY	Miss Meharry	Mrs. F. Harvie
SNAEFELL IMPERIAL ROSE OF	B	25 07 86	KELTINA FAN KANG OF SNAEFELL	CH. SNAEFELL IMPERIAL IMP	Mrs. A. Dadds	Mesdames Pickburn & Duke
JANMAYEN						
WEATSOM DRESSED TO KILL	B	05 03 89	CH. HARROPINE CHINA TOWN	WEATSOM SUGAR & SPICE	Mrs. M. Stangeland	Mrs. M. Stangeland
WENDOLYN WILDFIRE	D	02 07 88	CH. FIREFOX OF SANTOSHA	CH. WENDOLYN WILD GINGER	Mrs. W. Wood-Jones	Breeder
1993						
HARROPINE CHASING RAINBOWS	B	10 12 90	CH. HARROPINE CHINA TOWN	DRAGONFIRE'S SCARLET O'HARA	Mrs. D. & Mr. M. Harper	Breeders
HASHANAH NO JACKET REQUIRED	D	03 09 91	CH. WEATSOM LITTLE BIG MAN OF HASHANAH	CH. WEATSOM MY FAIR LADY OF HASHANAH	Mrs. J. Franks	Mrs. J. Franks
HEBOUCHON WONDER WOMAN	B	16 08 89	CH. SANTOSHA SUNKING	STARGEM YEH YING	Mr. & Mrs. C. Ripley	Breeders
HOT FAVOURITE AT HUXLOR	B	23 06 88	BASIL BRUSH OF THE GURNOS	WEATSOM GLIMPSE OF GOLD	Mrs. M. A. Hope	Mrs. P. Lord
MEIKWEI HAPPY GO LUCKY	B	17 07 86	KINGS RANSOM FOR LANSU	PATAJOHN GOLDEN SUNSHINE	Miss S. Brace	Miss S. Brace
SANTOSHA CHOCOLATE ORANGE	D	24 10 91	CH. ROSARIL THE CHIMNEY SWEEP	SANTOSHA MADAME BUTTERFLY OF PHINJANI	Mr. & Mrs. D. Crossley	Mr. & Mrs. D. Crossley

BIBLIOGRAPHY

Ackerman, Lowell, DVM. *Owners's Guide to Dog Health*, TFH Publications, 1995.

Aitchinson, James, `Incisor Dentitions of Short-muzzled Dogs', Veterinary Record, 1964, Volume 76.

American Shih Tzu Club Brochure, 1969.

American Shih Tzu Club Bulletin, 1972 (July).

American Shih Tzu Club Stud Book, 1963 (July).

Belfield, Wendell O. E.V.M. and Zucker, Martin. *How To Have A Healthier Dog*, Doubleday, 1981.

Burns, Marcia and Fraser, Margaret N, *Genetics of the Dog*, Agricultural Bureau, 1952; Oliver and Boyd 1966.

Collier, V W F, *Dogs of China and Japan in Nature and Art*, Heinemann 1921.

DePrisco, Andrew and Johnson, James. *The Canine Lexicon*, TFH Publications, 1993.

Dudgeon, Gene and Mollie, *Shih Tzu News*, Dudgeon, USA, passim. Kennel Gazette. October 1993.

Easton, Allan and Brearley, Joan McDonald. *This is the Shih Tzu*, TFH Publications, 1980.

Lauffer, Berthold, *Chinese Pottery of The Han Dynasty*, E J Brill, Leiden, 1909; Charles E Tuttle, Japan, 1962.

Lu Zee Yuen Nee, Madame, *The Lhasa Lion Dog*, Peking Kennel Club (International), n.d.; reprinted by Maples Press, Rugby, England, n.d.

Lyon, Kenneth, D.V.M. and Ackerman, Lowell, D.V.M., *Dog Owner's Guide to Proper Dental Care*, TFH Publications, 1993.

Manchu Shih Tzu Society, *Newsletter*, May/June 1968.

McCay, Clive M, *Nutrition of the Dog*, Comstock, Ithaca, New York, 1943 and 1949.

Scott, John Paul, and Fuller, John L, *Genetics and Social Behavior of the Dog*, University of Chicago Press, 1965 and 1971.

Shih Tzu Club, *Shih Tzu News*, England, passim.

Snellgrove and Richardson, *A Cultural History of Tibet*, Weidenfeld and Nicolson, 1968.

Stokard, Charles, `Inheritance of Localised Dwarfism and Achondroplasia in Dogs', American Journal of Anatomy, 38, 39.

Widdrington, Gay, *The Shih Tzu Handbook*, 1971.

Willis, Malcolm B. *Practical Genetics for Dog Breeders* , Witherby, 1992.

PEDIGREE FORM

NAME OF DOG ....

BREED ....

SEX ....

COLOUR & MARKINGS ....

DATE OF BIRTH ....

BREEDER ....

KENNEL CLUB No. ....

DATE OF REGISTRATION ....

KENNEL CLUB STUD No. ....

OWNER ....

ADDRESS ....

....

....

PARENTS	GRANDPARENTS	GREAT
SIRE Name	Sire	Sire
		Dam
Kennel Club No.		
Name and Address of Owner	Dam	Sire
		Dam
DAM Name	Sire	Sire
		Dam
Kennel Club No.		
Name and Address of Owner	Dam	Sire
		Dam

HONOU

I certify this Pedigree to be correct to the best of my knowledge.

FORM

ARENTS	GT: GT: GRANDPARENTS	GT: GT: GT: GRANDPARENTS
	Sire	*Sire*
		Dam
	Dam	*Sire*
		Dam
	Sire	*Sire*
		Dam
	Dam	*Sire*
		Dam
	Sire	*Sire*
		Dam
	Dam	*Sire*
		Dam
	Sire	*Sire*
		Dam
	Dam	*Sire*
		Dam
	Sire	*Sire*
		Dam
	Dam	*Sire*
		Dam
	Sire	*Sire*
		Dam
	Dam	*Sire*
		Dam
	Sire	*Sire*
		Dam
	Dam	*Sire*
		Dam
	Sire	*Sire*
		Dam
	Dam	*Sire*
		Dam

AINED

_____

_____

_____

Signed _____   *Date* _____

241

INDEX

INDEX

INDEX

INDEX

INDEX

INDEX

INDEX

INDEX

INDEX

INDEX

INDEX

INDEX

INDEX

INDEX

INDEX